The Center for South and Southeast Asia Studies of the University of California is the unifying organization for faculty members and students interested in South and Southeast Asia Studies, bringing together scholars from numerous disciplines. The Center's major aims are the development and support of research and language study. As part of this program the Center sponsors a publication series of books concerned with South and Southeast Asia. Manuscripts are considered from all campuses of the University of California as well as from any other individuals and institutions doing research in these areas.

PUBLICATIONS OF THE CENTER FOR SOUTH AND SOUTHEAST ASIA STUDIES:

Angela S. Burger
Opposition in a Dominant-Party System: A Study of the Jan Sangh, the Praja Socialist Party, and the Socialist Party in Uttar Pradesh, India (1969)

Robert L. Hardgrave, Jr.
Nadars of Tamilnad: The Political Culture of a Community in Change (1969)

Fugene F. Irschick
Political and Social Conflict in South India: The Non-Brahman Movement and Tamil Separatism, 1916–1929 (1969)

Briton Martin, Jr.
New India, 1885: *British Official Policy and the Emergence of the Indian National Congress* (1969)

James T. Siegel
The Rope of God (1969)

Jyotirindra Das Gupta
Language Conflict and National Development: Group Politics and National Language Policy in India (1970)

Gerald D. Berreman
Hindus of the Himalayas (Second Revised Edition, 1971)

Richard G. Fox
Kin, Clan, Raja, and Rule: State-Hinterland Relations in Preindustrial India (1971)

Robert N. Kearney
Trade Unions and Politics in Ceylon (1971)

David G. Marr
Vietnamese Anticolonialism, 1885-1925 (1971)

Leo E. Rose
Nepal—Strategy for Survival (1971)

Richard Sisson
The Congress Party in Rajasthan (1971)

Prakash Tandon
Beyond Punjab: A Sequel to Punjabi Century (1971)

Elizabeth Whitcombe
Agrarian Conditions in Northern India. Volume One: The United Provinces under British Rule, 1860–1900 (1971)

THE KĀPĀLIKAS AND KĀLĀMUKHAS

THE KĀPĀLIKAS AND KĀLĀMUKHAS

TWO LOST ŚAIVITE SECTS

David N. Lorenzen

UNIVERSITY OF CALIFORNIA PRESS
Berkeley and Los Angeles

Published in the United States by
The University of California Press
Berkeley and Los Angeles, California

Library of Congress Catalog Card Number 70-138509
International Standard Book Number 0-520-01842-7

First published in 1972 by Thomson Press (India) Limited, 19 Malcha Marg, New Delhi-21

Printed in India by Aroon Purie at Thomson Press (India) Limited, Faridabad, Haryana.

CONTENTS

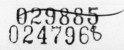

LIST OF ABBREVIATIONS

ABORI	:	*Annals of the Bhandarkar Oriental Research Institute* [Poona].
ARMAD	:	*Annual Report of the Mysore Archaeological Department.*
BSOS	:	*Bulletin of the School of Oriental Studies* [London].
CII	:	*Corpus Inscriptionum Indicarum.*
EC	:	*Epigraphia Carnatica.*
EI	:	*Epigraphia Indica.*
ERE	:	*Encyclopaedia of Religion and Ethics,* ed. James Hastings.
GSS	:	*Gorakṣa-siddhānta-saṃgraha,* ed. G.N. Kavirāja.
HAS	:	*Hyderabad Archaeological Series.*
HDS	:	*History of Dharmaśāstra* by P.V. Kane.
HTR	:	*Harvard Theological Review.*
IA	:	*Indian Antiquary.*
IHQ	:	*Indian Historical Quarterly* [Calcutta].
IIJ	:	*Indo-Iranian Journal* [The Hague].
JAnSB	:	*Journal of the Anthropological Society of Bombay.*
JAOS	:	*Journal of the American Oriental Society.*
JBBRAS	:	*Journal of the Bombay Branch of the Royal Asiatic Society.*
JBRS	:	*Journal of the Bihar Research Society.*
JGRS	:	*Journal of the Gujarat Research Society.*
JIH	:	*Journal of Indian History* [Trivandrum].
JOIB	:	*Journal of the Oriental Institute, Baroda.*
JORM	:	*Journal of Oriental Research, Madras.*
JRAS	:	*Journal of the Royal Asiatic Society* [London].
JRASB	:	*Journal of the Royal Asiatic Society of Bengal.*
QJMS	:	*Quarterly Journal of the Mythic Society* [Bangalore].
SBE	:	*Sacred Books of the East,* ed. F. Max Muller.
SII	:	*South Indian Inscriptions.*
TAS	:	*Travancore Archaeological Series.*

PREFACE

This study attempts to give as complete as possible a description of two extinct Śaivite sects—the Kāpālikas and the Kālāmukhas. In a Christian context the concept of a 'sect' embodies three essential features: a specific doctrine (including a prescribed mode of worship), a priesthood, and a well-defined and exclusive laity. The structure of Hindu 'sects' is in general much more amorphous than that of Christian ones. In most cases more emphasis is placed on doctrine and mode of worship than on organisation. The Sanskrit words most often used for the Kāpālika, Kālāmukha and Pāśupata 'sects'—the groups discussed in this study—are *darśana, samaya* and *mata*. The basic meaning of these words is 'doctrine.' Each of the three groups also had its own priesthood. That of the Kālāmukhas appears to have been the best organised. Several Kālāmukha monasteries *(maṭhas)*, each under a single head *(maṭha-pati)*, controlled temples in the regions surrounding them. It is doubtful, however, whether any of the three groups had its own exclusive laity. An ordinary farmer or merchant might have called himself a Buddhist, Jain, Vaiṣṇava, or Śaivite, but probably not a Kāpālika, Kālāmukha or Pāśupata. Records indicate that persons supported priesthoods of different and even hostile 'sects' without feeling disloyal. For this reason it might be more appropriate to speak of Kālāmukha, Pāśupata and Kāpālika 'monastic orders' rather than 'sects.' Since, however, the term 'monastic order' does not usually imply a separate doctrinal or philosophical position, we will remain content with the word 'sect.'

Unfortunately no religious texts of either the Kāpālikas or the Kālāmukhas have survived. Their portraits must be drawn from accounts by their opponents and, in the case of the Kālāmukhas, from the information contained in epigraphic grants to their temples. The comments on both sects by Yāmunācārya and his famous pupil Rāmānuja make the best starting point.

Many of the remarks by these two Vaiṣṇava sages about the Kāpālikas are confirmed and enlarged by the numerous descriptions of Kāpālika ascetics in Sanskrit literature. Of particular importance are two dramas—Bhavabhūti's *Mālatī-Mādhava* and Kṛṣṇamiśra's *Prabodhacandrodaya*—and two legendary accounts of the life of Śaṃkarācārya—Mādhavācārya's *Śaṃkara-digvijaya* and Ānandagiri's *Saṃkara-vijaya*. Although nearly all of the sources for the Kāpālikas are fictional and written from a hostile point of view, the overall picture they give is detailed enough and consistent enough to ensure that it is reasonably authentic. The discovery of two or three inscriptions from what must have been Kāpālika temples at least guarantees their existence.

Apart from the remarks of Yāmunācārya and Rāmānuja, the sources for the Kālāmukhas are nearly all epigraphic ones. The majority of the grants to Kālāmukha temples have been found in what is today Mysore State and date from the eleventh and twelfth centuries A.D. Most are written in Kannada, the language of the region. In general they provide more information about the history than the doctrine and cult of the sect. The religious information that they do contain tends to discredit rather than corroborate Yāmunācārya and Rāmānuja. Most importantly, the records indicate that the Kālāmukhas were an offshoot of the Pāśupatas, a sect about which a good deal is known from surviving religious texts as well as from inscriptions.

Few modern scholars have paid much attention to either the Kāpālikas or Kālāmukhas. One of the earliest reputable discussions of the two sects is in R.G. Bhandarkar's *Vaiṣṇavism, Śaivism and Minor Religious Systems* (1913). Bhandarkar limits himself to a brief summary of the accounts of Rāmānuja, Mādhavācārya, Ānandagiri, and Bhavabhūti. Although he admits that 'there appears to be a confusion between the sects of Kāpālikas and Kālāmukhas' in Rāmānuja's account, Bhandarkar seems to accept that the Kālāmukhas were 'the most extreme sect.' This view, which has been accepted by many subsequent writers, is, I feel, an incorrect one. For a truer picture of the Kālāmukhas one must look to their inscriptions. No comprehensive study of Kālāmukha epigraphy has so far been attempted, but worthwhile discussions of the Kālāmukha Śakti-pariṣad at Belagāve are found in J.F. Fleet's 'Inscriptions at Ablur' and in A.V. Subbiah's 'A Twelfth Century University in Mysore.' A great number of Kālāmukha inscriptions are edited and translated by B.L. Rice in *Epigraphia Carnatica*. Other inscriptions have been edited, and often translated, by various scholars in *Epigraphia Indica, South Indian Inscriptions, Indian Antiquary,* and other journals. For the Kāpālikas only one modern scholar merits special mention—K.K. Handiqui. He devotes several pages to the sect in his brilliant study of the tenth century background to Somadeva's *Yaśastilaka* and in a note on

Somasiddhānta in his translation of Śrīharṣa's *Naiṣadhacarita*. I have included a fairly comprehensive list of the many modern studies of the Pāśupatas at the beginning of chapter six.

In the present study I have attempted to gather together for the first time all the available source materials on the Kāpālikas and Kālāmukhas and to extract a coherent account of their history, doctrines and religious practices.

With the Kāpālikas I have first presented these source materials in as readable a form as possible and saved most of my analysis of them for a separate chapter. This arrangement has necessitated a good number of repetitions of important references for which I ask the reader's indulgence. The reconstruction of Kāpālika cult and doctrine is admittedly speculative owing to the distorted and fragmentary character of the evidence. For this reason I have had to repeatedly qualify my remarks with words and phrases such as 'probably,' 'possibly,' 'perhaps,' 'seems to,' 'tends to suggest,' etc. Of greatest importance is the identification and description of the peculiar vow of the Kāpālikas called the Mahāvrata. It is this vow, I believe, that provides the key to a proper understanding of many of their unorthodox ascetic practices.

The subject of tantric religion is potentially a rather controversial one, and some of my comments might raise the hackles of those concerned for the image of Indian religion. The axes I have to grind do not include the wilful denigration of things Indian, and I have tried at all times simply to draw the most reasonable conclusion the evidence afforded.

The presentation in a readable form of the profuse epigraphic evidence on the Kālāmukhas was a more difficult task. My main object has been to demonstrate the great importance of this sect in tenth to thirteenth century Mysore and to rescue it from the tantric limbo to which it was relegated by Rāmānuja, R.G. Bhandarkar and others.

The last chapter discusses the Pāśupata ancestry of the Kālāmukhas, particularly the date and life of the Pāśupata-Kālāmukha saint Lakulīśa. Many of my remarks are in the nature of criticisms and cautionary notes about the conclusions of modern scholars. Included, with some trepidation, is a criticism of Professor Ingalls' theory of the shamanistic origin of this sect.

Several technical details must be mentioned. The critical apparatus I have used is based for the most part on K.L. Turabian's *A Manual for Writers of Term Papers, Theses and Dissertations*. Brackets are mainly used for my additions to translations of other scholars. Additions to my own translations are put in parentheses. The words 'Śaivite' and 'Śaiva' are distinguished. The former is applied to anyone who specially worships the god Siva, the latter to a Śaivite who follows Śaiva-Siddhānta. The spelling of Indian place names is always a problem. In general I have used the versions given in the Government of India's *Road Map of India* (2d edition). For the names of small villages and other places not on this map, I have normally used the spellings given in my sources.

Sanskrit words are transliterated according to the system now used by most Indologists. Nasal-consonant combinations are transliterated as in Monier-Williams' *Sanskrit-English Dictionary*. Thus I have written 'Śaṃkara' not 'Śaṅkara.' In order to avoid confusion—especially between 'c' and 'ch'—I have also made uniform the spelling of Sanskrit words in quotes and translations of other scholars, though not in the titles of their books and articles. Translations from Sanskrit are my own unless otherwise specified. Since my knowledge of Kannada is more limited, I have normally relied on the translations of Rice, Fleet, Barnett, and others for the Kālāmukha epigraphy in this language. I have also had the help of Dr. H. Ullrich of Michigan State University and Professor H.S. Biligiri of Deccan College, Poona. I am particularly grateful for Professor Biligiri's excellent translation of the important record describing the exploits of Bonteyamuni of Hoṃbaḷ.

Several other persons have contributed suggestions, criticisms and linguistic assistance. I would specially like to thank Mr. Venugopalan of Deccan College; Professor J.W. de Jong, Dr. S.A.A. Rizvi and Dr. K.H.J. Gardiner of the Australian National University; and Dr. T.R. Trautman of the University of Michigan. For instruction and encouragement in the earlier stages of my study of ancient India I am indebted to Professor J.W. Spellman of Windsor University and to Dr. J.G. de Casparis and Mr. J.E.B. Gray of the School of Oriental and African Studies. By far my greatest debt of gratitude is owed to my mentor, Professor A.L. Basham. The present work is based on a thesis prepared under his supervision and for which he gave unstinting advice, assistance and encouragement.

Financial support for my studies has been provided by my parents, my wife, the American Institute of Indian Studies—which contributed an invaluable year in India—and the Australian National University. Neither the American Institute nor the Australian National University is to be held responsible for the contents of this work.

CHAPTER I

FOUR ŚAIVITE SECTS

Brahma-sūtra Commentaries

Several Sanskrit commentators on *Brahma-sūtra* ii. 2. 37 criticise the doctrines and practices of religious sects which preach devotion to Śiva and philosophical dualism. Śamkarācārya (*c*. 788–820) mentions only the Māheśvaras.[1] It is clear from his discussion that they are the same as the Pāśupatas. Vācaspati Miśra (*c*. 850) divides these Māheśvaras into four groups—Śaivas, Pāśupatas, Kāpālikas, and Kāruṇika-siddhāntins.[2] Bhāskarācārya (*c*. 850) repeats this division but replaces the Kāruṇika-siddhāntins with Kāṭhaka-siddhāntins.[3] Other commentators are said to call this last group Kāruka-siddhāntins.[4] Yāmunācārya (*c*. 1050), the teacher of Rāmānuja, lists together Śaivas, Pāśupatas, Kāpālas, and Kālāmukhas in his *Āgama-prāmāṇya*.[5] Rāmānuja (*c*. 1017–1137) repeats his preceptor's comments, in large part verbatim, in his *Śrī-bhāṣya*.[6] Most later commentators also seem to follow Yāmuna's classification. Although the Kāruka-, Kāruṇika-, Kāṭhaka-siddhāntins are only described very cursorily, they are apparently identical with the Kālāmukhas.

The comments of Yāmunācārya and Rāmānuja contain valuable information, but have been accepted too uncritically by modern scholars. In some places Rāmānuja's *Śrī-bhāṣya* is ambiguous and his remarks about the Kālāmukhas do not always harmonise with what is otherwise known about them.[7] Also, he does not maintain consistently clear distinctions between the four sects. Sometimes he seems to describe them collectively, at other times

---

[1] *Brahma-sūtra-bhāṣya*, ed. B. Śāstrī, ii. 2. 37.

[2] *Bhāmatī*, ed. B. Śāstrī, ii. 2. 37.

[3] *Brahma-sūtra-bhāṣya*, ed. V.P. Dvivedin, ii. 2. 37.

[4] R.G. Bhandarkar, *Vaiṣṇavism Śaivism and Minor Religious Systems*, p. 121. This name is also found in M. Monier-Williams' *Sanskrit-English Dictionary*, but we have not found a commentary containing it.

[5] Quoted in K.K. Handiqui's notes to Śrīharṣa's *Naiṣadhacarita*, p. 644.

[6] Ed. R.D. Karmarkar, ii. 2. 35–37.

[7] Since the full text of Yāmuna's *Āgama-prāmāṇya* was not available to us, we will follow Rāmānuja's *Śrī-bhāṣya*. The translations of this are our own.

individually. He first identifies the four sects which follow the doctrine of Paśupati and then adds :

> All these make an analysis of reality and a hypothesis about the attainment of bliss in this world and the next which are opposed to the Vedas. They make a distinction between the instrumental and material cause *(nimittopadānayor bhedam)* and designate Paśupati as the instrumental cause (but not the material cause of the Universe).[8]

In this respect the four sects appear to be the same. This is, no doubt, an oversimplification, but each may well have propounded a dualistic metaphysics.

Rāmānuja next discusses the main features of Kāpāla (Kāpālika) worship :

> As the Kāpālas declare: 'He who knows the essence of the six insignia *(mudrikā-ṣaṭka)*, who is proficient in the highest *mudrā*, and who meditates on the Self as seated in the vulva *(bhagāsana-stha)*, attains *nirvāṇa*.' They define the six insignia *(mudrā)* as the *kaṇṭhikā* (necklace),[9] the *rucaka* (another neck ornament), the *kuṇḍala* (earring), the *śikhā-maṇi* (crest-jewel), ashes, and the sacred thread. A person bearing these insignia is not born again in this world.[10]

Yāmunācārya makes the important addition that they have two secondary insignia *(upamudrā)*—the skull *(kapāla)* and the club *(khaṭvāṅga)*.[11] Most Śaivite ascetics smear their bodies with ashes and wear sacred threads, but the skull and *khaṭvāṅga* are mostly peculiar to the Kāpālikas. The term *kuṇḍala* is used for the earrings of the Kāpālikas in a number of sources, and in Bhavabhūti's *Mālatī-Mādhava* a female Kāpālika bears the name Kāpāla-kuṇḍalā.[12] Large earrings made of rhinoceros horn or other material are a distinguishing feature of a related group of tantric ascetics, the Kānphaṭā Yogins (*kān* = ear, *phaṭā* = split). Their earrings are of two basic types—a flat one called *darśana* and a round one called *kuṇḍala*. Both are known as *mudrās*.[13] Statues of Lakulīśa, the

---

[8] ii. 2. 35–37.

[9] Yāmunācārya reads *karṇikā* in place of *kaṇṭhikā*. Quoted in Śrīharṣa, p. 644.

[10] ii. 2. 35–37.

[11] Quoted in Śrīharṣa, p. 644.

[12] See below, pp . 56–57.

[13] G.S. Ghurye, *Indian Sadhus*, pp. 135–136.

Pāśupata-Kālāmukha saint, also commonly display large earrings. The other insignia in Rāmānuja's list, the neck ornaments and crest-jewel, are nowhere else specially connected with the Kāpālikas.

The phrase 'proficient in the highest *mudrā*' or 'most skilful in (the use of) *mudrās*' *(para-mudrā-viśārada)* is difficult to interpret. R.G. Bhandarkar explains it as he 'who is skilful in their [the six insignia's] use,'[14] but it is not easy to see how these insignia can be 'used'. In tantric literature the term *mudrā* is one of the five Ma-sounds which designate the principal ingredients of the central tantric ritual *(pañca-makāra-sādhanā)*: *madya* (liquor), *māṃsa* (meat), *matsya* (fish), *mudrā*, and *maithuna* (coition). Here *mudrā* has a variety of meanings. In Hindu tantras it usually denotes parched grain, kidney beans, or any cereal believed to possess aphrodisiac qualities.[15] In Buddhist tantric works, on the other hand, it usually refers to the female partner in the ritual. In Buddhist tantric yoga, the four stages in the production of *bodhi-citta* are also called *mudrās*. They are *karma-mudrā*, *dharma-mudrā*, *mahā-mudrā*, and *samaya-mudrā*.[16] In non-tantric religious usage, and often in tantric works as well, *mudrā* denotes various ritual gestures, especially ones made with the hands. More generally it simply means 'mark' or 'insignia' as in the 'set of six insignia' *(mudrā-ṣaṭka)* mentioned above. Bhandarkar's interpretation of Rāmānuja's phrase is still the best one, but most of the other meanings of *mudrā* are also possible.

The meditation on the 'Self as seated in the vulva'[17] is reminiscent of the Buddhist tantric maxim: 'Buddha-hood resides in the woman's vulva.'[18] The term *bhaga* (vulva) also has a variety of meanings, especially in the Buddhist Tantras. Many of these texts begin with the words: 'Once upon a time the Lord of all Tathāgatas . . . was dwelling in the vulvae of the *vajra*-women.'[19] This is an example of what Bharati calls afferent *sandhā*-terminology—the use of object words, frequently erotic ones, to 'intend' metaphysical or mystical concepts.[20] Here the commentators explain *bhaga* as

---

[14] p. 127.

[15] A. Bharati, *The Tantric Tradition*, p. 242.

[16] S.B. Dasgupta, *An Introduction to Tāntric Buddhism*, pp. 174–75.

[17] *Bhagāsana-stham ātmānaṃ dhyātvā.*

[18] Cited by L. de la Vallée Poussin, 'Tāntrism (Buddhist),' *ERE*, XII, 196.

[19] 'ekasmin samaye bhagavān sarva-tathāgata-kāya-vāk-citta-hṛdaya-vajra-yoṣit-bhageṣu vijahāra.' Trans. Bharati, p. 170.

[20] Ibid., p. 173.

the 'void-element' *(kha-dhātu)* or the 'void' *(śūnyatā)*, and also as Prajñā, the female personification of enlightenment.[21]

The use of the term *nirvāṇa* instead of its Hindu equivalent, *mokṣa* or *mukti,* is again suggestive of a Buddhist or Vajrayāṇa context although *nirvāṇa* is also used in some Śaivite tantric literature such as the famous, though admittedly late, *Mahānirvāṇa-tantra.* Another Buddhist connection is found in the vernacular songs *(caryās)* of the Sahajiyā Buddhist saint Kāṇhapāda. He elevates the Kāpālika to the rank of perfected yogin.[22] Vajrayāṇa literature also refers to ritual paraphernalia typical of Kāpālika worship—such as bones, blood, flesh, and skulls—more often than Hindu Tantras do.

Nonetheless, all Sanskrit sources claim that the Kāpālikas worship the Hindu deity Bhairava-Śiva and his consort. There is little doubt, therefore, that the Kāpālikas were a Śaivite sect. The Buddhist parallels indicate that they must have also had some connection with Buddhist tantrism, but, in the absence of additional evidence, it is useless to speculate about what this may have been. Yāmunācārya and Rāmānuja continue their discussion with some comments about the last of the four sects, the Kālāmukhas. Both authors should have been acquainted with these ascetics since the sect was influential in South India, particularly in the Mysore region, between the eleventh and thirteenth centuries. Yāmunācārya is believed to have spent most of his life in Kāñcī. His disciple divided most of his time between this city and Śrīraṅgam, about 150 miles to the south. He also made pilgrimages to other parts of India. Contemporary Kālāmukha monasteries in the Madras region existed at Tiruvānakkoyil in Chingleput District, Vēḍal in North Arcot District, Koyil Tēvarāyanpeṭṭai in Tanjore District, and Koḍumbāḷūr in Tiruchchirappali District—none very far from Kāñcī or Śrīraṅgam.[23]

Rāmānuja's portrait of the sect, however, is quite different from the one obtained from Kālāmukha epigraphs or from the works of their parent sect, the Pāśupatas. *Śrī-bhāṣya* ii. 2. 35–37 states :

> Likewise, the Kālāmukhas designate (the following) as the means of securing all desires in this world and the next : eating from a skullbowl, besmearing the body *(snāna)* with

---

[21]Dasgupta, pp. 105, 120–21.

[22]S.B. Dasgupta, *Obscure Religious Cults,* pp. 57–58, 90, 103–104.

[23]See below, pp. 165–67.

the ashes of a corpse, eating those (ashes), bearing a staff *(laguḍa),* keeping a pot of wine *(surā),* and using that pot for worship of the gods *(deva-pūjā),* etc.

Much of this description seems more appropriate to the Kāpālikas. Only two items are associated with the Kālāmukhas in other sources—the bath in ashes and the staff *(laguḍa).* The bath in ashes is one of the central rituals prescribed in the *Pāśupata-sūtra.*[24] The supposed author of this work, Lakulīśa, is held in equally high esteem by both the Pāśupatas and Kālāmukhas. His name indicates that he also carried a staff *(lakula).*[25] The words *lakula* and *laguḍa* are synonymous and etymologically identical. The Kāpālikas, on the other hand, normally carry a *khaṭvāṅga* or a trident *(triśūla).* Elsewhere in the *Āgama-prāmāṇya,* Yāmunācārya speaks of a fourfold division of the tantras: Śaiva, Pāśupata, Saumya, and Lāguḍa.[26] This clearly corresponds to the four sects: Śaiva, Pāśupata, Kāpāla, and Kālāmukha.

Eating from a skull bowl and worshipping the gods with a pot of wine are items especially associated with the Kāpālikas, not the Kālāmukhas. Sanskrit sources usually portray Kāpālikas as charlatan ascetics who wander about with a skull begging bowl and drink liquor freely for mundane as well as ritual purposes. They also wear the ashes of the dead although no source claims that they eat them.

The seeming confusion in Rāmānuja's account between the Kāpālikas and Kālāmukhas was noticed by R.G. Bhandarkar who concluded (p. 128) that 'people do not seem to have made a sharp distinction' between them. G.S. Ghurye has suggested (p. 128) that by the twelfth century, the time of the greatest number of Kālāmukha epigraphs, the sect 'had purged itself of, or had at least suppressed, the more objectionable practices.' Bhandarkar's theory is the more plausible one, but neither is very satisfactory. There were in fact considerable differences between the two sects, and Yāmuna and Rāmānuja must have known how to distinguish them. Ghurye's theory fails to account for the fact that the earliest Kālāmukha record, an inscription of A.D. 810, shows no more evidence of religious extremism than any of their later records. One might suggest a more sinister explanation. At the time of

---

[24]Ed. R.A. Sastri, i. 2.

[25]See below, p. 108.

[26]Quoted in Śrīharṣa, p. 643.

Yāmuna and Rāmānuja the Kālāmukhas were rapidly gaining popular and even royal support in South India. The two Vaiṣṇava priests may have purposely confused the two Śaivite sects in order to discredit their more important rivals.

Śrī-bhāṣya ii. 2. 35–37 next gives a list of religious paraphernalia prescribed in the *Śaivāgamas*: 'the rosary of *rudrākṣa* seeds in the hand, a single mass of matted hair on the head, the skull-bowl, the besmearing the body with ashes, etc.' Presumably Rāmānuja means to associate these items with the Śaiva sect, but with the exception of the skull-bowl, which does not belong with the Śaivas anyway, all the items are part of the costume of most types of Śaivite ascetics.

This list may be compared with the only significant epigraphic description of a Kālāmukha ascetic. A grant of A.D. 1252–53 from Munavaḷḷi in Belgaum District praises the Kālāmukha *rāyarājaguru* Sarveśvaradeva: 'whose body was sprinkled with ashes; who wore a small piece of cloth around the loins, and the hairy skin of an antelope; who carried a rosary of Rudrākṣas. . . .'[27] The loincloth and antelope skin as well as the ashes and *rudrākṣas* are standard equipment for most Śaivite ascetics. No mention is made of wine pots or skull bowls.

Rāmānuja's *Śrī-bhāṣya* ii. 2. 35–37 concludes with a disparaging description of the Kāpāla vow *(vrata)*:

> Likewise, they (?=the *Śaivāgamas,* the four sects, the Kāpālas) state that even men belonging to lower castes can attain the status of Brāhmaṇa and the highest *āśrama* (=*saṃnyāsa,* mendicancy) by means of certain special rites. (For it is said): 'One instantly becomes a Brāhmaṇa merely by the process of initiation. A man becomes a great ascetic *(yati)* by undertaking the Kāpāla vow.'

This may be compared with the following verse from the *Kulārṇava-tantra*: 'Gone is the Śūdra-hood of the Śūdra and the Brāhmaṇa-hood of the Brāhmaṇa *(vipra)*; there is no division into castes for one who is consecrated by initiation.'[28] Hostility to caste consciousness is a normal feature of tantric worship and is consistently espoused by Kāpālikas in Sanskrit literature. From a modern point

---

[27] J.F. Fleet (ed. and trans.), 'Sanskrit and Old Canarese Inscriptions Relating to Yādava Kings of Dēvagiri,' *JBBRAS,* XII (1876), 40.

[28] Ed. T. Vidyāratna, xiv. 91.

of view this hostility may be commended, but for orthodox Hindu writers such as Rāmānuja an attack on caste was an attack on the whole divinely ordained social order *(varṇāśrama-dharma)*.

There are also limitations to this tantric rejection of caste which Rāmānuja does not choose to note. In most tantric works the denial of caste occurs only in ritual situations. In day-to-day affairs, caste distinctions are still maintained. Thus *Kulārṇava-tantra* viii.101 says: 'In this *cakra* (circle of worship) there is no division into castes. Everyone (in it) is declared to be equal with Śiva.' Elsewhere, however, this text prescribes different lengths of studentship for members of different classes. The *Mahānirvāṇa-tantra* seems to accept class divisions without qualification.[29] The transcending of caste barriers in a ritual context has little or nothing to do with rational materialist arguments. It is part of a mystical reversal and revaluation of all values, *eine Umwertung aller Werte,* valid only in the sacred circle of worship. In the supra-mundane universe of the ritual, opposites coalesce and change places—the lowest is highest and the highest lowest.[30] In relation to caste, this mystical principle culminates with the apotheosis of the *ḍombī* (washerwoman) in Kāṇhapāda's tantric Buddhist songs.[31]

Purāṇas and Other Sources

Several Purāṇas and a few other works contain lists incorporating some or all of the sects in the fourfold classification of the *Brahma-sūtra*) commentators. The following table compares the commentaries with these other sources :

Bhāskarācārya[32]	Kāpālika Kāṭhaka-siddhāntin	Pāśupata Śaiva
Vācaspati Miśra[33]	Kāpālika Kāruṇika-siddhāntin	Pāśupata Śaiva

[29]Ed. and trans. J. Woodroffe, chap. viii.

[30]See Bharati, p. 234, and M. Eliade, *Yoga: Immortality and Freedom,* p. 261.

[31]See Dasgupta, *Obscure* . . ., pp. 57, 99, 102–106.

[32]*Brahma-sūtra-bhāṣya* ii. 2. 37.

[33]*Bhāmatī* ii. 2. 37.

Yāmunācārya[34] & Rāmānuja[35]	Kāpālika Kālāmukha	Pāśupata Śaiva	
Yāmunācārya[36]	Saumya Lāguḍa	Pāśupata Śaiva	
Kūrma Purāṇa	Kāpāla[37] Nākula or Lākula	Pāśupata	Also Vāma, Bhairava & Pañcarātra
	Soma[38] Lākura or Lāñjana or Vākula	Pāśupata	Also Vāma & Bhairava
	Soma[39] Lāṅgala (Lāguḍa)	Pāśupata	Also Vāma & Bhairava
Nārādīya P.[40]	Kāpāla Mahāvrata-dhara	Pāśupata Siddhānta-mārga	
Śiva P. Vāya-viya-saṃhitā[41]	Kāpāla Mahāvrata-dhara	Pāśupata Siddhānta-mārga	
Skanda P.[42]	Kaṅkāla Kālamukha	Pāśupta Śaiva	Also Mahāvrata

[34] *Āgama-prāmāṇya*, quoted in Śrīharṣa, p. 643.

[35] *Śrī-bhāṣya* ii. 35–37.

[36] Quoted in Śrīharṣa, p. 643.

[37] Ed. N. Mukhopadhyāya, i. 16 (p. 184).

[38] ii. 12 (p. 740). Lākura is probably a mistake for Lākula.

[39] *Uparibhāga*. 37. 147, cited by Handiqui, p. 463. We do not know from which edition of the Purāṇa this reference comes. Commenting on this verse, Appaya Dīkṣita (cited ibid.) reads Lāguḍa (holding a staff) for Lāṅgala (a plough). Lāguḍa is a better reading.

[40] *Uttarakhaṇḍa*. 31. 103, cited by A.P. Karmarkar, *The Vrātya or Dravidian Systems*, p. 220.

[41] Ed. Mallikārjunaśāstrī, ii. 24. 177.

[42] *Aruṇācala-Mā*. 10. 65, cited by Karmarkar, p. 220.

Skanda P. *Sūta-saṃhitā*[43]	Kāpāla Lākula	Pāśupata	Also Soma
Svayambhu P.[44]	Soma Vā(Lā)kula	Pāśupata Śaiva	
Vāmana P.	Kāpālika[45] Kāladamana	Pāśupata Śaiva	
	Mahāvratin[46] Kālāmukha	Pāśupata Śaiva	Also Mahāpāśupata & several others
Vaśiṣṭha & *Liṅga Ps.*[47]	Soma Nākula		Also Lokāyata & Bhairava
Ānandagiri[48]		Pāśupata Śaiva	Also Ugra, Raudra, Bhaṭṭa, & Jaṃgama
Rājaśekhara[49]	Mahāvrata- dhara Kālamukha	Pāśupata Śaiva	
Śaktisaṅgama- *tantra*[50]	 Kālāmukha	Pāśupata Śaiva	Also 6 others

[43]Ed. V.S. Paṇaśīkara, *Yajñavaibhavakhaṇḍa*. 22. 3.

[44]Quoted in *Īśāna-Śivaguru-paddhati*, Pt. III, *Kriyāpada*, chap. i, cited by V.S. Pathak, *History of Śaiva Cults in Northern India from Inscriptions*, p. 3.

[45]Veṅkateśvara Press edition, vi. 87.

[46]lxvii. 10–20.

[47]In a verse attributed to these two Purāṇas by the *Tantrādhikārinirṇaya*, cited by C. Chakravarti, *Tantras*: *Studies on their Religion and Literature*, p. 51.

[48]*Śaṃkara-vijaya*, cited by Pathak, p. 4.

[49]*Ṣaḍdarśana-samuccaya*, cited by Pathak, p. 21. On p. 2. Pathak incorrectly attributes this verse to Haribhadra's *Ṣaḍdarśana-samuccaya*.

[50]Ed. B. Bhattacharya, i. 5. 92–93.

Siddha-siddhānta-paddhati[51]	Kāpālika Kālāmukha	Pāśupata Śaiva	Also Mahāvrata-dhara & 5 others
Suprabhedāgama[52]	Sauma Lākula	Pāśupata Śaiva	
Malkāpuram Stone Inscri.[53]	Śivaśāsana Kālānana	Pāśupata Śaiva	

It is evident from this table that the sects had several alternate names. The most important variants are: Lākula, Nākula and Lāguḍa for Kālāmukha; Soma and Saumya for Kāpāla; and Mahāvrata-dhara for both Kāpāla and Kālāmukha. The term *Śivaśāsana* from the Malkāpuram inscription does not necessarily refer to the Kāpālikas since this identification is based merely on an analogy with the standard fourfold division.[54] The term *Kaṅkāla* (skeleton) from the *Skanda Purāṇa* almost certainly refers to the Kāpālika sect, but the fifth item of this list, Mahāvrata, often denotes this sect also. Kālānana (blackfaced) from the Malkāpuram inscription is merely a synonym for Kālāmukha. A tenth century grant to a Kālāmukha priest at Koḍumbāḷūr (Tiruchchirappali District) similarly mentions fifty Asitavaktra (black-faced) ascetics residing at his monastery.[55] Although the literal meaning of Kāladamana (time-subduing) from the *Vāmana Purāṇa* is considerably different, it is evidently another variant of Kālāmukha and Kālānana. The originator of the Kāladamaṇa doctrine was named Kālāsya (black-faced).[56]

Most of these sources merely enumerate the sects or say that their doctrines were revealed by Śiva. A few works openly condemn

[51]Cited by Pathak, p. 26.

[52]Cited by Pathak, p. 3.

[53]*Journal of the Andhra Historical Research Society*, IV, 147, cited by Pathak, p. 3.

[54]The verse reads: 'upeyuṣām Śaiva-tapodhanānāṃ Kālānanānāṃ Śivaśāsanānām/ vidyārthināṃ Pāśupata-vratānām apy anna-vastrādi-samarpaṇāya//.' Cited by Pathak, p. 3. Some of the four terms in this verse may be adjectives rather than nouns.

[55]K.A.N. Sastri, 'The Koḍumbāḷūr Inscription of Vikrama-Kēsarī,' *JORM*, VII (1933), 9.

[56]*Vāmana Purāṇa* vi. 90.

the sects. In the *Kūrma Purāṇa* Śiva says: 'I have declared other *śāstras* which are a source of confusion in this world and are opposed to the words of the Vedas. The Vāma, Pāśupata, Soma, Lāṅgala, and Bhairava *(śāstras)* are declared to be outside the Vedas and are not to be served.'[57] Yāmunācārya is equally critical: 'Śaiva, Pāśupata, Saumya, and Lāguḍa are designated as the fourfold division of the Tantras. One should not make a mixture (of these with Vedic rites).'[58] The *Skanda Purāṇa,* however, at one point declares that only five of the twenty-eight *āgamas* lead to the path of liberation: the Kālamukha, Kaṅkāla, Śaiva, Pāśupata, and Mahāvrata.[59]

The remarks of the *Vāmana Purāṇa* vi. 86–92 are the most interesting. It states that Brahmā created four groups which worshipped Hara (Śiva) and gave them each a *śāstra*: 'The first is known as Śaiva, then Pāśupata . . ., then the third Kāladamana, and the fourth Kāpālika.' The text then gives a pseudo-historical account of the origin of each:

> Śiva himself was Śakti, the beloved son of Vasiṣṭha. Gopāyana then became his pupil . . .
>
> Mahāpāśupata was the ascetic Bharadvāja. His pupil was the king Somakeśvara . . .
>
> Lord Kālāsya was the ascetic Āpastamba. His pupil was named Krātheśvara . . .
>
> Mahāvratin was Dhanada. His pupil was the powerful Arṇodara, a great ascetic and a Śūdra by birth.

The apparent associations of teachers and doctrines are Śakti and Śaiva, Bharadvāja and Pāśupata, Āpastamba and Kāladamana (Kālāmukha), and Dhanada and Kāpālika. The reasons behind this choice of religious founders are obscure. Śakti, Bharadvāja and Āpastamba are famous sages and Dhanada is the god of wealth. None are elsewhere connected with these sects with the possible exception of Āpastamba. An incomplete record from Vēḍal in North Arcot District, Madras, mentions a Kāḷamukha Daśapuriyan of the Hārita *gotra* and the Āpastamba *sūtra*.[60] The attribution of the Kāpālika *śāstra* to Dhanada and his powerful

---

57 *Uparibhāga*. 37. 146–47, cited by Handiqui, p. 463 (my translation).

58 Cited ibid.

59 *Aruṇācala-Mā*. 10. 65, cited by Karmarkar, p. 220.

60 See V. Rangacharya, *Inscriptions of the Madras Presidency,* II, 1162.

Śūdra disciple, Arṇodara, emphasizes the worldliness and debased status of this doctrine. The four disciples—Arṇodara, Gopāyana, Somakeśvara, and Krātheśvara—cannot be identified. Śiva, Mahāpāśupata, Kālāsya, and Mahāvratin are evidently forms of Śiva.

Vāmaṇa Purāṇa lxvii. 1–40 tells of a war between Śiva, aided by his *gaṇas* and *pramathas,* and the *asuras*. Śiva's allies included the Śaivas, Pāśupatas, Kālāmukhas, Mahāvratins, Nirāśrayas, and Mahāpāśupatas. Śiva extended a special welcome to the last group because they did not recognize a distinction between him and Viṣṇu. Here the Pāśupatas and Mahāpāśupatas seem to be separate groups.

CHAPTER II

KĀPĀLIKA SOURCES

Early Sources

The earliest occurrence of the word *kapālin* (one who bears a skull) is probably that in the *Yājñavalkya-smṛti* iii. 243 (*c.* A.D. 100–300). This *sūtra* prescribes the penance for one who has killed a Brāhmaṇa, a *Brahmahan*: 'With a skull *(śiraḥ-kapālī)* and a staff (in his hands), living on alms, announcing his deed (as he begs), and eating little food, the killer of a Brāhmaṇa may be purified after twelve years.'[1] Other law books prescribe much the same penance but do not use the term *kapālin*. An important connection between this penance and the Kāpālika faith does exist,[2] but in this passage *kapālin* has the sense only of 'bearing a skull' and does not imply the existence of a sect or order of Kapālins.

In the *Maitrāyaṇīya Upaniṣad* certain Kāpālins who hypocritically wear red robes *(kaṣāya)* and earrings *(kuṇḍala)* are mentioned among persons with whom it is improper to associate.[3] This seems to denote a member of the Kāpālika sect, but the relevant passage is definitely an interpolation or appendix to the original text and may be of fairly late date.[4]

The Prakrit *Gāthā-saptaśatī* is traditionally ascribed to the first century A.D. Sātavāhana king Hāla but was probably compiled sometime in the third to fifth centuries. It contains a verse describing a 'new' female Kāpālikā who incessantly besmears herself with ashes from the funeral pyre of her lover.[5] The word 'new' *(nava)*, unless it means simply 'young', suggests that her Kāpālika vow was taken at his death. This may well be the earliest reference to the Kāpālika sect.

A Buddhist text of the early centuries of the Christian era, the

---

[1]Ed. N.R. Acharya.

[2]See below, pp. 73–82.

[3]Ed. and trans. J.A.B. van Buitenen, vii. 8.

[4]Ibid. pp. 88–89.

[5]The Sanskrit *chāyā* reads: 'jāra-śmaśāna-samudbhava-bhūti-sukha-sparśa-sveda-śilāngyāḥ/ na samāpyate nava-Kāpālikyā uddhūlanārambhaḥ//' Kāvyamālā edition, vs. 408.

Lalitavistara, mentions certain 'fools' who seek purification by smearing their bodies with ashes, wearing red garments *(kaṣāya)*, shaving their heads, and carrying a triple-staff *(tridaṇḍa)*, a pot, a skull, and a *khaṭvāṅga*.[6] These must also be Kāpālikas.

By the sixth to seventh centuries references to Kāpālika ascetics become fairly commonplace. The astronomer-mathematician Varāhamihira (*c*. 500–575) refers to the Kāpāla vow in his *Bṛhatsaṃhitā* ix. 25: 'When the chariot of Rohiṇī (an asterism) is intercepted (by Venus), the earth (becomes) decorated with hair and pieces of bone and seems to keep the Kāpāla vow, as if it had committed sin.'[7] This might refer merely to the Brahmanhan penance, but verse lxxxvii. 22 of this work seems clearly to mention Kāpālika ascetics: 'When (a tranquil omen) is in the southwest (spoke of a 'Cycle of Quarters') the arrival of a cow, a sportsman *(krīḍaka)* or a Kāpālika is indicated, and one will obtain a bull. (There will also be) black gram, horse-gram, etc. and food.'

In his *Bṛhajjātaka* xv. 1, Varāhamihira enumerates seven classes of ascetics, each born under the influence of a different heavenly body.[8] He lists them as follows: the Śākyas under Mars, Ājīvikas under Mercury, Bhikṣus under Jupiter, Vṛddhas under the moon, Carakas under Venus, Nirgranthas under Saturn, and Vanyāśanas under the sun. The tenth century commentator Utpala (or Bhaṭṭotpala) says that the Vṛddhas are also known as Vṛddha-śrāvakas or Kāpālikas.[9] Utpala also mentions a similar classification made by the fifth century Jain authority, Kālakācārya. This connects the sun with Tapasvins, the moon with Kāpālins, Mars with Raktapaṭas, Mercury with Ekadaṇḍins, Jupiter with Yatis, Venus with Carakas, and Saturn with Kṣapaṇakas.[10] Again commenting on Varāhamirhira's text, Utpala says: 'Here the word Vṛddha-śrāvaka implies the wandering ascetics who seek refuge with Maheśvara, and the word Ājīvika those who seek refuge with

[6]Ed. P.L. Vaidya, chap. xvii (p. 183).

[7]Ed. H. Kern. A slightly different version of this verse is quoted in *Pañcatantra* i. 234 (ed. N.R. Acharya). This version reads 'Kāpālika vow' in place of 'Kāpāla vow' and 'ashes and pieces of bone' in place of 'hair and pieces of bone.'

[8]Ed. and trans. V.S. Sastri. See A.L. Basham, *History and Doctrines of the Ājīvikas*, pp. 168–71.

[9]'kṣapākaraś candro yadā Vṛddhaḥ Vṛddha-śrāvakaḥ Kāpālikaḥ vṛtta-bhaṅga-bhayāc chrāvaka-śabdo 'tra lupto draṣṭavyaḥ.' Commentary on *Bṛhajjātaka* xv. 1 (1863 Bombay edition).

[10]Ibid.

Nārāyaṇa.'[11] The attribution of Nārāyaṇa worship to the Ājīvikas is a mistake. It is apparently based on an attempt to equate them with Kālakācārya's Ekadaṇḍins.[12] If the identification of Vṛddhas or Vṛddha-śrāvakas with the Kāpālikas is correct, the claim that they worshipped Maheśvara is also correct. The Vṛddha-śrāvakas are again mentioned by Varāhamihira in his *Bṛhatsaṃhitā* li. 20 : 'When a fortune-teller is consulted by persons in the sight of a [Vṛddha-śrāvaka], they do so for the sake of friends or gambling; when in the sight of a friar of decent order [*suparivrāj*], their query concerns a courtesan, king or wife in childbed.'[13] H. Kern, the translator of this verse, renders Vṛddha-śrāvaka as 'skull-wearing Śaiva monk,' presumably on the basis of a commentary. We have found no other examples of Kāpālikas being called by this name.

The famous Chinese pilgrim Hsüan Tsang gives brief accounts of the relative strengths of the various types of Buddhists and other sects in the places he visited during his South Asian travels (*c.* A.D. 630–644). In Kāpiśā, modern Nuristan in eastern Afghanistan,[14] he found over a hundred Buddhist monasteries. In addition, he says, 'there are some ten temples of the Devas, and 1000 or so of heretics *(different ways of religion)*; there are naked ascetics, and others who cover themselves with ashes, and some who make chaplets of bones, which they wear as crowns on their heads.'[15] Beal identifies these heretics as Digambara Jains, Pāśupatas, and Kapāla-dhārins, i.e. Kāpālikas.[16] Elsewhere Hsüan Tsang gives a general description of various non-Buddhist ascetics he met in India proper :

> The dress and ornaments worn by non-believers are varied and mixed. Some wear peacocks' feathers; some wear as ornaments necklaces made of skull bones . . . ; some have no clothing, but go naked . . . ; some wear leaf or bark garments; some pull out their hair and cut off their moustaches; others have bushy whiskers and their hair braided

---

[11]Ibid. The text mistakenly reads 'Māheśvara' for 'Maheśvara.'

[12]See Basham, pp. 170–74.

[13]Trans. H. Kern, *JRAS*, n.s. VI (1873), 87. Kern believes that this chapter may be spurious.

[14]See T. Watters, *On Yuan Chwang's Travels in India*, I, 123–24.

[15]S. Beal (trans.), *Chinese Accounts of India*, I, 117–18.

[16]Ibid., p. 118.

> on the top of their heads. The costume is not uniform, and the colour, whether red or white, not constant.[17]

Those ascetics who wear peacocks' feathers, go about naked, and pull out their hair are probably Jains. Those who wear skull garlands, as Beal suggests, may well be Kāpālikas. The others are not easily identified.

Hsüan Tsang visited India during the reign of Harṣa-vardhana of Sthāṇvīśvara (A.D. 606–647). This king's contemporary biographer Bāṇabhaṭṭa vividly portrays the religious life of court and kingdom in his *Harṣa-carita* and *Kādambarī*. These works show that both primitive and developed types of tantric worship were already widespread in the seventh century. The most archaic level of tantric worship is represented in *Kādambarī* by the wild Śabara tribe of the Vindhya forest whose 'one religion is offering human flesh' to Caṇḍikā[18] and whose chief had shoulders that 'were rough with scars from keen weapons often used to make an offering of blood' to Caṇḍikā.[19] The incorporation of 'Hinduised' (Eliade) or 'Sanskritised' (Srinivas) forms into the rituals of tribesmen such as these probably amounted to little more than the identification of their tutelary gods and goddesses with Hindu ones such as Bhairava, Kālī and Caṇḍikā.

Elsewhere in *Kādambarī* Bāṇa describes various religious and philanthropic acts performed by Queen Vilāsavatī of Ujjayinī in order to acquire a son:

> She slept within the temples of [Caṇḍikā], dark with the smoke of *bdellium* [*guggulu*] ceaselessly burnt, on a bed of clubs covered with green grass . . . ; she stood in the midst of a circle drawn by [great magicians[20]], in a place where four roads meet, on the fourteenth night of the dark fortnight . . . .; she honoured the shrines of the siddhas and sought the houses of neighbouring Mātṛkās . . . ; she carried about little caskets of mantras filled with birch-leaves written over in yellow letters; . . . she daily threw out lumps of flesh in the evening for the jackals; she told pandits the

[17]Trans. ibid., II, 134.

[18]Trans. C.M. Ridding, p. 31. Ed. P.V. Kane, Vol. I, text p. 21.

[19]Trans. Ridding p. 28. Ed. Kane, Vol. I, text p. 20.

[20]*mahānarendra*. Ridding's translation, 'the king himself,' is unlikely.

> wonders of her dreams, and at the cross-roads she offered oblation to Śiva.[21]

Although these rituals display a greater degree of Sanskritisation than those of the Śabara tribesmen, many of her endeavours blend tantric worship with motifs of archaic fertility magic. Crossroads, for instance, are a focal point for fertility rituals and other religious ceremonies in many parts of the world.[22]

A much more sanguinary amalgam of archaic magic and tantric ritual is described in the *Harṣa-carita*. When Harṣa's father falls ill, the populace of the capital city undertake various penances in order to avert his death :

> Young nobles were burning themselves with lamps to propitiate the Mothers [Mātṛkās]. In one place a Dravidian was ready to solicit the Vampire [Vetāla] with the offering of a skull. In another an Andhra man was holding up his arms like a rampart to conciliate Caṇḍikā. Elsewhere young servants were pacifying Mahākāla by holding melting gum [*guggulu*] on their heads. In another place a group of relatives was intent on an oblation of their own flesh, which they severed with keen knives. Elsewhere, again, young courtiers were openly resorting to the sale of human flesh.[23]

The sale of human flesh to cremation ground demons is mentioned in Bhavabhūti's *Mālati-Mādhava*, in the *Kathāsaritsāgara*, and in other Sanskrit works. Somadeva's *Yaśastilaka* (A.D. 959) mentions Mahāvratin heroes who sell human flesh cut from their own bodies.[24] The term *Mahāvratin* is normally used to denote Kāpālikas.[25] The Dravidian in the above passage who offers a skull to a Vetāla must also represent a Kāpālika or closely related type of ascetic.

A tantric ascetic from South India is described in great detail in *Kādambarī*. This *Draviḍa-dhārmika* superintends a temple of Caṇḍikā located on the road to Ujjayinī. In one spot the temple

---

[21]Trans. Ridding, pp. 55–56. Ed. Kane, Vol. I, text pp. 42–43.

[22]For a discussion of worship at the crossroads, see D.D. Kosambi, *Myth and Reality*, chap. iii. In ancient Greece Hermes was the leading god of the crossroads and also a god of fertility. See N.O. Brown, *Hermes the Thief*.

[23]Trans. E.B. Cowell and F.W. Thomas, pp. 135–36. Ed. P.V. Kane, Part II, text p. 21.

[24]See K.K. Handiqui, pp. 358–59.

[25]See below, pp. 73–82.

'displays the slaying of (animal) sacrifices . . . with heaps of skulls (that are) like fruits'.[26] The *dhārmika* is crippled and maimed as a result of foolish penances and fights with travellers and wild animals. The tantric character of his worship is emphasised in some of the following epithets :

> He had a tumor growing on his forehead that was blackened by (constantly) falling at the feet of Ambikā (the idol of Caṇḍikā) . . . He had brought on himself premature fever with improperly prepared mercurial medicines. Although old, he troubled Durgā with requests for the boon of sovereignty over the Deccan . . . He had made a collection of manuscripts of jugglery, Tantras and *mantras* (which were written) in letters of red lac on palm leaves (tinged with) smoke. He had written down the doctrine of Mahākāla, which is the ancient teaching of the Mahāpāśupatas . . . He manifested the disease of talking (continually about the nine) treasures (of Kubera) and became very windy (on the subject) of alchemy . . . He had increased his grasp on the *mantra-sādhana* for becoming invisible and knew thousands of wonderful stories about Śrīparvata . . . He had many times employed woman-subduing powders on old female ascetics from foreign countries who stayed (at the temple) . . .[27]

This remarkable passage contains one of the earliest references to Tantra manuscripts as well as to alchemy *(dhātuvāda)* and mercurial medicines for prolonging life *(rasāyana)*. *Mantra-sādhana* (performance of mantras) is a typical tantric term. These facts show that tantric worship was fully developed by Bāṇa's time and was apparently centered mainly in South India.

From our point of view the references to the teachings of the Mahāpāśupatas and to the mountain Śrīparvata are of special interest since they both tend to connect this devotee with the Kāpālikas and Kālāmukhas. We have noted that the *Vāmana Purāṇa* seems to mention Mahāpāśupata as the form of Śiva who incarnated himself as Bharadvāja for the propagation of the Pāśupata doctrine, but that elsewhere it mentions Śaivas, Pāśu-

---

[26]Ed. Kane, Vol. II, text p. 67.

[27]Ed. Kane, Vol. II, text pp. 68–69. My translation is loosely based on the renderings in Kane's English notes.

patas, Kālamukhas, Mahāvratins, Nirāśrayas, and Mahāpāśupatas, as separate groups.[28] Several other sources lend weight to the suggestion that the Mahāpāśupatas were at least partly distinct from the ordinary Pāśupatas. Handiqui points out (p. 241) that the Mahāpāśupatas are mentioned by Udayana (late tenth century) and that Varadarāja (eleventh century) and Śaṃkara Miśra (*c*. 1600) both identify them as those Pāśupatas who practised the Mahāvrata. A South Indian drama approximately contemporary with *Kādambarī*, Mahendravarman's *Mattavilāsa*, seems to address a Kāpālika as Mahāpāśupata.[29] A verse found in two Kannada inscriptions from Belgaum District dated A.D. 1148 and 1219–20 seems to identify Kālāmukhas as both Mahāpāśupatas and Mahāvratins.[30] A few other inscriptions also called Kālāmukha priests Mahāvratins. This is a source of some confusion since Kāpālikas are usually given this title, but it is likely that the Kālāmukha and Kāpālika Mahāvratas were quite different vows.[31] Since the Kālāmukhas were closely related to the ordinary Pāśupatas, we feel that it is in general best to connect the Mahāpāśupatas with the Kālāmukhas and not with the Kāpālikas or Pāśupatas. There is no evidence, however, that either the Kālāmukha or Pāśupata faiths were markedly tantric in character. For this reason it is quite possible that the Mahāpāśupata teachings written down by Bāṇa's Draviḍa-dhārmika were Kāpālika and not Kālāmukha doctrines. This would also agree with the *Mattavilāsa* reference. The conflicting claims of the Kālāmukhas, Kāpālikas and Pāśupatas to the title Mahāpāśupata cannot be completely resolved without further evidence.

Somewhat the same problem is encountered in the reference to the Draviḍa-dhārmika's wonderful stories about Śrīparvata. This famous pilgrimage site in Kurnool District, Andhra Pradesh, is the home of the Kāpālikas in Bhavabhūti's *Mālatī-Mādhava*

---

[28]See above, pp. 11–12.

[29]Ed. T.G. Śāstrī, p. 26. Trans. L.D. Barnett, *BSOS*, V (1930), 715. Barnett did not recognize the significance of the term and translated it as 'noble Pāśupata.' In so doing he assumed that it referred to the Pāśupata who appears in the play, but the context makes this unlikely.

[30]R.S. Panchamukhi (ed.), *Karnatak Inscriptions*, I, 34 and J.F. Fleet, 'A Series of Sanskrit and Old Canarese Inscriptions Relating to the Raṭṭa Chieftains of Saundatti and Beḷgaum,' *JBBRAS*, X (1871–74), 247.

[31]See below, pp. 73–82.

but is mentioned in eleventh century inscriptions as a Kālāmukha shrine.[32]

Bāṇa gives a more sympathetic portrait of a Śaivite ascetic in his *Harṣa-carita*. Bhairavācārya, the saint who befriended Harṣa's ancestor Puṣpabhūti, was also from South India *(dākṣiṇatya)* and also performed a tantric ritual appropriate for a Kāpālika. One of his three disciples, Karṇatāla, was a *Drāviḍa* and another, Tīṭibha, carried a skull begging bowl *(bhikṣā-kāpālika)* in a box made of *kharjūra* wood.[33] Bhairavācārya's name indicates that he worshipped Śiva as Bhairava, the form of the god held in especial esteem by tantric groups such as the Kāpālikas. Bāṇa introduces him as the 'great Śaiva saint named Bhairavācārya, almost a second overthrower of Dakṣa's sacrifice, who belonged to the Deckan [*sic*], but whose powers, made famous by his excellence in multifarious sciences, were, like his many thousands of disciples, spread abroad over the whole sphere of humanity.'[34]

The word here translated as 'great Śaiva saint' *(mahāśaiva)* does not seem to denote a specific sect or ascetic order. It is simply a descriptive term showing his strong devotion to Śiva. The original overthrower of Dakṣa's sacrifice was Śiva himself. In at least one source, the *Vāmana-Purāṇa,* Dakṣa is said to have refused to invite Śiva to his sacrifice because the god had become a Kapālin after cutting off the fifth head of Brahmā.[35] Śiva-Kapālin or Kapāleśvara is the divine archetype of the Kāpālika ascetic.[36]

When King Puṣpabhūti, a devout worshipper of Śiva *(parama-māheśvara)*, learned of this great saint Bhairavācārya, he expressed a desire to pay him homage. A meeting was arranged and Puṣpabhūti went to see him in a Bilva tree plantation near an old temple of the Mothers (Mātṛs). The description of the saint which follows is too long to quote in full, but a few of its more interesting features should be noted.[37] Puṣpabhūti saw Bhairavācārya 'seated on a

---

[32]See below, pp. 50–51.

[33]Ed. Kane, Part I, text p. 46.

[34]Trans. Cowell and Thomas, p. 85. Ed. Kane, Part I, text p. 45.

[35]ii. 17 to iv. 1. In Somadeva's *Kathāsaritsāgara* i. 1. 23 ff. (ed. Durgaprasād and K.P. Parab), Śiva is not invited because he wears a necklace of skulls. Similar explanations are given in the *Padma* and *Bhāgavata Purāṇas*. See *Viṣṇu Purāṇa,* H.H. Wilson (trans.), pp. 55–56.

[36]See below, pp. 77–81.

[37]The translations are from Cowell and Thomas, pp. 263–65. The text is edited by Kane, Part I, text pp. 46–47.

tiger-skin, which was stretched on ground smeared with green cow-dung, and whose outline was marked by a boundary ridge of ashes.' The flashing luster of his body was like red arsenic paste 'purchased by the sale of human flesh.' His hair was twisted together *(jaṭī-kṛta)* in ascetic fashion and was festooned with rosary beads *(rudrākṣa)* and shells. He had a 'slanting forehead-mark, made with ashes.' His lip hung down a bit 'as if overweighted by the whole Śaivite canon [*Śaiva-saṃhitā*] resting on the tip of his tongue.' He wore a pair of crystal earrings *(sphāṭika-kuṇḍala)* and 'upon one forearm, having an iron bracelet and bound with the line of charm-thread [*mantra-sūtra*] of various herbs, ... a bit of shell like one of Pūṣan's teeth broken by holy Śiva.'[38] He revolved a rosary in his right hand like a water wheel. He had a thick beard and wore a loincloth *(kaupīna)* and ascetic's shawl *(yoga-paṭṭaka)*. 'Constant at his side was a bamboo staff[39] with a barb of iron inserted in the end' which was like the goad for driving away Gaṇeśa. He had observed the vow of celibacy since childhood.[40] 'Supreme in austerities' and 'surpassing in wisdom,' he was 'like Kailāsa, having his head purified by the dust of Paśupati's feet; like Śiva's heaven, the resort of Māheśvara throngs.'

One day Bhairavācārya asked the king to assist him in the completion of the powerful spell *(mahāmantra)* called Mahākāla-hṛdaya. He had previously begun its performance in the great cemetery 'by a crore of muttered prayers ... in garlands, clothes, and unguents all of black as enjoined in the Kalpa.' The object was to subdue a Vetāla. The king agreed to help and duly arrived at 'the empty house near the great cemetery ... on the approaching fourteenth night of the dark fortnight':[41]

> In the centre of a great circle of ashes white as lotus pollen Bhairavācārya could be seen ... Seated on the breast of a corpse which lay supine anointed with red sandal and arrayed in garlands, clothes and ornaments all of red, himself with a black turban, black unguents, black amulet [*pratisara*], and black garments, he had begun a fire rite [*agnikārya*] in the corpse's mouth, where a flame was burning.

---

[38]Pūṣan lost his tooth during the destruction of Dakṣa's sacrifice.

[39]*vaiṇavena viśākhikādaṇḍena*. The meaning of *viśākhikā* is unclear.

[40]*kumāra-brahmacāriṇam*. Cowell and Thomas incorrectly translate this as 'chaste as a boy.'

[41]Trans. Cowell and Thomas, pp. 90–91. Ed. Kane, Part I, text pp. 49–50.

> As he offered some black sesamum seeds, it seemed as though in eagerness to become a Vidyādhara he were annihilating the atoms of defilement which caused his mortal condition.[42]

As he muttered the syllables of his charms, his three disciples and the king stationed themselves about him in the four quarters. Suddenly a spirit *(puruṣa)* rose up from a chasm in the earth. This spirit, the Nāga Śrīkaṇṭha, attacked the king and Bhairavācārya's three disciples. The king used the sword Aṭṭahāsa given to him by Bhairavācārya to fell this Nāga. The king refrained from administering the final blow, however, because the spirit wore a sacred thread. Lakṣmī rewarded the king for his piety with the promise that he would become the founder of a mighty line of kings. Having completed the rite, Bhairavācārya acquired 'the hair-lock, diadem, earring, necklace, armlet, girdle, hammer, and sword' and became a Vidyādhara.[43]

The powerful spell called Mahākāla-hṛdaya (Heart of Mahākāla-Śiva) is not mentioned elsewhere in Sanskrit literature to our knowledge. From the vividness of his description, however, it seems certain that Bāṇa had some real ceremony in mind. Most remarkable is the fact that Bāṇa portrays Bhairavācārya sympathetically. He is not a wicked magician but a worthy ascetic and a friend and confidant of the founder of the house of Bāṇa's patron. From this fact we can only infer that by the seventh century tantric religion, even of the so-called 'left-hand observance' *(vāmācāra)* type, was accepted and supported by many persons of learning and high social status. As a corollary to this, it must also be assumed that the behaviour of most of these ascetics was considerably more circumspect than their critics would have us believe. Two epigraphs from western India show that even the Kāpālikas had at least some official support in the early mediaeval period.[44] Another indication of public support for this sect is found in Bhavabhūti's *Mālatī-Mādhava*. Although the two major villains of the play are Kāpālikas, one of the heroes, the *yoginī* Saudāminī, is also said to observe the vow of a Kāpālika.[45]

A wicked counterpart to Bāṇa's Bhairavācārya appears in Daṇḍin's *Daśakumāra-carita* (seventh century).[46] Prince Mantra-

---

[42]Trans. Cowell and Thomas, p. 92. Ed. Kane, Part I, text p. 51.

[43]Trans. Cowell and Thomas, pp. 93–97. Ed. Kane, Part I, text pp. 51–54.

[44]See below, pp. 27–31.

[45]Ed. and trans. C.R. Devadhar and N.G. Suru, Act I, after vs. 15.

[46]Ed. and trans. V. Satakopan, V. Anantacharya, and N. Bhaktavatsalam.

gupta, one of the ten princes of the title, met this evil ascetic in a forest near the cremation ground outside of the capital of Kaliṅga. The prince overheard a servant couple complaining that their master, a black magician *(dagdha-siddha)*, gave them no time to enjoy each other's company. They called out for someone to be an 'obstacle to the magical power of this vile wizard.'[47] Prince Mantragupta followed them in order to discover who was this *siddha* and what was his *siddhi*. After going a short way the prince saw him. His body was decorated with ornaments made of pieces of human bones and smeared with ashes; his hair, matted in ascetic fashion *(jaṭā)*, shone like lightning; and with his left hand he continually threw crackling sesame and mustard seeds into a fire. The magician ordered his servant to fetch Kanakalekhā, the daughter of the king of Kaliṅga. When the servant had done this, the magician attempted to decapitate the princess with his sword. Mantragupta rushed forth, seized the sword, and decapitated the magician instead.[48] This story may have been the basis for the similar Kāpālika episode in Bhavabhūti's *Mālatī-Mādhava*.[49]

Several sources attest to the early presence of Kāpālikas and similar tantric ascetics in South India. We have already noted the references in Bāṇa's works and the association of Kāpālikas with Śrīparvata in *Mālatī-Mādhava*. The most important South Indian source is the *Mattavilāsa*. This one act farce *(prahasana)* was composed by the Pallava king Mahendravarman, who ruled at Kāñcī between about A.D. 600 and 630. The leading character in the drama is a Kapālin ascetic who lives at the temple of Ekāmbiranātha near the capital. We will discuss this work in more detail below.[50] A contemporary of Mahendravarman, the Śaivite *nāyaṉār* Appar, refers to Śaivas, Pāśupatas and Kāpālikas in his vernacular songs.[51] The Kapālīśvara temple at Mylapore, a suburb of Madras is the subject of a song by Sambandar (*c.* A.D. 644–660), another of the *nāyaṉārs*.[52] The sixth or seventh century Tamil epic *Maṇimekalai*

47'asyāṇaka-narendrasya . . . siddhy-antarāyaḥ.' Ed. ibid., text pp. 213–14.

48Ibid., text pp. 213–15.

49See below, pp. 56–57.

50See below, pp. 54–55.

51See M.A.D. Rangaswamy, *The Religion and Philosophy of Tēvāram,* Book I, p. 392.

52*Tēvāram* ii. 183, cited by T.V. Mahalingam, 'The Pāśupatas in South India,' *JIH,* XXVII (1949), 47.

contains another brief reference to Kāpālika ascetics.[53]

Kāpālikas are mentioned disparagingly in several Purāṇas. Although it is impossible to date these composite texts accurately, some of them—such as the *Brahmāṇḍa, Vāyu* and *Matsya*—date back to the third to seventh centuries A.D. The *Vāyu, Brahmāṇḍa* and *Kūrma Purāṇas* assert that when the *Kali-yuga* is in full sway Kāṣāyins, Nirgranthas, Kāpālikas, Veda sellers, *tīrtha* sellers, and other heretics opposed to *varṇāsrama-dharma* will arise.[54] *Brahmāṇḍa* ii. 29. 116–17 claims that Svayambhū (Śiva) created Pāśupata Yoga first and Kāpāla Yoga last. The *Skanda Purāṇa* prescribes, as part of the worship of the goddess Parameśvarī, the distribution of pots of wine *(surāsava)* to Kāpālikas and male and female slaves.[55]

Kāpālika Epigraphy

The epigraphical sources regarding the Kāpālikas are very few. Only two inscriptions register donations to Mahāvratin ascetics who are fairly certain to have been Kāpālikas. The term Kāpālika itself, however, appears in three inscriptions from southern Mysore State dedicated to their arch rivals, the Jains. Two are from famous Shravan Belgola and one from Tirumakūḍal-Narsipur Taluk in Mysore District. The earliest is from the former site and records the death by the Jain rite of *sallekhanā* (fast unto death) of the Western Gaṅga king Mārasiṃha III (A.D. 960–974).[56] It is written in Sanskrit and Old Kannada. The author compares Mārasiṃha to Śiva, Lord of the Kāpālikas :

> Famous was the glory of Maṇḍalika-Triṇetra (a Triṇetra or Śiva among the *maṇḍalikas* or chieftains) as if to make the . . . Kāpālikas arrange in a string all the newly cut off heads of the Pallavas and firmly proclaim to hostile chieftains—'Aho! Do not allow your newly cut off heads to be added to this string; have audience and live happily in the ranks of his servants.'[57]

[53]vi. 86, cited by K.A.N. Sastri, *The Cōḷas*, p. 94. See S.K. Aiyangar, *Maṇimēkhalai in its Historical Setting*, p. 126.

[54]*Vāyu Purāṇa*, Ānandāśrama edition, lviii. 64–65; *Brahmāṇḍa Purāṇa*, Veṅkateśvara Press edition, ii. 31. 64–66; and *Kūrma Purāṇa* i. 30 (p. 304). Kāpālins are included among the denizens of the *Kali-yuga* in *Matsya Purāṇa* (Ānandāśrama edition, cxliv. 40).

[55]Veṅkaṭeśvara Press edition, *Prabhāsakhaṇḍa*. 87. 51–52.

[56]Ed. and trans. R. Narasimhachar, *EC*, Vol. II (rev. ed.), no. 59. Also Ed. and trans. J.F. Fleet, Sravana Belgola Epitaph of Mārasiṃha II, *EI*, V (1898–99), 151–80.

[57]Trans. Narasimhachar. The text is in Kannada.

The evident intent of this remarkable passage is to show the king's ferocity against his traditional enemies, the Pallavas. It does not necessarily imply any sympathy with Śaivism. The Kāpālikas seem to be either religious mercenaries or simply battlefield scavengers. The possibility that they were militant religious mercenaries is strengthened by the description of a warlike Kāpālika band in Mādhavācārya's *Śaṃkara-digvijaya*.[58] The strings on which the Kāpālikas of the inscription arrange the heads of the king's Pallava enemies are apparently the traditional skull garlands of these ascetics.

The other two inscriptions, both written in Sanskrit, date from the twelfth century. The Shravan Belgola record commemorates the death by *sallekhanā* of the Jain preceptor Malliṣeṇa-Maladhārideva in A.D. 1129.[59] The inscription from Tirumakūḍal-Narsipur Taluk, dated A.D. 1183, commemorates the death in the same manner of a preceptor named Candraprabha.[60] Both records give a lengthy priestly genealogy of the teachers whose deaths they honor. The genealogies show that both preceptors belonged to the same priestly line. Malliṣeṇa's name does not appear in the later record, however, unless it has been defaced. Both records quote a verse about an earlier teacher named Vimalacandra who hung up a letter—presumably a polemic document of some kind—addressed to the Kāpālikas and other opponents :

> To the gate of the spacious palace of Śatrubhayaṃkara which is constantly thronged with passing troops of horses and numbers of mighty elephants of various kings, the high-minded Āśāmbara (*i.e.* Digambara) Vimalacandra eagerly affixed a letter (addressed) to the Śaivas, the Pāśupatas, the sons of Tathāgata (*i.e.* Buddha), the Kāpālikas, (and) the Kāpilas.[61]

Śatrubhayaṃkara, if this is a proper name, cannot be identified. Consequently, the date of Vimalacandra is uncertain. To add to the difficulties, the list of teachers 'is not a connected and complete account, and cannot even be proved to be in strict chronological

[58]See below, pp. 39–46.

[59]Ed. and trans. R. Narasimhachar, *EC*, Vol. II (rev. ed.), no. 67. Also ed. and trans. E. Hultzsch, 'Sravana Belgola Epitaph of Mallishena,' *EI*, III (1894–95), 184–207.

[60]Ed. and trans. B.L. Rice, *EC*, III, no. TN. 105.

[61]Trans. Hultzsch, *EI*, III, vs. 26.

order.'[62] For the most part, however, the list does seem to be in order since a few of the teachers can be dated. Vimalacandra is the nineteenth of forty teachers named in the Mallisena epitaph. The *Pārśvanātha-carita,* composed by Vādirāja in A.D. 1025, says that Vimalacandra was the disciple of Matisāgara, who was the disciple of Śrīpāla of Siṃhapura.[63] In the epitaph list, however, the eighteenth teacher is one Puṣpasena, who was a contemporary of number seventeen, Akalaṅka. Three verses which Akalaṅka addressed to a king named Sāhasatuṅga are quoted. In the last verse he claims that 'in the court of the shrewd king Himaśītala, I overcome all the crowds of Bauddhas.'[64] Akalaṅka's exploits are described in other Jain works such as the *Rājāvali-kathe,* the *Akalaṅka-carita,* the *Akalaṅka-stotra,* and Jinasena's *Ādipurāṇa.*[65] These works identify Himaśītala's capital as Kāñcī. According to the *Akalaṅka-carita,* Akalaṅka defeated the Buddhists in year 700 of an era referred to as Vikramārka-Śakābdīya.[66] This obscure term might denote either the Vikrama or Śaka eras. If the latter—the era most often used in the region—the date would be equivalent to A.D. 777–78. If the former, it would be A.D. 642–43. Another work dates his victory sometime after the year Śālivāhana-Śaka 710 during the reign of 'Himasitala-mahārāja.'[67] This is equivalent to A.D. 787–88. B.L. Rice claims that 'the Jains have for the date [of Akalaṅka's victory] the memorial sentence *sapta-śailādra* which gives 777 Śaka = 855 A.D.'[68] This chronogram is probably merely a mystical number. If the suggested date for Jinasena's *Ādipurāṇa* (between A.D. 782 and 838)[69] is correct, A.D. 855 is too late for Akalaṅka. The Pallavas ruled at Kāñcī during the eighth century, but none of their kings was called Himaśītala. Nonetheless it is best to place Akalaṅka in this period. The king named Sāhasatuṅga to whom Akalaṅka made his claim might then be the Rāṣṭrakūṭa king Dantidurga (*c.* A.D. 733–758).[70] If Vimalacandra came not long after Akalaṅka, he must have lived in about the first half

[62] Ibid., p. 185.
[63] Narasimhachar, *EC,* II (rev, ed,), intro. p. 84.
[64] Trans. ibid., no. 67.
[65] See Hultzsch, *EI,* III, 187.
[66] See Narasimhachar, *EC,* II (rev. ed.), intro. p. 84.
[67] W. Taylor, *Catalogue,* III, 436f., cited by Hultzsch, *EI,* III, 187.
[68] *EC,* II, intro, p. 45.
[69] Hultzsch, *EI,* III, 187.
[70] See B.A. Saletore, *Mediaeval Jainism,* pp. 34–37.

of the ninth century. Teacher number 21 in the Malliṣeṇa list, Paravādimalla, is said to have spoken in the presence of a king named Kṛṣṇarāja. This might be the Rāṣṭrakūṭa king Kṛṣṇa II, who ruled between A.D. 877 and 913.[71]

The three inscriptions thus indicate that Kāpālikas were present in southern Mysore during the ninth and tenth centuries. This helps to give credence to the legend of Śaṃkarācārya's encounter with some of these ascetics in the Karṇāṭa region.[72] We know from Mahendravarman's *Mattavilāsa* that Kāpālikas already existed elsewhere in South India at the beginning of the seventh century.[73]

The two grants which register donations to Mahāvratin ascetics who must have been Kāpālikas are from western India. Both connect these ascetics with the god Śiva in his Kapālin or Kāpāleśvara form. The earlier grant is a copper plate issued by the early Cālukya Nāgavardhana, son of Jayasiṃha and nephew of Pulakeśin II, sometime about the middle of the seventh century.[74] It was found in the possession of a resident of Nirpaṇ near Igatpuri in Nasik District. Nāgavardhana informed all present and future kings :

> Be it known to you that . . . the village of Balegrāma, which lies in the district of Goparāṣṭra, has been given by us, at the request of Balāmma-Ṭhakkura, . . . for the purpose of the (rite called) Guggula-pūjā of the temple of (the god) Kāpāleśvara, and . . . to the great ascetics [Mahāvratins] who reside at that (temple).[75]

Balegrāma has been identified as modern Belgaum-Tarāḷhā about twelve miles north-east of Igatpuri.[76] The fact that the god is called Kāpāleśvara (Lord of the Kāpālas) and not Kapāḷeśvara (Lord of the Skull) helps to confirm that the Mahāvratins of the temple were Kāpālikas. The term Guggula-pūjā probably denotes the penance of placing hot or burning *guggula* (bdellium, a fragrant gum) on one's head. We have noted how the subjects of Harṣa's

---

71See Rice, *EC,* II, intro. p. 47.

72See below, p. 43.

73See above, p. 23.

74Ed. and trans. J.F. Fleet, 'Sanskrit and Old Canarese Inscriptions,' *IA,* IX (1880), 123–25. Also ed. and trans. R.G. Bhandarkar, 'A Revised Transcript and Translation of a Chālukya Copper-plate Grant,' *JBBRAS,* XIV (1878–80), 16–28.

75Trans. Fleet, *IA,* IX, 125.

76Ibid., 123.

father performed this penance to avert his death.[77] Bhairavācārya, the priest of Harṣa's ancestor Puṣpabhūti, also practised it.[78] In Somadeva's *Yaśastilaka* a temple of Caṇḍamārī is said to contain devotees who were burning *guggula* on their heads and also Mahāvratikas who were selling flesh cut from their own bodies.[79]

The second Kāpālika grant, another copper plate, was found in the bed of the Narmadā at Tilakwādā in Baroda District.[80] It registers the gift of a village named Viluhaja for a temple of Śrīghaṇṭeśvara and was issued from the temple of Maṇeśvara at the confluence of the Maṇā and Narmadā rivers. The donation was made in A.D. 1047 by a feudatory or officer of the Paramāra king Bhoja. The donee was 'the *muni* named Dinakara, a Mahāvratadhara who was like the Kapālin, Śaṃkara, in bodily form.'[81] We know that Kāpālikas continued to exist in Gujarat until at least the twelfth century from the *Moharājaparājaya* of Yaśaḥpāla.[82]

Several inscriptions from various other parts of India mention Kapāleśvara temples, but none of these temples are said to contain Mahāvratin or Kāpālika ascetics. A copper plate grant of the *mahāsāmanta* and *mahārāja* Samudrasena, found in Nirmaṇḍ village in Kāṅgara District of Himachal Pradesh, records the donation of a village to a group of *Atharva Veda* Brāhmaṇas in Nirmaṇḍa *agrahāra*.[83] The gift was to support worship of Śiva in the form of Mihireśvara at a temple dedicated to Kapāleśvara. A king named Śarvavarman is said to have given land 'at the former installation of the god Kapāleśvara.' Fleet could not identify any of these kings but guessed that the grant belongs roughly to about the seventh century A.D. E.A. Pires has suggested that Śarvavarman might be identical with the Maukhari king of this name who ruled *c.* A.D. 576–580.[84] If the *Atharva Veda* Brāhmaṇas were in fact Kāpālikas, it would appear that the sect claimed to follow this Veda. Many Śaivite Tantras trace their authority to it.[85]

---

[77]See above, p. 17.

[78]Ed. Kane, Part I, text p. 46.

[79]See K.K. Handiqui, pp. 22, 358.

[80]Ed. and trans. J.S. Kudalkar, 'A Note on Tilakwādā Copper-plate of the Time of King Bhoja Paramāra of Mālwā,' in All India Oriental Conference, *Proceedings and Transactions of* 1*st Session, Poona,* 1919, II, 319–326.

[81]Ibid., p. 324 (my translation).

[82]See below, p. 52.

[83]Ed. and trans. J.F. Fleet, *CII,* III, 286–91.

[84]*The Maukharis,* p. 91.

[85]See Chakravarti, pp. 10–14.

A Kannada inscription from Lakkunda village in Hassan District, Mysore, records the establishment of an image of Vāsantikādevī by a certain Mallideva who was an 'ornament to the Brahman family, *brahmādhirāya,* (and) *mūliga* of Kapāleśvara-devaru of Nekunda [=Lakkunda] in Nedunāḍ.'[86] The inscription is dated Śaka 777, but the paleography is typical of the tenth century.

An inscription from a modern temple of Kavāljī (Kapālin) in former Kotah principality of Rajasthan contains an introductory verse to Gaṇeśa and Kapālīśvara.[87] The record is dated A.D. 1288 during the reign of Hammīra, a Cāhamāna king of Ranthambhor. The half verse in praise of Kapālīśvara, written in corrupt Sanskrit, shows that the god had special powers over disfiguring diseases :

> May the god Kapālīśvara through compassion manifest that which is desired of (i.e. by) men and destroy the pain of bodies spoilt by leprosy, elephantiasis, and cutaneous eruptions.[88]

Three thirteenth century inscriptions from the Kavileśvara temple at Ambale in Mysore District contain dedications to Kapāleśvara.[89] The Huzur Treasury Plates from a Viṣṇu temple at Tiruvalla, or Tiruvallavāḷ, a *taluk* centre in Kerala, mention a village called Kapālimaṅgalam and a temple of Kāpālīśvara at another village named Veḷūr.[90] A record of about A.D. 1100 from the former Bastar State refers to a village called Kapālika.[91]

The most famous Kapāleśvara temple is located at Mylapore, a suburb of Madras. The seventh century Śaivite saint Tiruñānasambandar is said to have revived at this place a dead girl whose bones had been kept in a pot by her father.[92] The present temple is of comparatively recent construction.

A holy place especially associated with the purāṇic myth of Śiva-Kapālin, or Kapāleśvara, is the Kapālamocana *tīrtha* on the

---

86Ed. in *ARMAD* 1940, pp. 145–46.

87Ed. R.R. Haldar, 'Inscription of the Time of Hammir of Ranthambhor, dated (V.S.) 1345,' *EI,* XIX, 45–52.

88'dadru-ślīpada-kuṣṭha-duṣṭa-vapu[ṣ]ām ā[dh]i[ṃ] vini[gh] na[nn]ṛṇāṃ kāruṇyena samīhitaṃ vitanutāṃ [de]vaḥ Kapālīśvaraḥ.' Ed. ibid., p. 49.

89Ed. and trans. B.L. Rice, *EC,* IV, Part II, nos. Yl. 6, 7 and 8.

90Ed. T.A.G. Rao, 'The Huzur Treasury Plates Belonging to the Vishṇu Temple at Tiruvalla,' *TAS,* II, 156 and 142.

91Ed. R.B.H. Lal, 'Kuruspāl Stone Inscription of Someśvaradeva,' *EI,* X, 25–31.

92See V. Venkayya, 'Triplicane Inscription of Dantivarman,' *EI,* VIII, 290.

Ganges at Varanasi. It was here that Śiva was released from his curse and allowed to abandon his skull begging bowl.[93] A copper plate grant of the Gāhaḍavāla king Govinda-candra (A.D. 1114–54) states that the king bathed at this place and then donated a village to a Brāhmaṇa named Vyāsa.[94]

K.C. Panigrahi argues that the well-known Vaitāl temple in Bhubaneshwar, Orissa, was originally a Kāpālika shrine.[95] This temple, built in about the eighth century, has Cāmuṇḍā as its presiding deity. In all likelihood it was originally named after this goddess. The *Svarṇṇādri-mahodaya* states that 'the venerable goddess Cāmuṇḍā garlanded with skulls exists at a spot on the west not far from the tank . . . ,' and that 'she is of terrific form and is known as Kāpālinī.'[96] This must refer to the Vaitāl temple. Although this solitary reference to Cāmuṇḍā as Kāpālinī cannot be taken as conclusive evidence of Kāpālika worship, other features of the temple—such as the fierce deities sculptured around the inner shrine and a panel of erotic couples between the walls and roof—at least indicate tantric influence.

Another temple which may have been associated at one time with the Kāpālikas is the famous Paśupati temple near Kathmandu in Nepal. An inscription from this temple, written in Sanskrit and belonging to the reign of King Jiṣṇugupta (*c.* A.D. 630), records a gift to 'Vārāhasvāmin, Dharma . . . and to the Somakhaḍḍukas in the congregation of the Muṇḍaśṛṅkhalika-Pāśupatācārya . . .'[97] The term *Muṇḍaśṛṅkhalika* (Wearing a Chain of Heads) is more appropriate for a Kāpālika than a Pāśupata. The term *Somakhaḍḍuka* (Wearing Moon Bracelets) is unique but reminds one of *Soma-siddhānta,* the name of the Kāpālika doctrine.[98]

Sculptures of the god Kapāleśvara or Kapāla-Bhairava and the goddess Kāpālikā or Kapāla-Bhairavī are found in many early medieval temples, particularly in South India.[99] Neither the

---

93See below, pp. 77–80.

94Ed. F. Kielhorn, 'Twenty-one Copper-plates of the Kings of Kanauj; (Vikrama-) Samvat 1171–1233,' *EI,* IV, 97–129. (plate no. H).

95*Archaeological Remains at Bhubaneswar,* pp. 61, 233–34.

96Quoted ibid., p. 233.

97Ed. and trans. B. Indraji and G. Bühler, 'Inscriptions from Nepal,' *IA,* IX (1880), 174.

98See below, pp. 82–83.

99See *ARMAD* 1930, pp. 20, 46; *ARMAD* 1932, p. 11; *ARMAD* 1933, pp. 46–47, 95; *ARMAD* 1934, p. 41; *ARMAD* 1935, pp. 44–45, 48; *ARMAD* 1936, p. 32;

presence of such sculpture nor even the dedication of an entire temple to Kapāleśvara is proof of Kāpālika influence, but the copper plate grants from Nasik and Baroda districts show that at least some Kapāleśvara temples were at one time staffed by these ascetics.

Śaṃkarācārya and the Kāpālikas

Some of the most valuable material about the Kāpālikas appears in the legendary biographies of the great Śaṃkarācārya (*c.* A.D. 788–820). The most important, and probably the earliest, of the extant biographies are the *Śaṃkara-vijaya,* attributed to his disciple Ānandagiri,[100] and the *Śaṃkara-digvijaya,* attributed to the famous Vijayanagar sage Mādhavācārya alias Vidyāraṇya.[101] Dhanapatisūri's *Ḍiṇḍima* commentary on the latter work adds some extra detail but is mainly extracted from Ānandagiri's account. A significantly different version of one of the legends is contained in a Kānphaṭā work, the *Gorakṣa-siddhānta-saṃgraha.*[102] None of these sources can lay much claim to historical accuracy. They are collections of stories handed down, embellished and invented during several centuries between the great theologian's death and their final redaction. Most modern authorities agree that the author of the *Śaṃkara-vijaya* was not Śaṃkara's disciple Ānandagiri but an obscure author of about the fifteenth century. Many scholars also believe that the author of the *Śaṃkara-digvijaya* was not Mādhavācārya, the Vijayanagar *rājaguru,* but a later author who wrote under his name.[103] Śaṃkara's disciple could not have written the *Śaṃkara-vijaya,* but we can see no significant objection to Mādhava-Vidyāraṇya being the author of the *Śaṃkara-digvijaya,* particularly since the quality of its Sanskrit verse is excellent.

ARMAD 1937, pp. 3, 45, 58; *ARMAD* 1938, p. 5; *ARMAD* 1939, pp. 55, 57, 72; *ARMAD* 1940, p. 34; *ARMAD* 1945, p. 33.

[100]Ed. J. Tarkapanchānana.

[101]Ed. with Dhanapatisūri's *Ḍiṇḍima* commentary, Ānandāśrama edition. There are several other such biographies of Śaṃkara but they are mostly inferior and of later date. Few have been published so far. One which has, the *Śaṃkara-vijaya* of Vyāsācala (ed. T. Chandrasekharan), borrows most of its verses from Mādhava, often rearranging them in illogical order.

[102]Ed. G.N. Kavirāja. The work is ascribed to Gorakhnāth but is a collection of essays and stories by various later authors.

[103]Sarkar, *A History of Dasnami Naga Sanyasis* [*sic*], p. 20. G.S. Ghurye (*Indian Sadhus,* pp. 82–83) accepts Mādhava-Vidyāraṇya's authorship and places the *Śaṃkara-vijaya* Ānandagiri in the eleventh to twelfth centuries.

The *Ḍiṇḍima* commentary must be later than both these works. The *Gorakṣa-siddhānta-saṃgraha* (henceforth *GSS*) dates from sometime in the later mediaeval period.

There are three separate legends. The first of these, the story of Śaṃkara's encounter with a treacherous Kāpālika named Ugra-Bhairava, appears in Mādhava's work and in the *GSS*; the second, Śaṃkara's battle with the militant Krakaca of Karṇāṭaka, appears in the works of Mādhava and Ānandagiri; and the third, Śaṃkara's debate with the casteless hedonist Unmatta-Bhairava, appears in Ānandagiri and is repeated in similar wording by Dhanapatisūri.

Śaṃkara and Ugra-Bhairava

Śaṃkara's meeting with Ugra-Bhairava seems to have occurred somewhere along the Krishna River, perhaps at a spot near Śrīśaila (=Śrīparvata).[104] Mādhavācārya begins his tale (xi. 1–2) :

> Once a certain Kāpālika there, who hid his own wickedness by adopting the disguise of a *sādhu* like Paulastya (=Rāvaṇa, in the abduction of Sītā) and had not yet completed what he had set out to accomplish, saw the *muni* (Śaṃkara) whose magical power *(māyā)* was limitless.

Thinking that his own ambition was as good as achieved, Ugra-Bhairava approached Śaṃkara and greeted him with fulsome praise. The Kāpālika then explained what he had 'set out to accomplish' (xi. 9–12) :

> I will endeavour to please Kapālin (Śiva) and thereby achieve my own object.
>
> I gratified Ugra (Śiva) with arduous and severe penances for a full one-hundred years in order to go to Kailāsa with this body to sport with Īśa (Śiva).
>
> Pleased, Giriśa (Śiva) said to me: 'You will attain the (ultimate) goal which men desire if, for the sake of pleasing me, you sacrifice in the sacrificial fire either the head of an omniscient sage or the head of a king.'

---

[104]The location is not explicitly stated. In the previous *sarga,* however, Śaṃkara is said to have been travelling along this river from Śrīśaila. The Kāpālika's name is not mentioned in Mādhava's text but appears in the commentary and in the *GSS.*

> Having said this, Maheśa hid himself. From that time on I have wandered about, my hope fixed on obtaining that, but I have not yet found a (willing) king nor a (willing) omniscient sage.

There is little doubt who he had in mind.

In order to persuade Śaṃkara to accede to his implicit demand, Ugra-Bhairava then extolled the great benefits of self-sacrifice (xi. 13–16):

> By good fortune I have now seen you, an omniscient sage, travelling about for the welfare of the world. Soon the rest (of my object) will be accomplished, for the bondage of men has its termination in correct vision *(saṃdarśanānta)*.
>
> The skull of an anointed king or a lord of *munis* is the prerequisite for my success *(siddhi)*. The former, however, I cannot even conceive of (obtaining). Therefore, it is up to you.
>
> In offering your head you will acquire wondrous fame in the world, and I will acquire success *(siddhi)*. After meditating on the transience of the body, O Best of Men, you should do what is propitious.
>
> I cannot dare to ask (*lit.,* my mind cannot ask) for that. Who will (willingly) abandon his own body, the fulfiller of desires? (But) you are indifferent (to worldly desires) and care nothing for the body. (You have) assumed your own body (only) for the benefit of others.

Here he even attempts to turn Śaṃkara's own Vedāntic doctrines against him.

Ugra-Bhairava then compared himself, with specious modesty, to those men who are ignorant of the pain of others and think only of their own ends. Such men, he said, are like Indra, who stole a bone from the sage Dadhyañc to use as an axe to slay the ninety-nine Vṛtras. Men like Dadhyañc, who abandon their transient bodies for the sake of others, acquire an immutable body of fame *(yaśaḥ-śarira)*. Their priceless virtues delight all mankind. After several more verses in the same vein, Ugra-Bhairava finally made his request (xi. 24): 'You should bestow (your) head (on me). O Lord, homage to you!' Śaṃkara was apparently moved by the Kāpālika's plea and agreed to grant him his desire. 'What true sage,' said Śaṃkara (xi. 25), 'who knows the human body here in this world (to be subject to) decay, would not fulfill the request of a supplicant?' Śaṃkara had to abide by the principles of his theology. Since the soul *(ātman)* is the only ultimate reality, it matters little what becomes of the body. It is merely the creation of *māyā*. Realizing that his pupils would never allow such idealistic foolhardiness, however, Śaṃkara advised Ugra-Bhairava to visit him in secret. The two sealed their pact and Śaṃkara retired to an isolated spot hidden from his pupils.

In full Kāpālika regalia, Ugra-Bhairava again approached to collect his reward (xi. 30, 32) :

> (Holding) a trident, with three horizontal lines (drawn across his forehead), looking about (cautiously, wearing) ornaments made of garlands of bones, with his eyes inflamed and rolling about through intoxication, the *yogin* (Ugra-Bhairava) went to the dwelling place of the teacher . . .
>
> Beholding that (Kāpālika) in the form of Bhairava, the teacher resolved himself to abandon his body

Śaṃkara then 'yoked himself with the *ātman (ātmānam ātmany udayunkta)*.' Sitting in the proper yogic position *(siddhāsana)*, he (xi. 35) 'forgot the whole world of creation in *samādhi*.' When Ugra-Bhairava saw him seated in this position, his fears were dispelled and he prepared to strike with his trident. No sooner did he come near to Śaṃkara, however, than that sage's disciple Padmapada magically knew it (xi. 38, 42) :

> Then, remembering the supreme power of the Man-lion (Viṣṇu's Nṛsiṃha incarnation) held by Prahlāda, which removes the affliction of those who call it to mind, that (Padmapada), well-versed in *mantras (mantra-siddha)*, became the Man-lion (incarnate) and saw the ill-intentioned endeavour of (Ugra-Bhairava) . . .
>
> Running up with great speed he . . . tore open with his claws . . . the breast of (the Kāpālika) who was striking with his trident.

This ends Mādhava's version of the encounter.

The *Gorakṣa-siddhānta-saṃgraha* belongs to the Kānphaṭā or Gorakhnāth (Gorakṣa-nātha) tradition, sometimes called the religion of the Nāth Siddhas. Many of the tantric practices of its adherents resemble those attributed to the Kāpālikas. According to the *GSS* (p. 16), its philosophy is 'above dualism and monism *(dvaitādvaita-vivarjita)*.' In these circumstances it is not surprising that the *GSS* version of the legend of Śaṃkara and Ugra-Bhairava reflects less favourably on the *advaita* sage. Here the god Śrī-Bhairava himself assumed the form of Ugra-Bhairava in order to challenge Śaṃkara's religious beliefs and test their sincerity. The disguised god approached him and said (p. 16) : 'Sir, you are a *saṃnyāsin* (and hence) impartial to friend and foe alike and indifferent to the (opposite) senses of word pairs such as bliss and sorrow, etc.' He immediately requested the sage's head as an offering to Śrī-Bhairava. By this means he would fulfill his vow *(pratijñā)*. Śaṃkara carefully considered the alternatives (p. 16) :

> If it is not done (as the Kāpālika demands), then there will be the ruin of monism *(advaita-hāni)* since there will not be impartiality towards friend and foe. If it is so done, defeat is (equally certain). Even in this twofold thought there is defeat (of pure non-duality).

These unhappy alternatives completely baffled the great sage, and he could say nothing. Mādhava posed more or less the same problem but avoided carrying matters to their final philosophical absurdity by the commonsense intervention of Padmapada. The *GSS* retains this episode but refuses to let it go at that. After he was struck by Padmapāda-Nṛsiṃha,[105] Ugra-Bhairava manifested his true identity as the god Śrī-Bhairava. He then addressed Śaṃkara in a voice as deep as thunder :

> Sir, (this is) a defeat for *advaita*. What has become of that which you said about friend and foe? As a wrestler causes his opponent to fall by falling himself, (I have) accomplished the ruin of (my) opponent's (i.e. your) doctrine through the loss of my own body. Moreover, now you yourself will also meet your doom. Stand up, stand up! You should fight![106]

---

[105]The third vowel in Padmapada's name is lengthened in the *GSS*.

[106]Pp. 16–17. The Sanskrit of this and the following passage is particularly barbaric, and some of the rendering is quite free.

Śaṃkara was completely dumbfounded (p. 17) :

> Thinking, 'Then (if I fight), there will be an interruption of the work (I have) commenced since, in the doctrine of the *nyāsins* (=*saṃnyāsins,* i.e. my own doctrine), *kriyā-karaṇa* (action or performance of rites) is not a (proper) doctrine,' he became powerless to fight as commanded by the Kāpālika. (Thinking), 'In my own doctrine *akriyā* ([inaction] is proper),' he stood (motionless) in accordance with his devotion to *advaita.*

The Kāpālika then created a magical power of Yoga *(yoga-māyā)* and employed it to cut off the heads of Śaṃkara and his four disciples. Afterwards, however, they were revived. 'Then,' says the *GSS* (p. 17), 'true detachment arose.'

Although it is clear that the author of the *GSS* wishes to condemn Śaṃkara's insistence on *akriyā* (inaction or non-performance of rites), he never really proposes any practical alternative. Whether Śaṃkara stood up and fought or not, his doom was equally certain. In a sense this paradoxical dilemma is well-suited to a doctrine which says it is 'beyond *dvaita* and *advaita.*' Similar statements are found in other tantric texts. In the *Kulārṇava-tantra,* for example, Śiva declares : 'Some accept *dvaita* and others accept *advaita,* (but) they do not know my essence which is beyond *dvaita* and *advaita.*'[107] Neither the Tantras nor related Kānphaṭā literature contain much systematic philosophical speculation. For the most part they are content to loosely synthesise the arguments and hypotheses of the orthodox systems. To a certain extent phrases such as 'beyond *dvaita* and *advaita*' merely proclaim the *religious* superiority of tantric doctrine. They do not necessarily imply any rational philosophical position. In a sense they are rejections of all rational metaphysics. It is not knowledge, but ritual, devotion and psycho-physical discipline (Yoga) which these schools emphasise. In this context, there is no need for the *GSS* to propose an alternative course of action. The author needs only to point out the inadequacy of Śaṃkara's position. The command to stand up and fight may be interpreted simply as a demand to symbolically acknowledge the self-defeating nature of the doctrine of *akriyā.* Śaṃkara's beheading is therefore the occasion for the appearance of true detachment *(virāga).*[108]

[107]Ed. T. Vidyāratna, i. 110.

[108]It seems from this that the *GSS* not only wishes to criticize Śaṃkara but also

The attitude of the *GSS* towards the Kāpālika Ugra-Bhairava is ambiguous. Śrī-Bhairava assumes this form to challenge Śaṃkara, but Ugra-Bhairava himself is neither praised nor condemned. Since both the Kāpālika and Kānphaṭā schools belong to the tantric tradition, however, one might expect that the Kānphaṭā attitude would be broadly favorable. That this is the case is made clear by some subsequent passages in the *GSS*. In the first of these the author asserts the superiority of the doctrine of the Nāth Siddhas but allows the Kāpālika faith a qualified validity (p. 18) :

> Indeed, some people believe that these (Siddhas) hold the Kāpālika doctrine on account of the mention of the devotion of the Kāpālika,[109] but that is not actually (the case). Our doctrine is beyond all worldly ties *(avadhūta)*.
>
> Nonetheless, the Kāpālika doctrine was also revealed by Nātha (Śiva). Nātha was the revealer of this path.

The author then quotes from the *Śābara-tantra* a list of twelve sages to whom the Kāpālika doctrine was revealed: Ādinātha, Anādi, Kāla, Atikālaka,[110] Karāla, Vikarāla, Mahākāla, Kāla-bhairavanātha, Baṭuka, Bhūtanātha, Vīranātha, and Śrīkaṇṭha. These twelve had twelve disciples: Nāgārjuna, Jaḍabharata, Hariścandra, Satyanātha, Bhīmanātha, Gorakṣa, Carpaṭa, Avadya, Vairāgya, Kanthādhārin, Jalandhara, and Malayārjuna. These pupils were the original 'promoters of the (Kāpālika) path *(mārga-pravartakas)*.'[111] Several of these names recur in traditional Kānphaṭā lists of the eighty-four Siddhas and nine Nāthas, most notably the name of Gorakhnāth (Gorakṣa) himself.[112] On the basis of this statement and the common features in Kāpālika and Kānphaṭā worship, some modern authorities believe that the latter

to claim him for the Kānphaṭā side. The section which immediately follows this passage describes Śaṃkara's spiritual advancement through Viṣṇu, Śiva and Śakti worship to his final enlightenment by the Mahāsiddhas and his adoption of the Path of the Nāthas *(Nātha-mārga)*.

[109]This apparently refers to the preceding Ugra-Bhairava episode.

[110]S.B. Dasgupta (*Obscure* . . ., p. 207) replaces Atikālaka with Vaikālika. We do not know from where he got this reading.

[111]*GSS*, pp. 18–19.

[112]For a summary of the various Kānphaṭā lists, see S.B. Dasgupta, *Obscure* . . ., pp. 202–10.

school was a later 'transformation' of the older Kāpālika order.[113] As a historical document, however, the late *GSS* is virtually useless, and the similarities between the two schools—such as meat eating, drinking wine, attainment of magical powers through Yoga, dwelling in cremation grounds, and the like—are common to the whole of the tantric tradition. We feel, therefore, that such historical speculations are of little value.

The author of the *GSS* next poses the question (p. 20) : 'For what reason was the Kāpālika path revealed?' The answer is found in a myth. Once the twenty-four *avatāras* of Viṣṇu became intoxicated with pride (*mada,* also = wine). As mortal creatures amuse themselves, so Varāha (Boar), Nṛsiṃha (Man-lion), and the other *avatāras* began splitting the earth, frightening wild animals, oppressing towns and villages, and doing other mischief. Kṛṣṇa was filled with adulterous emotions, and Paraśurāma destroyed a great number of *kṣatriyas* to punish the sin of only one of them. Nātha became exceedingly angered by these wicked actions and assumed the form of twenty-four Kāpālikas.[114] In the ensuing battle the Kāpālikas cut off the heads of the *avatāras* and carried the skulls about in their hands. This was how the school of Kāpālikas (Skull-men) arose. The loss of their heads caused the *avatāras* to lose their pride as well. As a result they were granted a boon. Nātha replaced the skulls and returned them to life.[115]

The Ugra-Bhairava legend, whatever its historical value, and this myth both reflect the very real hostility between the tantric sects and Brāhmaṇic orthodoxy. The fact that the author of the *GSS* chooses the Kāpālikas instead of the Siddhas to represent the Kānphaṭā side of the dispute suggests not only that the two sects were on friendly terms, but also that the stories were already in popular circulation. Mādhavācārya's Vedāntic version of the Ugra-Bhairava legend is certainly older than the *GSS*'s Kānphaṭā account.

The battle between the Viṣṇu's *avatāras* and the twenty-four Kāpālikas may reflect an extension of the conflict between the

---

[113]Ghurye, p. 128. See also G.W. Briggs, *Gorakhnāth and the Kānphaṭā Yogīs,* p. 218. Eliade gives a somewhat more realistic appraisal of the situation in his work on Yoga (p. 218).

[114]These are presumably the same twelve teachers and twelve pupils mentioned earlier.

[115]*GSS,* p. 20. Note that Kṛṣṇa is singled out for his adulterous emotions *(vyabhicāri-bhāva),* a charge more frequently aimed at the Tāntrikas themselves.

Jains and Kāpālikas which is described in earlier sources. In many parts of India the Vaiṣṇavas replaced the Jains in popularity and influence and in the process absorbed many Jain beliefs and practices, including hostility to the excesses of tantric Śaivism.[116]

Śaṃkara and Krakaca or Bodholbaṇa-nityānanda

This legend also has two versions—one by Mādhava and the other by Ānandagiri. Although the broad outlines of the two accounts are identical, several important differences indicate that they may have originated from separate traditions. Ānandagiri sets his story in Ujjain while Mādhava sets his somewhere in Karṇāṭaka. Mādhava calls Śaṃkara's Kāpālika antagonist Krakaca and Ānandagiri calls him Bodholbaṇa-nityānanda. The latter Kāpālika also has a disciple named Baṭuka-nātha. Ānandagiri begins his account with a lengthy debate between Śaṃkara and Bodholbaṇa-nityānanda which is omitted by Mādhava,[117] and Mādhava includes some semi-historical and martial detail omitted by Ānandagiri. Since Mādhava's version is generally more coherent and complete, we will base most of our discussion on it.

According to this version, Śaṃkara had begun a march to Setu (Rāmeśvaram) in extreme South India accompanied by his best pupils and a king named Sudhanvan. This was the start of a conquest of the four quarters *(digvijaya)*. At Rameśvaram they met a number of non-Brāhmaṇical and non-Āryan Śāktas whom Śaṃkara defeated in a great debate. The sage honored Lord Rāmanātha and converted the Colas, Pāṇḍyas and Draviḍas. Next he proceeded north to Kāñcī, constructed a beautiful temple there, and suppressed the Tāntrikas by spreading Goddess worship in a form authorized by the scriptures *(śruti-saṃmata)*. Proceeding towards the Northeast he passed through Andhra, paid homage to the Lord of the Veṅkaṭa hills (Veṅkaṭācaleśa), and eventually arrived at the capital of the Vidarbha kingdom (eastern Maharashtra) (xv. 1–7):

[116]The most obvious example of Jain influence on later Vaiṣṇava attitudes is found in the philosophy of M.K. Gandhi. Although some of Gandhiji's ideas were inspired in part by European precedents, others—such as his faith in *ahiṃsā,* asceticism, cleanliness and vegetarianism—owe more to his Gujarati Vaiṣṇava background. From quite early times Gujarat has been a centre of Jain influence, and all these beliefs derive their original impetus more from Jainism than Hinduism.

[117]This debate contains much religious information and will be discussed below, pp. 83–85.

> There the king of the Kratha-Kaiśikas (Vidarbhas) approached him with reverence and offered his worship. (Śaṃkara then) caused his pupils to suppress the heretical views of the followers of the *Bhairava-tantra.*

These 'followers of the *Bhairava-tantra*' are not identified, but they might be Kāpālikas since many authors depict Kāpālika ascetics as worshippers of Śiva in his terrific Bhairava form. Krakaca himself is subsequently said to 'prattle the essence of the *Bhairavāgamas*.' At the least, these *Bhairava-tantra* followers must have belonged to some similar group of Tāntrikas. Mādhava continues (xv. 8–9) :

> Then the king of Vidarbha bowed (to Śaṃkara, who) desired to proceed to the Karṇāṭa region, and said : 'That region is unsuitable for your visit since (it is filled) with many crowds of Kapālins,
>
> 'I say (this) since they cannot endure your fame and have a secret hatred towards the scriptures *(śrutis)*. They revel in the misfortunes of the world and bear hostility against honoured men.'

Śaṃkara's royal disciple Sudhanvan guaranteed the sage protection, however, and they advanced 'to conquer the multitude of Kāpālikas' (xv. 10–14) :

> When Krakaca, the foremost of the Kapālin teachers, learned of (Śaṃkara's) arrival, he came to meet him.
>
> Smeared with ashes from a cremation ground *(pitṛ-kānana-bhasman)*, carrying a skull-bowl in his hand, weilding a trident, and accompanied by many whose appearance matched his own, that conceited and proud (Kāpālika) spoke thus :
>
> 'Although properly ashes are worn (by you),[118] for what reason do you hold that impure (clay) bowl and renounce this pure and fitting skull? Why is not Kapālin worshipped (by you)?

[118]Śaṃkara was a nominal devotee of Śiva and therefore wore the traditional Śaivite ashes.

> 'If He (Kapālin-Śiva) does not receive Bhairava worship with liquor *(madhu)* and blood-smeared lotuses which are human heads, how can he attain joy when his body is embraced by the lotus-eyed Umā, who is his equal?'

After Krakaca 'had prattled thus the essence of the *Bhairavāgamas,*' King Sudhanvan ordered his officials to send him away. The enraged Kāpālika soon returned with his followers to seek retribution for this insult. As they approached he shouted: 'I am not Krakaca (= a saw) if I do not cut off your heads' (xv. 15–17):

> He sent out the countless crowds *(kulas)* of angered Kapālins whose cries were as terrifying as the clouds of the deluge. They attacked with weapons held aloft.

The Brāhmaṇa followers of Śaṃkara were terrified, but the faithful Sudhanvan countered the Kāpālika advance and drove them back. Krakaca then shifted the battle to another part of the field and again threw the Brāhmaṇas into confusion. In desperation they sought Śaṃkara's protection (xv. 21):

> The king of ascetics (then) reduced those (Kāpālikas) . . . to ashes in an instant through the fire which arose from his *huṃkāra* (the sound *hum,* a *mantra).*

Sudhanvan rejoined Śaṃkara and slaughtered a thousand more of their enemies. Seeing his army routed, Krakaca again approached Śaṃkara and said (xv. 24–25):

> 'O Devotee of Evil Doctrines, behold my power! Now you will reap the fruit of this action *(karman).*' Closing his eyes, (Krakaca) placed a skull in the palm of his hand and briefly meditated.
>
> After that master of the *Bhairavāgamas* had thus meditated, the skull was immediately filled with liquor *(surā).* After drinking half of it, he held the (remaining) half and thought of Bhairava.

This god instantly appeared in the form of Mahākapālin. He wore a garland of human skulls and his hair was a flaming mass of matted locks *(jaṭā)*. He held a trident and uttered loud and dreadful laughter. Krakaca commanded him (xv. 27) :

> 'O God, you should destroy the enemy of your devotee with your (fierce) gaze.' Instead the enraged (Mahākapālin declared), 'How dare you offend against my own self (i.e. Śaṃkara),' and cut off the head of Krakaca.

This ends Mādhava's account. Dhanapatisūri's *Ḍiṇḍima* commentary, following Ānandagiri almost verbatim, continues the story to the final conversion of the Kāpālika's disciples. In this version the god Saṃhāra-Bhairava did not immediately kill Bodholbaṇa-nityānanda. When the god appeared Śaṃkara paid him homage and set forth his own philosophy in order to justify his action against the Kāpālika and his disciples. Bhairava was pleased by the sage's statements, however, and commanded him : 'You should make those Kāpālikas embrace the faith of the Brāhmaṇas.'[120] The god explained that he had become manifest because he was bound by the *mantra (mantra-baddha)* used by Bodholbaṇa, not because of any merit of that ascetic *(na dharmatas)*. Saṃhāra-Bhairava then vanished and the followers of the Kāpālika doctrine *(Kāpālika-matānugas)*—who were of twelve sorts, Baṭukas, etc.—bowed down to Śaṃkara. The sage was filled with compassion and instructed Padmapāda and his other disciples to convert the repentant heretics.[121]

Unfortunately neither the commentator nor Ānandagiri identifies the 'twelve sorts *(dvādaśadhā)* of Kāpālikas beginning with the Baṭukas.' Baṭuka, however, appears as one of the twelve original Kāpālika sages in the *Śābara-tantra* list quoted in the *Gorakṣa-*

---

[119]xv. 26. Ānandagiri's account of this episode is worth comparing. Seeing that he and his pupils had been beaten by Śaṃkara, Bodholbaṇa-nityānanda approached the sage and said (chap. xxiii): '"Saṃhāra-Bhairava is to be honored by me. I will cause him to appear by means of *mantras*. He will quickly devour you and your retinue." Saying this and again uttering (the sound) *huṃ*; holding a human skull with his left hand; filling that with liquor by means of a *mantra*; drinking half (of it) himself and giving the remainder to his pupils; and looking into the middle of the sky with round and reddened eyes—he said: "(You), who are Saṃhāra-kāla (Destruction-time), Bhairava, Prabhu, and Iśvara, should come and speedily devour the *saṃnyāsin* and his retinue.' "

[120]*Ḍiṇḍima* commentary, vs. 8, on Mādhavācārya, xv. 28.

[121]Ibid., vss. 1–14.

siddhānta-saṃgraha.[122] Evidently these twelve sages were considered to be the founders of twelve divisions of the Kāpālika sect. The presence of this tradition in such unrelated sources suggests that there may have been some factual justification for it.

The personalities of the two legendary Kāpālikas, Krakaca and Ugra-Bhairava, are quite distinct—where the latter used guile the former chose brute force—but in appearance Krakaca, like Ugra-Bhairava, is a typical Kāpālika. He smears his body with the ashes of the dead; he carries a trident and a skull bowl; he worships Bhairava and Mahākapālin; his text is the *Bhairavāgama*; he honours this god with liquor and offerings of human heads; and he imagines salvation as the indescribable bliss of an endless embrace in the arms of Umā.

Both the location and the large size of Krakaca's Kāpālika battalions merit additional comment. In Mādhavācārya's version the Vidarbha king warned Śaṃkara against going to the Karṇāṭa region because it was populated by 'many crowds of Kapālins.'[123] Dhanapatisūri glosses this location as the town Ujjayanī *(sic)*, but this cannot be correct. He apparently relies for this identification on Ānandagiri, who begins his version (chap. xxiii) : 'Travelling along the northern road, Śrī-Śaṃkarācārya ... saw the city named Ujjayinī which was filled with (persons) devoted to the Kāpālika observance.' The Karṇāṭa region approximately corresponds with modern Mysore State and never included the famous Mālava city, Ujjain.[124] Evidently there were two separate traditions. Reasons exist for both these places to be associated with the Kāpālikas.

Neither Mādhavācārya's *Śaṃkara-digvijaya* nor Ānandagiri's *Śaṃkara-vijaya* can claim much historical accuracy. Both are products of about the fourteenth or fifteenth century and both tend to shed as much light on the religious life of India during the century or two preceding their composition as on the religious life of

---

[122]See above, pp. 37–38.

[123]Mādhavācārya xv. 11.

[124]It is tempting to identify the Ujjayinī of Ānandagiri and Dhanapatisūri with the town by that name in Bellary District, Mysore, where one of the five chief *maṭhas* of the Vīraśaivas is located. The *maṭha* at this place was supposedly founded by Marulasiddha, one of the five great *ācāryas* of Vīraśaiva tradition. See M.R. Sakhare, *History and Philosophy of Lingayat Religion*, pp. 361–62. Unfortunately Ānandagiri's statement that Śaṃkara reached Ujjayinī 'travelling along the northern road' makes this identification less likely.

the time of Śaṃkarācārya. The Karṇāṭaka region, which seems to have been the home of Ugra-Bhairava as well as Krakaca, was dominated by the Kālāmukhas during the eleventh to thirteenth centuries. Since no lesser authorities than Yāmunācārya and Rāmānuja associate, and perhaps confuse, the two sects, there is at least a *prima facie* case that Mādhava did the same. Krakaca's dress, behaviour and religious beliefs are definitely those of a Kāpālika, not a Kālāmukha, but in one important respect he and his followers have more affinity with the latter sect.

In Mādhava's story Krakaca is said to command vast legions of Kāpālikas *(Kapāli-jālāḥ, Kāpālika-jālakaḥ, Kapālināṃ kulāni)*. Nearly every other story featuring Kāpālikas describes them as solitary peripatetic ascetics, occasionally joined by a single female disciple. This absence of organization may help to explain the relative lack of Kāpālika epigraphy. The Kālāmukhas, on the other hand, usually established themselves in large monastic communities. It seems quite likely that Mādhava was modelling his Kāpālika legions on the brotherhoods of the Kālāmukha *maṭhas*. As in the accounts of Yāmunācārya and Rāmānuja, the confusion between the two sects may have been intentional. This would help explain the absence of any mention of Kālāmukhas in Mādhava's work.

Although in each chapter of Ānandagiri's *Śaṃkara-vijaya* Śaṃkara debates a different rival sect, the Kālāmukhas do not appear in this work either. Since the Mālava Ujjain was never a center of the Kālāmukhas, however, it is less likely that Ānandagiri was confusing the two sects. There is a tenuous connection between this town and the Kāpālikas in the fact that Bhavabhūti wrote his *Mālatī-Mādhava* for the festival of Lord Kālapriya, who is usually identified with the god Mahākāla of Ujjain. The play is set, however, in Padmāvatī, a town which scholars locate some 220 miles north of Ujjain near modern Narvār.[125] Today Ujjain is an important center of the Kānphaṭā yogins.[126] If Gorakhnāth's commonly accepted date, *c.* A.D. 1200, is correct, this town may well have been a Kānphaṭā center by the time of Ānandagiri (about the fifteenth century).[127] Since Kānphaṭā Yogins also organise them-

[125]See the introduction to Devadhar and Suru's edition of the play, p. 4.

[126]Ghurye, p. 137.

[127]Although Ānandagiri's date is not certain he seems to have lived sometime after Mādhavācārya. Since the Kālāmukhas were already rapidly declining in Mādhava's time, this is another reason why it is unlikely that Ānandagiri was confusing them with the Kāpālikas.

selves into monastic communities, Ānandagiri might have confused them and the Kāpālikas.

Whether Krakaca's ascetic legions are modelled on the organization of the Kālāmukhas, Kānphaṭās, or Kāpālikas themselves, their militancy is quite striking. Military orders of religion were not unknown, however, either in mediaeval India, mediaeval Europe, or sixteenth century Japan. In Europe the Crusades produced several military orders, the most famous being the Templars and the Hospitallers. These orders not only fought against the Muslim princes of the Holy Land but also on occasion joined forces with these very princes against each other.[128] In the sixteenth century Japan witnessed the Ikko Ikki or Fanatic Risings by monks of the Pure Land (Jodo) sect, who fought with their sectarian enemies and in many places even challenged the authority of the feudal lords.[129]

Although the mutual tolerance shown by religious groups native to India has always been remarkable, rivalry among them, especially for royal patronage, sometimes led to violence. In ancient times competition usually took the form of great public debates which often became miracle contests. One such contest between Buddha and the Ājīvika teacher Pūraṇa Kassapa took place at Śrāvasti in North India. It seems to have ended with some sort of riot in which the Ājīvikas were expelled.[130] In some cases defeat in debate led to royal persecution. According to a South Indian legend, the famous *nāyaṉār* Ñānasambandar once vanquished the Jains in debate and converted the Pāṇḍya king to Śaivism. The king then executed 8,000 Jains by impalement.[131] The Kālāmukhas are frequently extolled for their debating skill, but most of their debates—like that between Bonteyamuni and some rival logicians[132] —seem to have been peaceful ones. In about A.D. 1160, a debate *cum* miracle contest between the Vīraśaiva leader Ēkāntada Rāmayya and the Jains at Ablūr in Dharwar District, Mysore, ended with the defeat of the latter. When the losers refused to abide by a previous agreement to set up a Śiva idol in place of their Jina, Ēkāntada Rāmayya marched on their temple, defeated

---

[128] A.S. Atiya, *Crusade, Commerce and Culture*, pp. 67–68.

[129] G.B. Sansom, *Japan : A Short Cultural History* (rev. ed.), pp. 374–76.

[130] See Basham, pp. 84–87.

[131] See K.A.N. Sastri, *A History of South India*, p. 413,

[132] See below, p. 132.

its defenders and demolished all the buildings.[133] The six major *ākhāḍās* of the Daśanāmi Nāgās are the earliest recorded examples of true religious military orders in India. These *ākhāḍās* (regiments) are still in existence. Nominally at least, their members belong to one or other of the ten orders of Śaivite ascetics reputedly founded by Śaṃkarācārya (the Daśanāmis) .The Junā Ākhāḍā (Old Regiment) was formerly known as the Bhairava Ākhāḍā. Its present tutelary deity is Dattātreya but originally must have been Bhairava. The traditional date for its establishment is A.D. 1146, but Ghurye (p. 104) believes that it is descended from an older sect of Śaivites, namely the Kāpālikas. This is a tempting suggestion, particularly since one of the *ākhāḍā's* centers is at Ujjain. It is difficult to see, however, how it could have survived a transition from the Kāpālika faith to Vedānta. The traditional dates for the foundation of some of the other *ākhāḍās* go back to as early as A.D. 647, but the earliest reasonably verifiable date for an actual battle involving Nāgā Saṃnyāsins is A.D. 1266. Most of their recorded activity belongs to the sixteenth to eighteenth centuries and culminates in a great victory over the Vaiṣṇava Bairāgis at Hardwar in 1760.[134]

The preceding discussion suggests an interesting but admittedly hypothetical chain of events. An original historical debate between Śaṃkara and some Kāpālika ascetics either at Ujjain or somewhere in Mysore ended in a riot during which the Kāpālikas were put to flight and some possibly converted. In succeeding centuries this story was gradually elaborated until the original antagonists became a vast army of warlike monks modelled in part either on the Kālāmukha monastic orders (Mādhava) or on the newly emerging military orders of medieval India (Ānandagiri).

Śaṃkara and Unmatta-Bhairava

This legend appears in Ānandagiri's *Śaṃkara-vijaya,* chapter xxiv, and in Dhanapatisūri's *Ḍiṇḍima* commentary on Mādhava's *Śaṃkara-digvijaya* xv. 28. The two accounts are almost the same and show the commentator's debt to Ānandagiri. Since the published text of Ānandagiri's work is corrupt, we will follow the commentary wherever possible. The introduction to the story is found only in Ānandagiri's account :[135]

[133]See J.F. Fleet, 'Inscriptions at Ablur, '*EI,* V, 213–65 (inscription no. E).

[134]Ghurye, pp. 103–112.

[135]Dhanapatisūri omits this passage and grafts his story directly onto the Krakaca legend.

> After they had been thus repudiated, the various groups *(varṇas)*—Kāpālikas, Cārvākas, Saugatas, Kṣapaṇakas, Jainas, and Bauddhas—reappeared in another town. A certain Kāpālika of the Śūdra caste *(jāti)* named Unmatta-Bhairava (lived) there. His body was covered with ashes from a funeral pyre; his neck was ringed with a garland of human skulls; (three horizontal) streaks of lamp-black were drawn across his forehead; all his hair was fashioned into a top-knot *(jaṭā-jūṭa)*; his waistband and loincloth were made from a tiger skin; a skull-bowl adorned his left hand; his right hand held a loudly ringing bell *(ghaṇṭā)*; and he was chattering repeatedly 'O Śambhu-Bhairava! Aho, Kālīśa!'

This classic description of a Kāpālika ascetic is followed by a derisive exposition of his hedonistic doctrine, a doctrine more suitable for a Cārvāka or Lokāyatika than a Kāpālika. Unmatta-Bhairava came to meet Śaṃkara and proclaimed to him the superiority of the Kāpālika faith over all others. He lamented the fall of Baṭukanātha, Bodholbaṇa's disciple, and the other Kāpālikas from the true faith and said: 'Their undoing (was their reliance on) being of the Brāhmaṇa caste. I will have nothing to do with caste.'[136] He then gave a materialistic justification for his rejection of caste and suggested that there are only two real castes, the male-caste and the female-caste. He also asserted that promiscuity is the proper rule of conduct between them since the joy *(ānanda)* of sexual union is the true form of Bhairava, and the attainment of that joy at death is salvation *(mokṣa)*.[137]

Śaṃkara listened politely to the Kāpālika's blasphemy and said (vs. 23): 'O Kāpālika, this was well said. (But) the truth should be told. Whose daughter is your mother?' Unmatta-Bhairava retorted that his mother was the daughter of a *dīkṣita* (initiated priest) and explained his contention thus (vss. 23–28):

> O sage, He (my mother's father) extracts the toddy *(surā)* of the best palm trees. Though he knows well its taste, he does not wish to drink it himself but with due devotion

---

[136]Dhanapatisūri, vss. 15–16. The name Baṭukanātha is from Ānandagiri. The commentary reads 'Baṭukas and others.'

[137]Dhanapatisūri, vss. 17–22. See below, pp. 90–92.

> *(śīlavān)* sells it. Therefore people always call him *dīkṣita*.[138] His daughter became my mother. By making an offering of her own body, O sage, she always caused men, who had come (to her) for the sake of pleasure, to be immersed in an ocean of bliss. Know this (person) named Unmatta-Bhairava (to be) her son. My father was also a liquor maker.[139] Even the gods *(suras)* approach him here on earth, and they by no means run away (because they are) averse to the smell of liquor.

Having tricked Unmatta-Bhairava into this self-condemnation, Śaṃkara good-naturedly ordered him to leave and wander about wherever he wished. To his own disciples Śaṃkara explained (vss. 28–30): 'I have come only to punish Brāhmaṇas who have embraced a bad faith and not others. This man is not to be spoken to. Take him away quickly.'

This legend provides a good example of the accusations of hedonistic licentiousness which orthodox writers are fond of leveling against tantric ascetics. These accusations have some factual basis. Sex and alcohol, for instance, do play an important part in tantric ritual. In the *dakṣiṇācāra* tradition symbolic equivalents are substituted or the rituals sublimated into mere mental exercises, but in the *vāmācāra* tradition of the Kāpālikas real women and wine were employed. Nonetheless, the assertion that the Kāpālikas were hedonists and that they justified this hedonism with a thoroughly materialistic philosophy cannot be accepted. Materialistic hedonism falls within the province of Lokāyata and Cārvāka philosophy, not tantricism. This is not to say, of course, that many tantric ascetics were not licentious. Unmatta-Bhairava's orgasmic conception of *mokṣa* and his rejection of caste, however, are at least partly confirmed by other sources and will be discussed in more detail elsewhere.[140]

Kāpālikas in Sanskrit Drama

Villainous Kāpālika ascetics appear in a number of Sanskrit dramas and stories. The dramas include: (1) *Mattavilāsa* by the

---

[138]A *dīkṣita* makes sacrificial offerings to the gods which he does not himself consume. Unmatta's maternal grandfather sells liquor but does not drink it.

[139]There is an implied pun on the words *surā-kara* (liquor maker) and *sura-ākara* (treasure of the gods).

[140]See below, pp. 90–92. and above, pp. 6–7.

Pallava king Mahendravarman (*c.* A.D. 600–630); (2) *Mālatī-Mādhava* by Bhavabhūti (*c.* 725); (3) *Caṇḍakauśika* by Kṣemīśvara (*c.* 900–950); (4) *Prabodhacandrodaya* by Kṛṣṇamiśra (*c.* 1050–1100); (5) *Laṭamelaka* by *kavirāja* Śaṅkhadhara (*c.* 1110–50); (6) *Kaumudīmitrānanda* by Rāmacandra (*c.* 1143–75); (7) *Nalavilāsa* by the same author; and (8) *Moharājaparājaya* by Yaśaḥpāla (*c.* 1175).[141] Two very late works in which these ascetics appear are the *Amṛtodaya* of Gokulanātha (A.D. 1693)[142] and the *Vidyāpariṇayana* attributed to Ānandarāyamakhin (*c.* 1700).[143] They are also mentioned in Kavikarṇapūra's *Caitanyacandrodaya* (*c.* 1550).[144] The Prakrit drama *Karpūramañjarī* by Rājaśekhara (*c.* 900) features a tantric 'master magician' named Bhairavānanda, who 'follows the *kula* path.'[145] The *Rucikaraṭīkā* on Kṛṣṇamiśra's *Prabodhacandrodaya* claims that Rājaśekhara's Bhairavānanda followed *Somasiddhānta*, the doctrine of the Kāpālikas.[146] This is not strictly correct. 'The *kula* path' refers to the doctrine of the Kaulas, not the Kāpālikas. Both these sects belonged to the Vāmācāra tradition, however, and had many similarities. Kaulas also appear in Yaśaḥpāla's *Moharājaparājaya* and Śaṅkhadhara's *Laṭamelaka*.

None of these dramatists had much sympathy for the Kāpālikas. According to tradition, Mahendra, the royal author of *Mattavilāsa*, was converted from Jainism to Śaivism by the famous Tamil *nāyaṉār*, Appar.[147] The king's own Tiruchchirappalli (Trichinopoly)

---

[141] A.B. Keith (*The Sanskrit Drama*, p. 254) places Yaśaḥpāla during the time of 'Abhayadeva or Abhayapāla, who reigned after Kumārapāla from A.D. 1229–32.' C.D. Dalal, in his introduction to Chaturavijayaji's edition of the *Moharājaparājaya*, places Yaśaḥpāla during the time of Ajayadeva or Ajayapāla, who 'reigned from A.D. 1229 to 1232.' Ajayapāla, the Caulukya king of Gujarat, ruled from A.D. 1172 to *c.* 1176. The dates given by Dalal and apparently copied by Keith belong to the Vikrama era, not the Christian era. We do not know why Keith read the king's name as Abhayapāla rather than Ajayapāla.

[142] Keith (p. 343) dates this author in the sixteenth century, but this is incorrect.

[143] Handiqui (*Śrīharṣa*, p. 641) follows a brief note in Śivadatta and Parab's edition of the play (p. 1) and dates Ānandarāyamakhin in the first half of the seventeenth century. Keith (p. 253) gives the correct date. See M.D. Aiyangar's introduction to his edition of Ānandarāya's *Jīvānanda*.

[144] Ed. Kedāranātha and W.L.S. Paṇśīkar, pp. 24–25.

[145] Ed. S. Konow and trans. C.R. Lanman. See especially Act I, vss. 22–25 and Act IV, vs. 19.

[146] Cited in G. Tucci, 'Animadversiones Indicae,' *JRASB*, n.s. XXVI (1930), 131.

[147] R. Sathianathaier, K.R.S. Iyengar, and T.M.P. Mahadevan (all in R.C. Majumdar [ed.], *The Classical Age*) seem to accept this tradition without question. K.A.N. Sastri, in his *Development of Religion in South India* (p. 42), points out that the identification is based on slender evidence.

record indicates that he turned to Śaivism from some other faith.[148] Even if he wrote his play after his conversion, he could not be expected to favor a heretical sect such as the Kāpālikas. Bhavabhūti was an orthodox Brāhmaṇa from a family which followed the *Taittirīya* branch of the *Yajurveda*. He may have had some Śaivite leanings but was not a strict sectarian.[149] It is likely that Kṣemīśvara, the author of *Caṇḍakauśika,* was also an orthodox Brāhmaṇa. Kṛṣṇamiśra used his allegorical *Prabodhacandrodaya* to extol the merits of *advaita* Vaiṣṇavism. Śaṅkhadhara seems to have favored some moderate form of Śaivism since his *Laṭamelaka* opens with introductory verses to Gaurī and Śiva. Rāmacandra and Yaśaḥpāla were both devout Jains.

All these writers express their contempt for the orgiastic and sadistic features of the Kāpālika cult. This is particularly true of the Jains, whose extreme asceticism made them natural enemies of tantricism. The distain of the orthodox Śaivite writers, on the other hand, probably reflects a desire to disavow any association with their heretical brethren. It is significant, perhaps, that Kṛṣṇamiśra, a strong Vaiṣṇava, attacks a Cārvāka, a Digambara, a Buddhist, and a Kāpālika but neglects to mention any of the more respectable Śaivite sects.

The dramas provide some important additional information about the geographical distribution of the Kāpālikas. The *Mattavilāsa* is set in Kāñcī, the capital of Mahendra. The Kāpālika ascetic of the play is said to live at Ekambam *(eaṃvvavāsī)*.[150] This must refer to the Ekāmbira-nātha temple, which is still one of the major temples of Kanchipuram. In its present form, however, the building dates from a later time than Mahendra's. Bhavabhūti's *Mālatī-Mādhava,* as we have noted, is set in Padmāvatī, a town which was probably located about 100 miles south of Agra. The Kāpālika Aghoraghaṇṭa operates from a temple of Karālā situated in the cremation ground of that town, but his home is said to be the mountain Śrīparvata.[151] Another character, the virtuous *yoginī* Saudāminī, is said to be 'observing the vow of a Kāpālika on Śrīparvata.'[152] The heroine Mālatī is eventually abducted to this place by Aghoraghaṇṭa's female disciple, Kapālakuṇḍalā.

[148]See ibid.

[149]Bhavabhūti's name means either 'wealth of Śiva' or 'ashes of Śiva.'

[150]Ed. T.G. Śāstrī, p. 13. Trans. L.D. Barnett, *BSOS,* V, 707.

[151]Act I, after vs. 15.

[152]Ibid.

The famous holy center Śrīparvata (also called Śrīśailam) is located in Kurnool District of Andhra Pradesh. It is mentioned in the *Mahābhārata* as a place sacred to Śiva and Devī.[153] In *Matsya Purāṇa* clxxxi. 28–29, it is listed as one of eight secret places sacred to Śiva. The Mallikārjuna *liṅga* at the site is one of the twelve *jyotirliṅgas* of Śiva.[154] Today the shrine is held in especial esteem by the Vīraśaivas. The earliest references to Mallikārjuna worship on Śrīparvata are found in Subandhu's *Vāsavadattā* (*c.* A.D. 600)[155] and the *Padma Purāṇa*.[156] Mādhavācārya claims that Śaṃkarācārya himself visited the shrine of this god on Śrīśaila.[157] In A.D. 1090 a Kālāmukha priest of the Parvatāvali named Rāmeśvara-paṇḍita was the head of the Mallikārjuna-śilā-maṭha on this mountain.[158] A few years earlier, in 1057, the Western Cālukya king Someśvara I came to Śrīśaila and washed the feet of the Kālāmukha teacher Sureśvara-paṇḍita in the presence of the god Mallikārjuna.[159] In Bāṇabhaṭṭa's *Kādambarī*, as we have seen,[160] the South Indian tantric priest who lived in the Caṇḍikā temple near Ujjain is said to know 'thousands of wonderful stories about Śrīparvata.' In his *Harṣa-carita*, Bāṇa calls Harṣa a 'Śrīparvata of magical powers (*siddhis*).'[161] These two references by Bāṇa indicate that Śrīparvata was already famous as a center of tantric worship by the first half of the seventh century, but Kalhaṇa is the only author besides Bhavabhūti to specifically connect it with the Kāpālikas.[162] Sometime before the eleventh century the temple of Mallikārjuna came into the hands of the Kālāmukhas. We do not know what sort of relations, if any, they maintained with the Kāpālikas. It is not likely that the two sects were ever on very friendly terms. By about the fourteenth century the Kālāmukhas had been replaced by the Vīraśaivas. The Kāpālikas seem to have become virtually extinct by this time.

Most of the other dramatists lived in northern and western India.

---

[153] *Āraṇyakaparvan*, ed. V.S. Sukthankar, iii, 83. 16–17.

[154] See P.V. Kane, *HDS*, IV, 678.

[155] Trans. L.H. Gray, p. 68.

[156] *Uttarakhaṇḍa*, chap. xix, cited by Handiqui, p. 359.

[157] *Śaṃkara-digvijaya*, x. 7–12.

[158] See inscription ed. and trans. by P. Sreenivasachar, *HAS*, No. 13, Part II, pp. 25–31.

[159] See inscription ed. by R.S. Sastry and N.L. Rao, *SII*, IX, Part I, no. 119.

[160] See above, p. 18.

[161] Ed. Kane, Part I, text p. 2.

[162] See below, pp. 66–67.

Kṣemīśvara, the author of *Caṇḍakauśika*, dedicated his play to Mahīpāla, who may best be identified with Mahīpāla I (*c.* 912–942), the Pratīhāra king of Kanauj. This king was also the patron of Rājaśekhara. Kṛṣṇamiśra composed the *Prabodhacandrodaya* for Kīrttivarman (*c.* 1070–90), a Candella king of Jejakābhukti (modern Bundelkhand region). Śaṅkhadhara's *Laṭamelaka* was written during the time of Govindacandra (*c.* 1114–54), a Gāhaḍavāla king of Kanauj. Rāmacandra and Yaśaḥpāla both lived in northern Gujarat during the reign of the Caulukya king Ajayapāla (*c.* 1172–76). Yaśaḥpāla's *Moharājaparājaya* describes the conversion to Jainism of Ajayapāla's predecessor, Kumārapāla (*c.* 1143–72). A Kāpālika is included among the enemies of this king. In Rāmacandra's *Nalavilāsa*, a reworking of the Nala-Damayantī legend, some Kāpālikas appear as spies of Citrasena, a Kalacuri-Cedi king. This king is probably modeled on one of the Kalacuri kings of Tripuri (near Jabalpur, Madhya Pradesh) since one or more of these kings is believed to have fought with Kumārapāla.[163] The play is set in Vidarbha.

If all the information about the distribution and dates of the Kāpālikas is collated, we find that they existed throughout most of the Deccan plateau as early as the eighth century. They are connected specifically with Kāñcī, parts of Mysore, western and central Maharashtra, Ujjain, the Gwalior region of Madhya Pradesh, and Kurnool District in Andhra Pradesh. They may also have been found in Orissa (Bhubaneswar) by this date. Sources later than the eighth century indicate their presence in Gujarat, Bundelkhand, the Vindhya hills, and other parts of India.[164] According to Bhavabhūti, Śrīparvata in Kurnool District was a particularly important Kāpālika center in his time. In later centuries, however, they were replaced at this site by the Kālāmukhas. Areas from which we have no pre-ninth century records of Kāpālikas include Bihar, Uttar Pradesh (except Varanasi), Rajasthan, Punjab, Kashmir, and West Pakistan—the whole of ancient Āryāvarta. Bengal, traditionally a stronghold of tantric worship, is unrepresented in early records, but Kāṇhapāda, in his famous Old Bengali songs, calls himself a Kāpālika.[165] Nowadays Kāpālikas are still rumored to inhabit the jungles of northern Bengal and

163R.C. Majumdar (ed.), *The Struggle for Empire*, p. 64.

164See below, pp. 63–71.

165See below, pp. 69–71.

parts of Assam. These rumors are undoubtedly little more than old wives' tales, but some Vāmācāra ascetics do survive in this region.

Although the evidence is very scanty, it appears likely that the Kāpālikas originated in South India or the Deccan. This is not surprising since the region south of the Vindhyas was dominated by Śaivism from very early times. The earliest epigraphical reference to tantric worship occurs in Viśvavarman's A.D. 423–424 record from Gangdhar in south-eastern Rajasthan near Ujjain.[166] Further south, in Tamil country, the early inhabitants worshipped the god Murugaṉ with rites which might be called tantric in character.[167] Murugaṉ was later identified with Śiva's warlike son Skanda.

The precise date of the foundation of the Kāpālika order is impossible to establish. It is unlikely however, that these ascetics existed more than a century or two before the time of Mahendra, the author of the *Mattavilāsa*. This period, the fifth to the sixth century A.D., also marks the time of the first development of tantric literature in the subcontinent. The Kāpālikas appear to have virtually died out by about the fourteenth century. The sect was perhaps absorbed by other Śaiviṭe tantric orders such as the Kānphaṭās and the Aghorīs.[168]

Kāpālika characters have important roles in only four of the dramas—*Mattavilāsa, Mālatī-Mādhava, Caṇḍakauśika,* and *Prabodhacandrodaya*. The Kāpālika Satyasoma in Mahendra's *Mattavilāsa* is a wholly comic creation, reminiscent in many respects of the Kāpālika hedonist Unmatta-Bhairava. The Kāpālikas in *Mālatī-Mādhava* and *Caṇḍakauśika,* on the other hand, are nefarious rogues similar to Krakaca and Ugra-Bhairava. In the *Prabodhacandrodaya* the Kāpālika Somasiddhānta displays both comic and horrific traits.

To some extent dramatic requirements, both practical and theoretical, have influenced the differing treatments of these ascetics. The classical theory of eight primary sentiments *(rasas)*, which correspond to the eight basic emotions *(bhāvas)*, encouraged

---

166Ed. and trans. J.F. Fleet, *CII,* III, 72–79.

167See A.L. Basham, *The Wonder That Was India,* p. 314. See also J.M.N. Pillai's translation of the famous early Tamil poem 'Tirumurugaṉaṟṟupadai' in J.M.S. Pillai's *Two Thousand Years of Tamil Literature,* pp. 55–81.

168For the Aghorīs, see H.W. Barrow, 'On Aghorīs and Aghorapanthīs,' *Journal of the Anthropological Society of Bombay,* III (1893), 197–251 and also W. Crooke, 'Aghorī,' *ERE,* I, 210–13.

Sanskrit dramatists to imbue each act and character with a specific sentiment.[169] In skilful hands this technique could achieve striking ritualistic effects, but it also militated against any form of realistic expression. As a result, the plots of many dramas are recapitulations and elaborations of popular legends and myths, and the characters are representatives of ideal types and sentiments, not people. The influence of the *rasa* theory is particularly noticeable in *Mālatī-Mādhava*. The act in which the Kāpālikas appear is meant to evoke the sentiments of terror (*bhayānaka,* based on the emotion of terror, *bhaya*) and horror (*bībhatsa,* based on disgust, *jugupsā*), and these sentiments are embodied in them.

The *Mattavilāsa* is a one act farce *(prahasana)* in which the comic sentiment *(hāsya)* naturally predominates. Satyasoma, a drunken Kapālin or Kāpālika and his equally tipsy wench, Devasomā, engage in some classic slapstick and clever banter with a Buddhist friar, a Pāśupata monk, and a raving madman. As they enter the stage, Devasomā finds that she is too drunk to stand upright and calls for Satyasoma's assistance. Equally drunk, he falls as he lifts her up. In his befuzzlement Satyasoma calls Devasomā Somadevā and is accused by her of having another mistress. He offers to forswear liquor to atone for his mistake, but she protests: 'O, master! Don't for my sake ruin your holy life [*tapas*] by breaking your vow.' He joyfully embraces her and exlaims:

> *Dhṛrṇa dhṛrṇa*! Reverence to Śiva! My dear—
> Ho, don a right jolly and quaint attire,
> Drink brandy [*surā*] and gaze in your wenches' eyes:
> Long life to our Lord of the Trident, who found
> That the road to salvation this way lies![170]

Satyasoma next makes a witty attack on the asceticism of the Jains, and the two proceed to a Kāñcī liquor shop. He elaborately compares the shop with a sacrifice-yard where 'the brandy is the Soma, the tipplers are the priests' and 'the keeper of the brandy shop is the master of the sacrifice' (shades of Unmatta-Bhairava's grandfather!). The two Kāpālikas are offered liquid alms, but Satyasoma discovers that his skull bowl is missing. After consi-

[169]See Keith, pp. 314–26.

[170]Trans. Barnett, *BSOS,* V, 703, Ed. T.G. Śāstrī, vs. 7. *Dhṛrṇa* is some sort of religious exclamation, probably one invented by Mahendra. The translations which follow are all by Barnett.

dering the problem for a moment, he decides to follow the 'law of necessity' *(āpad-dharma)* and takes the gift in a cow's horn. Without the skull bowl, however, he fears he will lose the title of Kapālin (Skull-bearer). Even worse, the skull had some nice roast meat in it. As they set off in search of the skull, a Buddhist friar passes by on his way to the King's Monastery with a full alms bowl hidden under his robe. The friar's favorite pastime is looking for an 'uncorrupted original text' wherein the Buddha sanctions 'possession of women and use of strong drink.' Satyasoma and Devasomā see that he is hiding something and accuse him of taking their skull. The Buddha, Satyasoma taunts, is superior even to Kharapaṭa, the author of the Thieves' Hand-book, for :

> Your Buddha, while the Brahmans' eyes were closed,
> Filled up his granary by filching notions
> From Mahābhāratam and from Vedāntas.[171]

Devasomā offers her master a drink and he passes the cow's horn to the friar. Even though this fellow has wronged us, Satyasoma declares, nonetheless 'our doctrine lays chief weight on sharing our goods.' Visibly licking his chops, the friar is forced to refuse because he is afraid someone might see. The argument becomes more and more heated and Satyasoma finally threatens to make the friar's own head into an alms bowl. They begin to fight but are stopped by Babhrukalpa, the Pāśupata monk, who agrees to act as mediator. In reality, however, he is more interested in winning Devasomā than in settling the dispute. The friar is at last forced to show the bowl which he had hidden in his robe. Satyasoma and Devasomā refuse to admit that it is not their skull and claim that the friar merely changed its color and shape. Babhrukalpa suggests they take the matter to court, but before they can do so the madman enters carrying the skull bowl which he had taken from 'a most respectable dog belonging to a Caṇḍāla.' He offers the skull to Babhrukalpa, who rejects it, but refuses to give it to its rightful owner, Satyasoma. They all attempt to trick the madman into giving it up, but he is adamant. Finally, when the friar calls him a madman, he tells Satyasoma to 'take this skull and show me the madman.' Satyasoma obligingly misdirects him and everyone parts the best of friends.

[171] Trans. Barnett, *BSOS*, V, 708 (vs. 12).

Bhavabhūti's *Mālatī-Mādhava* is a love story, and the erotic sentiment *(śṛṅgāra-rasa)* consequently predominates. For the purpose of dramatic contrast, and also to display his own virtuosity, however, the author imbues several acts with differing sentiments.[172] Much of the plot seems to have been borrowed from the story of Madirāvatī in the *Kathāsaritsāgara*.[173]

The hero and heroine of the drama, Mādhava and Mālatī, are children of the ministers of the kings of Vidarbha and Padmāvatī respectively. Although both parents want to see Mālatī and Mādhava wed to each other, a close companion of the king of Padmāvatī also desires the lovely heroine. The Buddhist nun Kāmandakī, an old friend of the two ministers, arranges for Mālatī and Mādhava to meet and fall in love and plans to get them married in secret. Meanwhile, the king summons Mālatī to the palace for her marriage with his companion. In desperation Mādhava resolves to offer human flesh to the ghouls of the cremation ground in exchange for a boon. Act five opens with the entrance, by an aerial path, of Kapālakuṇḍalā, the female disciple of the Kāpālika Aghoraghaṇṭa. She offers homage to Śiva, Lord of Śakti, and describes her flight to the cremation ground :

> The speed of my flight through the sky endows me with a great and charming tumultuousness. Shrill small bells jangle as they strike against the garland of skulls swinging to and fro about my neck. My pile of matted locks, though fastened by firm knots, streams out in every direction. The bell on my *khaṭvāṅga* staff seems to ring out with a continuous piercing scream as it whirls round and round. The wind whistling through the hollows of the row of bare skulls constantly jingles the small bells and causes my banners to flap about.[174]

Looking at the place around her, she says :

> This is the temple of Karālā. I can tell that the nearby enclosure of the great cremation area is in front of me by the smoke from the funeral pyres which smells like the

[172]See the introduction to Devadhar and Suru's edition of the play, pp. 35–36.
[173]See ibid., pp. 14–20.
[174]Act V, vss. 3–4 (my translation).

> frying of garlic smeared with old *nimba* oil. My teacher Aghoraghaṇṭa has completed the performance of incantations *(mantra-sādhana)* and has commanded me today to bring together here all the necessities of worship *(pūjā)*.[175]

Aghoraghaṇṭa has told her, she says, that today he must offer to Karālā the previously promised 'woman-gem' who dwells in this very city. Kapālakuṇḍalā then notices the forlorn Mādhava wandering about the cremation ground. In his left hand he holds a 'glistening chunk of human flesh dripping with clotted blood.' As the Kāpālika woman exits Mādhava enters. He laments his separation from Mālatī and offers the flesh for sale to the fiendish local residents. His lengthy description of their loathsome activities serves as Bhavabhūti'a vehicle for expressing the sentiment of horror *(bībhatsa)*. As Mādhava passes near the temple of Karālā, he hears a voice crying out in distress and goes to investigate.

Kapālakuṇḍalā and Aghoraghaṇṭa then enter with Mālatī, who wears the marks of a sacrificial victim. The Kāpālikas offer obeisance to the goddess Cāmuṇḍā and describe her fearful dance as they themselves dance about the stage. Mālatī's last wish—that Mādhava should remember her even in death—wins the sympathy of the cruel Kapālakuṇḍalā, but Aghoraghaṇṭa remains pitiless. Raising his weapon, he calls upon Cāmuṇḍā to accept his offering. In the nick of time Mādhava rushes forward to save Mālatī. As the two men prepare to fight, soldiers are heard approaching the temple looking for her. This ends the fifth act called 'Description of the Cremation Ground.'

In act six Kapālakuṇḍalā tells how Mādhava has killed her *guru* and swears revenge. Much later, when Malatī and Mādhava are again briefly separated as they are about to be secretly married, Kapālakuṇḍalā has her chance. She captures the heroine and flies off to Śrīparvata with her. Act nine opens with the entrance of the *yoginī* Saudāminī, a former pupil of the go-between Kāmandakī. The *yoginī,* who has just flown up from Śrīparvata, finds the deseparate Mādhava and tells him that she has intercepted Kapālakuṇḍalā and rescued his precious Mālatī. The lovers are eventually reunited and all ends happily.

The *Caṇḍakauśika (Angry Kauśika)* by Kṣemīśvara is an adaptation of the purāṇic myth about King Hariścandra and the

---

[175]Act V, after vs. 4 (my translation).

irascible sage Viśvāmitra Kauśika.[176] One day the king accidentally interrupted the sage's meditation. As reparation he offered his whole kingdom, but the sage was still not satisfied and demanded a final fee *(dakṣiṇā)* as well. The king set out for Varanasi to earn it. In this city he resolved to sell himself into slavery. His virtuous wife, who had followed him to the market, rushed forward ahead of him and sold herself as a domestic slave to a Brahman teacher. Kauśika was not placated by her self-sacrifice, however, and the king in desperation declared that he would sell himself even to a Caṇḍāla. The god Dharma immediately appeared in the disguise of a Caṇḍāla and purchased the king as a keeper.

Act four, like the fifth act of *Mālatī-Mādhava,* takes place in the cremation ground. Hariścandra's duty was to take the blankets from the dead for his new master. Dharma entered, this time disguised as a Kāpālika, and said :

> Here am I, sir—
>
> Subsisting on alms given without asking for them and calmed by control over the five senses, I have crossed the great cremation ground of transmigratory existence *(saṃsāra)* and now roam this disgusting cremation ground.
>
> *(Reflecting).* It is quite suitable that divine Rudra performed the Mahāvrata. Supreme indeed is this excellence of (those who) roam at will. But—
>
> Being exclusively devoted to alms alone, penance alone, and rites alone—all this is easy to obtain. (Being intent upon) the Self alone, however, (is a state) difficult to obtain.[177]

The king greeted the ascetic: 'Welcome to the performer of the Mahāvrata who has undertaken a vow of lifelong chastity *(naiṣṭhika).*' The Kāpālika held several magical powers: control over a Vetāla and a thunderbolt *(vajra)*; possession of magical pills, ointments and foot salve; command over Daitya women; and knowledge of the elixer of life *(rasāyana)* and alchemy *(dhātuvāda).*[178] He requested the king to guard these from interference

[176] Ed. and trans. S.D. Gupta.

[177] Act IV, vss. 26–27 (my translation).

[178] Act IV, vs. 31. The purpose of these items is not altogether clear. According to one commentator, the Vetāla (a corpse animated by a demon spirit) serves as a

(vighnas). The king agreed to do so as long as there was no conflict with the aims of his master, the Caṇḍāla. While the king warded off the vighnas, the Kāpālika left in search of a great treasure of magical quicksilver *(siddharasa)* located somewhere nearby. The female Sciences (Vidyās) then appeared and offered their services to the king, but he told them to wait upon the revered Viśvāmitra Kauśika instead. Meanwhile the Kāpālika returned with a Vetāla who carried the treasure of magical quicksilver on his shoulder. This treasure, the Kāpālika claimed, could bestow immortality :

> Driving away death through its use and at once attaining the path to the immortal world, the Perfected Ones (Siddhas) enjoy themselves on the peaks of Meru, where the wishing tree *(kalpa-druma)* bears clusters of blossoms.[179]

He offered it to the king who refused to accept it for himself since this would be inconsistent with his condition of slavery. He requested the Kāpālika to give the treasure to the Caṇḍāla.

Hariścandra was given one more great test of character. His wife entered the cremation ground bearing the body of their son, and the king was forced to demand the funeral blanket as his master's due. After he had snatched it away, flowers fell from the sky and the gods sang his praises. The child revived and was crowned king of his father's empire. Hariścandra and his wife ascended to heaven amidst great rejoicing.

The *Prabodhacandrodaya* of Kṛṣṇamiśra[180] is an allegorical *nāṭaka* dedicated to the defense of *advaita* Vaiṣṇavism. Most of the characters are personifications of abstract qualities such as Discrimination *(viveka)*, Confusion *(moha)*, Falsity *(dambha)*, and Faith *(śraddhā)*. The third act introduces four heretical sectarians who are the friends and auxiliaries of Passion *(mahāmoha)* : a Materialist (Cārvāka), a Jain (Digambara or Kṣapaṇaka) a Buddhist monk (Bhikṣu), and a Kāpālika called Somasiddhānta. Two virtuous maidens, Tranquility *(śānti)* and Compassion *(karuṇā)*, enter in search of Tranquility's mother, Faith. They first meet the Jain who calls upon Faith in the form of a female

---

slave, the thunderbolt can be directed at will, the foot salve bestows power to walk on water or fly. We are not certain what the pills and ointment *(guṭikāñjana)* are supposed to accomplish.

[179]Act IV, vs. 34 (my translation).

[180]Ed. V.L. Paṇśīkar.

Digambara. Tranquility cannot accept this as her mother. Next the Buddhist introduces his own version of Faith, but this is also unacceptable to Tranquility. Somasiddhānta then enters extolling his own virtues (act III, vs. 12) :

> My charming ornaments are made from garlands of human bones. I dwell in the cremation ground and eat my food from a human skull. I view the world as alternately (or mutually) separate and not separate from God (Īśvara) through eyes that are made clear by the ointment of Yoga.

The Jain Kṣapaṇaka, curious to hear about the Kāpālika vow *(vrata)*, asks Somasiddhānta to explain his conception of *dharma* and *mokṣa*. Somasiddhānta eagerly complies (act III, vs. 13) :

> O Kṣapaṇaka, you should certainly consider our *dharma*. We offer oblations of human flesh mixed with brains, entrails and marrow. We conclude our fast by drinking liquor *(surā)* from the skull of a Brahman (or Brahmā). At that time the god Mahābhairava should be worshipped with offerings of awe-inspiring human sacrifices from whose severed throats blood flows in torrents.

When the Kṣapaṇaka fiercely repudiates this grim *dharma,* Somasiddhānta castigates him in return (act III, vs. 14) :

> Ah, Evil one, outcast among heretics, you whose bald head has a single tuft of hair on the top, you whose hair is pulled out (at the roots)! So, the divine Lord of Bhavānī, He who creates, preserves and destroys the fourteen worlds, He the greatness of whose doctrine is revealed in the Vedānta (or Upaniṣads), is a deceiver! I control the gods headed by Hari, Hara and the Eldest of gods (Brahmā). I can even halt the progress of the stars travelling in the sky. Know that I can submerge this earth with its mountains and towns under water and then drink up all that water again in an instant.

The Kṣapaṇaka again condemns the Kāpālika *dharma*, and Somasiddhānta threatens to gladden the Wife of Bharga (Durgā) and her troop of demons with the blood from his severed neck.

With the help of the Buddhist Bhikṣu, the Kṣapaṇaka succeeds in calming his adversary and asks him about the Kāpālika conception of *mokṣa*. Somasiddhānta replies that *mokṣa* is a condition of sensual bliss and is achieved by the union of the worshipper and his wife, who are the earthly counterparts of Śiva and Śakti.[181] When the Jain and the Buddhist again declare his doctrine to be false, Somasiddhānta summons his own Faith in the form of a beautiful Kāpālinī. At the command of her master she embraces first the Buddhist and then the Jain. The resistance of both is soon shipwrecked on the shore of lust. They plead with Somasiddhānta to initiate them into the most excellent doctrine of Mahābhairava. He orders them to sit and takes up a vessel of liquor. He drinks from it and offers the remainder to his new disciples (act III, vs. 20) :

> Drink this purifying nectar. It is the remedy prescribed by Bhairava against (transmigratory) existence. It is the means of cutting away the bonds of creaturehood *(paśu-pāśa)*.

They at first refuse this polluted and improper drink, but when Faith takes a sip they can contain their eagerness no longer and together imbibe the wine, which is made 'fragrant with the liquor from the mouth of the Kāpālinī.' The two are soon drunk. Pleased with his work, the Kāpālika says to his Faith : 'Love, we have obtained a pair of slaves purchased without capital. Let us now dance.' As they all dance about, he extols his doctrine in which the eight great powers *(mahāsiddhis)* are won without having to abandon the objects of the senses.[182] The Ksapaṇaka then praises his new 'king of teachers' and *kulācārya*.[183] The Bhikṣu sees that the Jain is drunk and asks Somasiddhānta to sober him up. Somasiddhānta does this by giving the Jain some half-chewed betel nut. The three heretics then draw up a plan to capture Faith for their king, Passion, but they soon discover that she has been joined by Viṣṇu-devotion and Dharma and has entered the ranks of their enemy, the good king Discrimination. Tranquility and Compassion are overjoyed at this news and set off again in search of Faith.

Kāpālikas have relatively minor roles in the other plays we have noted. Śaṅkhadhara's *Laṭamelaka*[184] is a one act farce *(prahasana)*,

[181]Act II, vs. 16. See also below, pp. 90–92.

[182]Act III, vs. 22.

[183]The title *kulācārya* again shows the close relation between the Kaula and Kāpālika faiths.

[184]Ed. Durgāprasād.

like the *Mattavilāsa*. The Kāpālika in it is called Ajñānarāśi (Ignorance-heap) and has an intelligence to match. He spends his time arguing with a Digambara monk named Jaṭāsura. In Rāmacandra's *Kaumudīmitrānanda*[185] a Kāpālika offers oblations of human intestines in a fire and revives a corpse. One of the heroes of the play causes the revived corpse to strike down the Kāpālika. The same author's *Nalavilāsa*[186] features two Kāpālikas—Lambodara (Hanging-belly) alias Koṣṭhaka (Stomach) alias Bhasmaka (Ashes) and his teacher Ghoraghona (Horrible-snout) alias Meṣamukha (Sheep-face). Both are spies for Ciṭrasena, a Kalacuri-Cedi king. The spies are devious but rather amusing. In Yaśaḥpāla's *Moharājaparājaya*[187] five heretics—a Kaula, a Rahamāṇa (Muslim), a Ghaṭacaṭaka, a Nihilist (Nāstika), and a Kāpālika—each give a one verse summary of their faith. The Kāpālika says : 'It has been declared by Narakāpālin (Human-skull-bearer, = Śiva) that whosoever always eats human meat from the skull of an excellent man obtains the place of Śiva *(Śivasthāna)*.'[188]

Between the rather ghoulish Kāpālikas of some of these works and the bibulous Satyasoma of the *Mattavilāsa* there is a wide gulf, but this need not imply that either description is completely false. Tantric religion contains an amalgam of hedonistic and sadistic elements. The playwrights have simply emphasised one or other of these two elements in accordance with their artistic purposes and religious prejudices. Since hedonism lends itself easily to comic treatment, farces such as *Mattavilāsa* and *Laṭamelaka* feature Kāpālika sybarites. Those authors whose aim is to horrify lay stress on the more sinister aspects of the cult. One work, the *Prabodhacandrodaya,* includes both elements. Although the account in this play is still highly tendentious and distorted, it is in many respects the most informative. We must postpone a fuller discussion of Kāpālika religion until after we have reviewed the descriptions of these ascetics in religious and narrative literature.

Miscellaneous Later Sources

Stories about Kāpālikas occur frequently in *kathā* collections such as Somadeva's *Kathāsaritsāgara* (*c.* 1063–81). In this work

[185]We could not locate a copy of this work, It is summarised by Handiqui, p. 358 and by Keith, p. 259.

[186]Ed. G.K. Shrigondekar and L.B. Gandhi.

[187]Ed. Chaturavijayaji.

[188]Act IV, vs. 23. The Ghaṭacaṭaka cannot be satisfactorily identified.

the story of Madanamañjarī pits a Kāpālika against the illustrious king Vikramāditya.[189] Madanamañjarī, the daughter of the king of the Yakṣas and wife of Kubera's brother, was amusing herself one day in a garden in Ujjayinī. She was seen there by a 'hypocritical Kāpālika.'[190] He immediately fell in love with her and retired to a cremation ground to attempt to make her his wife by means of a spell *(mantra)* and burnt offering. Madanamañjarī learned of his plan through her magical power but was helpless against his Yakṣa-subduing spells. Drawn by these spells she reached 'the terrible cremation ground which was filled with bones and skulls and frequented by demons.' There she saw the wicked Kāpālika. He had made a fire for oblations and a ritual circle *(maṇḍala)* in which he worshipped a supine corpse.[191] Madanamañjarī invoked the protection of king Vikramāditya who immediately appeared accompanied by a Vetāla named Agniśikha. The king ordered the Vetāla to 'kill and eat this evil Kāpālika who has carried off another's wife.' The Vetāla entered the corpse which rose up and quickly dispatched the Kāpālika.

Another lecherous Kāpālika appears in the story of a young Brahman named Candrasvāmin.[192] One day this Brahman went to town on an errand. Meanwhile a Kāpālika came to Candrasvāmin's house and happened to see his beautiful wife. The lady immediately contracted a fever and died that evening. By the time Candrasvāmin returned, his wife's relations had already placed her body on a funeral pyre. As he approached the blazing pyre he saw the Kāpālika. On his shoulder the ascetic carried a 'dancing' *khaṭvāṅga* staff, and in his hands he held a thundering *ḍamaruka* drum. When he threw ashes on the fire, the lady stood up uninjured. Drawn by his magical power *(siddhi)*, she ran away with him to a cave on the bank of the Ganga. In the cave were two captive maidens. After putting down his *khaṭvāṅga*, the Kāpālika exclaimed to them: 'My vow has attained success *(siddhi)*. I have now obtained her without whom I could not enjoy you two even though I had obtained you.' The lady's husband Candrasvāmin had followed them there, however, and, seeing his chance, he threw the *khaṭvāṅga* into the

---

189Ed. Durgāprasād and K.P. Parab, xviii. 2. 1–33 and 209–214.

190*khaṇḍa-Kāpālika*. This is how Tawney renders this strange term. Böhtlinck and Roth *(Sanskrit Wörterbuch)* translate 'ein Quasi-kāpālika.'

191xviii. 2. 15. To a certain extent this ceremony resembles the Mahākāla-hṛdaya performed by Bhairavācārya in the *Harṣa-carita*.

192Ibid., xviii. 5. 1–22.

Ganga. Without the magic of his staff, the Kāpālika was powerless. He tried to flee but was killed by one of Candrasvāmin's poison arrows. 'Thus,' says Somadeva (xviii. 5. 16), 'heretics, who make a mockery of the *Śivāgamas* for the pleasure of evil accomplishments, fall (into ruin), just as they had already fallen (into sin).' Candrasvāmin released the two bewitched maidens and returned home with his wife.

Another story from the *Kathāsaritsāgara,* that of the Brahman gambler Devadatta (v. 3. 196ff.), has as one of its central characters a Mahāvratin named Jālapāda. One day Devadatta gambled away all his possessions, even his clothes, and was unable to return home to his father's house. He entered an empty temple where he saw the solitary Mahāvratin, whose magic had accomplished many things, muttering *mantras*. Devadatta greeted him respectfully and recited his tale of woe. The Mahāvratin offered to restore Devadatta's fortunes if the gambler would assist him in becoming a Vidyādhara. The following day the Mahāvratin came and sat under a banyan tree in a corner of the cremation ground. That night he did *pūjā*, offered rice boiled in milk, and scattered food offerings in the four quarters. He told his new assistant to perform the same worship every day in the same spot while saying: 'O Vidyutprabhā, you should accept this *pūjā*.'[193] Eventually their efforts were rewarded with success.

In *Kathāsaritsāgara* v. 2. 81 Somadeva mentions a 'Mahāvratin Kapālin' who wears matted hair, smears himself with white ashes, and has a half moon like Śiva's drawn on his forehead. In yet another story (iii. 5. 74–77) a group of spies in Varanasi disguise themselves as ascetics who 'observed the Kāpālika vow.' One of them assumes the role of teacher while the others become his disciples. These disciples then go about saying: 'This teacher knows the present, past and future.' And they make sure that any predictions their teacher makes, come true. By this infallible method the spy-ascetic quickly wins the notice and confidence of the king.

The Jain legend of Prince Brahmadatta is found in Devendra Gaṇī's eleventh century commentary on the *Uttarādhyayana*[194] and in Hemacandra's (1088–1172) *Triṣaṣṭiśalākapuruṣacaritra.*[195] At one point in this story, the prince's friend Varadhanu is forced

[193]v. 3. 207. Vidyutprabhā was the daughter of a Yakṣa king.
[194]Trans. J.J. Meyer, *Hindu Tales,* pp. 23ff.
[195]Trans. H.M. Johnson, V. 335ff.

to disguise himself as a Kāpālika in order to rescue his mother from the Caṇḍāla quarter of a town.

Several other early mediaeval works by Jain authors contain stories about Kāpālika ascetics or at least briefly mention them. In Haribhadra's (*c.* 750–800) Prakrit *Samarāiccakahā,* the gambler Maheśvaradatta becomes a Kāpālika and an expert in snakebite charms *(gāruḍa-mantras)*.[196] In the *Pārśvanātha-caritra* the goddess Kālī priases a Kāpālika who collects skulls for her. When she obtains her 108th skull she is to 'fulfill her purpose.'[197] Vinayacandra's (*c.* 1300) *Mallinātha-caritra* tells how Prince Ratnacandra finds a Kāpālika 'eagerly dancing with a sharp sword' in front of a young woman who is tied to a post. The prince rescues her and kills the ascetic.[198] The story of King Devapāla in the *Kathākośa,* a collection of uncertain date, mentions a Kāpālika who carries a bundle of wood on his head. When the queen sees him, she recognises him as her husband from a former life. She had worshipped the Jina and become a queen. He had refused to do so and attained the 'miserable condition' of a Kāpālika.[199] In Jambhaladatta's version of the *Vetālapañcaviṁśati,*[200] written sometime before 1500, the ascetic whom King Vikramakeśarin agrees to assist is called a Kāpālika. The king is requested to carry an unmutilated dead man from a tree on the bank of a river to the cremation ground where the Kāpālika is to perform a magic rite. 'When you have come,' the Kāpālika tells him, 'then here in a circle [*maṇḍala*] furnished with the various instruments of worship, when I have washed the corpse and worshipped the gods and muttered a great incantation [*mahāmantra*], I shall attain magic power [*siddhi*].'[201] The ascetic's actual aim is to sacrifice the king, but the dead man, really a Vetāla, warns the king and the Kāpālika is killed instead.

Many references to these ascetics take the form of poetic metaphors or similes. Thus Trivikrama-bhaṭṭa's (*c.* 915) *Nalacampū,* a Jain version of the famous legend, compares the trees of the

---

[196]Cited by Handiqui, p. 358.

[197]ii. 288, cited by M. Bloomfield, 'On False Ascetics and Nuns in Hindu Fiction,' *JAOS,* XLIV (1924), 203. There are several works by this name. We have not been able to locate Bloomfield's source.

[198]Ed. Hargovinddas and Bechardas, i. 40–62. This is again reminiscent of the episodes in Daṇḍin's *Daśakumāracarita* and Bhavabhūti's *Mālatī-Mādhava.*

[199]Ed. J.L. Shastri, p. 4.

[200]Ed. and trans. M.B. Emeneau. The earlier versions of this cycle do not specifically call the ascetic a Kāpālika.

[201]Trans. ibid., p. 11.

Vindhya forest to the *khaṭvāṅga* staffs of Kāpālikas.[202] The fourteenth century Muslim poet Abdul Rahmān uses the Kāpālika as a symbol of an absent and wandering husband in his Apabhraṃśa *Saṃdeśa-rāsaka.*[203]

Kalhaṇa's *Rājataraṅgiṇī,* written between 1150 and 1160, contains several such poetic allusions. During a severe famine in Kashmir the ground is said to have become covered with fragments of skulls and 'to observe, as it were, the custom of skull-carrying ascetics *(kāpālika).*'[204] After the burning of the temple of Cakradhara (Viṣṇu) in about A.D. 1125, says Kalhaṇa, '*Maṅkha,* a Dāmara from *Naunagara,* searched the dead bodies like a Kāpālika, and gratified himself with the objects found upon them.'[205] Bhandreśvara, a rapacious tax official in the service of Saṃgrāmarāja (1003–1028), is unfavorably compared to 'a fear-inspiring Kāpālika, who lives on corpses, [but] gives maintenance to his own people.'[206]

More interesting is an episode in the *Rājataraṅgiṇī* which seems to identify the Pāśupatas and the Kāpālikas and to connect them both with Śrīparvata. This is the legend of the kings Vikramāditya-Harṣa, Pravarasena II and Mātṛgupta.[207] Pravarasena, son of Toramāṇa and heir to the throne of Kashmir, went on a lengthy pilgrimage during which the throne fell vacant. King Vikramāditya-Harṣa, who was apparently overlord of the region, sent his court poet Mātṛgupta to fill the post. Pravarasena, still on pilgrimage, learned of this usurpation and sought to gain the kingship himself. When he arrived at Śrīparvata, 'a saint [Siddha] called *Aśvapāda,* who appeared in the guise of a Pāśupata ascetic, offered him food prepared from roots.'[208] Aśvapāda said that the prince had been his attendant in a former life and that on a certain occasion the ascetic had offered his servant a boon. Pravarasena had asked for a kingdom. Śiva had then appeared and promised to fulfill this wish in another life. After imparting this information, Aśvapāda disappeared. The prince stayed at Śrīparvata and performed penances in order to win the favor of Śiva. Eventually Śiva granted

---

[202]Ed. Durgāprasād and Śivadatta, p. 165.

[203]Ed. and trans. J.V. Muni, ii. 86 and iii. 185.

[204]Trans. M.A. Stein, Vol. II, viii. 1211. Ed. M.A. Stein (same verse numbers).

[205]Trans. Stein, Vol. II, viii. 995.

[206]Trans. Stein, Vol. II, vii. 44.

[207]Trans. Stein, Vol. I, iii. 125–378.

[208]Trans. Stein, Vol. I, iii. 267.

the promised boon and Mātṛgupta peacefully abdicated in favor of Pravarasena. At the end of Pravarasena's long reign, Aśvapāda ordered his new disciple Jayanta, a Kashmiri Brahman, to take a letter to the king. When Jayanta complained that he was too exhausted from travelling to start on the great journey back to Kashmir, Aśvapāda said: 'Then bathe to-day, since I who am of the *Kāpālin* sect, have touched you who are a Brahman.'[209] Aśvapāda then threw him into a pond. When Jayanta opened his eyes he was standing near Pravarasena's palace. The letter was quickly delivered. It instructed the king to 'go and betake yourself to Śiva's abode.'[210] With a great burst of light the king rose into the heavens.

There has been much speculation about the identity of these three kings. It can be safely said only that they lived sometime between the fifth and eighth centuries. The legend about them is apocryphal in any case. From our point of view the important fact is that a Pāśupata ascetic who lives at Śrīparvata calls himself a member of the Kāpālin sect. Kalhaṇa's apparent identification of the two sects is undoubtedly a mistake, but it is an understandable one since Śrīparvata is associated both with the Pāśupatas, through their offshoot the Kālāmukhas, and with the Kāpālikas. In the time of the three kings, the site was probably controlled by the Kāpālikas. In Kalhaṇa's time it was a Kālāmukha center. This might be the source of his confusion.

The idea of contact with Kāpālikas causing pollution recurs in several sources. In view of their strange habits, this is not surprising. Kṣemendra (*c*. 1050–75), the Kashmiri polymath, includes a restriction against drinking with Kāpālikas in an attack against the tantric *gurus* of the Kali-yuga: 'The *gurus* claim that *mukti* (is obtained) by drinking (wine) in one vessel with artisans—such as washermen, weavers, leather makers, and Kāpālikas—during *cakra-pūjā*,[211] by having a feast of unhesitating sexual pleasure, and by (generally leading) a festive life.'[212] It is not clear why

[209] Trans. Stein, Vol. I, iii. 369.

[210] Trans. Stein, Vol. I, iii. 373.

[211] During *cakra-pūjā* tantric adepts are required to partake of the five Ma-sounds—wine, meat, fish, *mudrā*, and sexual intercourse.

[212] *Daśāvatāra-carita*, ed. Durgāprasād and K.P. Parab, x. 26. In Kṣemendra's *Deśopadeśa* (ed. M.K. Shāstrī, iv. 3), a procuress is said to have the 'form of the great skeleton of the Kāpālika of Death.' A Mahāvratin appears with some heretics and rogues in Kṣemendra's *Narmamālā* (ed. M.K. Shāstrī, iii. 15).

Kāpālikas are included in a list of artisans *(śilpins)*. Somadeva's *Yaśastilaka* (A.D. 959) prescribes the following penance for a Jain monk who comes into contact with a Kāpālika: 'When there is contact with a Kāpālika, a menstruating woman, a Caṇḍāla, a Śabara, or other (such persons), as a penance one should duly bathe, fast, and mutter a *mantra*.'[213] Devaṇṇa Bhaṭṭa (*c*. 1200) quotes a similar passage from the *Ṣaṭtriṃśanmata*: 'When one touches Bauddhas, Pāśupatas, Jains, Lokāyatikas, Kāpilas, or Brahmans who perform prohibited acts, one should enter the water still dressed. In case of contact with Kāpālikas, restraint of the breath *(prāṇāyāma)* is also prescribed.[214] The *Uśana-saṃhitā* includes Kāpālikas in a list of heretics with whom food should not be eaten.[215]

Two fairly late works, the *Bārhaspati-sūtra* and Guṇaratna's fourteenth century commentary on Haribhadra's *Ṣaḍdarśana-samuccaya,* stress the hedonistic element of the Kāpālika faith. Guṇaratna claims that the Kāpālikas are identical with the Nāstikas or Lokāyatikas who enjoy wine, meat and illicit intercourse.[216] The *Bārhaspati-sūtra* distinguishes Kāpālikas from Lokāyatikas but seconds Guṇaratna's charge of dissoluteness.[217]

A fourteenth century Tamil work, the *Śivaprakāśam* of Umāpati, contains a brief disquisition on seven sects which hold that *mukti* is the removal of *mala* (impurity). These include the Pāśupata, the Mahāvratin and the Kāpālika.[218] Here Mahāvratin probably denotes the Kālāmukhas. Another Tamil work, the *Tiruvoṟṟiyūr Purāṇam*. seems to refer to Mahāvratins in this sense.[219] The twelfth century Tamil author Śēkkiḻār describes a Mahāvratin ascetic who might be either a Kāpālika or a Kālāmukha. This ascetic is Śiva himself in disguise. Three lines of ashes are drawn across his forehead; his head is shaved except for a tuft tied up

---

[213]vi. 3, cited by Handiqui, p. 356 (my translation). Elsewhere in this work Somadeva describes a certain bad minister as one whose 'fame has been spread in the world by religious mendicants, snake-charmers, Kāpālikas, jugglers and consummate thugs' (iii. 183, trans. Handiqui, p. 66).

[214]*Smṛticandrikā,* ed. L. Srinivasacharya, II, 310.

[215]Chap. iv, vss. 23–26, cited by T.V. Mahalingam, 'The Pāśupatas in South India,' *JIH,* XXVII (1949), 46.

[216]Ed. L. Suali, p. 300.

[217]Ed. and trans. F.W. Thomas, ii. 6, 9, 13, 18–21.

[218]Trans. H.R. Hoisington, *JAOS,* IV (1854), 125–244.

[219]See V. Raghavan, 'Tiruvoṟṟiyūr Inscription of Chaturānana Paṇḍita: 20th Year of Kṛishṇa III,' *EI,* XXVII, 300.

with a garland of bone beads; he wears *kuṇḍala* earrings; he has a necklace or garland of shining bone beads and a shoulder strap for yogic postures; his sacred thread is a rope of black hair; he is smeared with ashes and carries a sack of them with him; on one wrist a single bead is tied with a string *(sūtra)*; his genitals are covered only by a loincloth; and the five marks *(mudrās)* of greatness shine on his feet.[220]

Important references to Kāpālikas occur in three Old Bengali songs *(caryāpadas)* by the Sahajiyā Buddhist saint Kāṇhapāda (Sanskrit, Kṛṣṇapāda).[221] Kāṇha in fact calls himself a Kāpālin although the context makes it probable that he intends this in a symbolic sense. Two of the Kāpālin songs are addressed to the Ḍombī (Washerwoman) who, in symbolic terms, is the goddess Nairātmyā (Essencelessness) and Buddhist counterpart to the Hindu Kula-kuṇḍalinī Śakti.[222] In the form of a Kāpālin yogin, Kāṇha becomes the lover or husband of the Ḍombī :

> Outside the city, O Ḍombī, is thy cottage; thou goest just touching the Brahmins and the shaven-headed (and never reveal [*sic*] thyself to them). O Ḍombī, I shall keep company with thee and it is for this purpose that I have become a naked Kāpālī without aversions. . . . Thou art the Ḍombī and I am the Kāpālī, for thee have I put on a garland of bones. The Ḍombī destroys the lake and eats up the lotus-stalk. I shall kill thee, Ḍombī, and take thy life.[223]

As the earthly Ḍombī should not be touched by the orthodox, so the divine Ḍombī is inaccessible to them. She lives outside the 'city' (the world of the senses). Unless she is killed (i.e. controlled) she spoils the lake (the body) and eats the lotus stalk (the *bodhicitta* or mind of enlightenment).[224] The second song expresses similar sentiments :

> Of what nature is, O Ḍombī, thy cleverness?—the aristocrats are outside thee and the Kāpālīs are within . . . Thou art

[220]Paraphrase of translation by Rangaswamy in his *The Religion and Philosophy of Tēvāram*, I, 385.

[221]Ed. and trans. M. Shahidullah, *Les Chants Mystiques*, songs no. 10, 11 and 18 (Śāstrī's numbers). Some of Kāṇha's songs are translated into English by S. Dasgupta in his *Obscure Religious Cults*.

[222]See Dasgupta, ibid., pp. 96–106.

[223]Song no. 10, trans. ibid., pp. 103–104.

[224]See ibid., p. 104.

the *Kāma-caṇḍālī,*—there is no woman more cunning and unfaithful than the Ḍombī.[225]

The 'aristocrats' *(kuliṇa jaṇa)* are the orthodox priests. It is only the Kāpālins who can realise Nairātmyā.[226]

In the third song Kāṇha symbolically explains the essence of the true Kāpālin : 'the yogin Kāṇha has become a Kāpālī, and has entered into the practices of yoga, and he is sporting in the city of his body in a non-dual form.'[227] His anklets and bell *(ghaṇṭā)* are the *āli* and *kāli*—'the principles of all kinds of duality.'[228] His earrings *(kuṇḍala)* are the sun and the moon (Upāya and Prajñā, equivalent to Śiva and Śakti). The ashes he smears on his body are the ashes of passion *(rāga)*, aversion *(deśa,* Sanskrit *dveṣa),* and error *(moha)*. His pearl necklace is supreme salvation *(parama mokha)*. The song ends with a paradoxical verse typical of tantric 'intentional language' *(sandhā-bhāṣā)* : 'Ayant tué la belle-mère (=le souffle) le beau-frère et la belle-soeur [=the senses] dans la maison et ayant tué la mère (=l'illusion) Kāṇha est devenu porteur de crânes [*kabāli,* = *kapālin*].'[229]

In these songs the Kāpālin symbolizes the perfected yogin precisely because on a mundane level he is the most debased of ascetics. The verse about his murder of his mother and various relatives suggests that Kāṇha may also have been aware of the connection between the Kapālin and the Brahmahatyā vow of the law books.[230] But just as one must not suppose that Kāṇha actually killed his mother and relatives, it is unlikely that he actually became a Kāpālika. The Kapālin, like the Ḍombī, is a symbolic representative of the mystical doctrine of the identity of opposites. It is just possible, however, that Kaṇha gave this doctrine concrete embodiment and assumed the dress and habits of a Kāpālika.[231] The connection between the Kāpālika vow and the penance of

[225]Song no. 18, trans. ibid., pp. 104–105.

[226]Ibid.

[227]Song no. 11, trans. ibid., p. 90. Dasgupta notes that here the Sanskrit commentator derives the word Kāpālika as follows : *kaṃ mahā-sukhaṃ pālayati'ti kāpālikaḥ,* 'He who nurses Ka which means Mahā-sukha is a Kāpālika.'

[228]Ibid., p. 58. Dasgupta paraphrases the song on pp. 57–58.

[229]Trans. Shahidullah, p. 118.

[230]See below, pp. 73–82.

[231]Kāṇhapāda is often identified with the Nāth Siddha Kānupā. If correct, this identification would help to bridge the gap between Kāṇha's tantric Buddhism and the tantric Śaivism of the Kāpālikas. *Kāṇha* and *Kānu* are both venacular variants

the Brahmahan is itself an example of the operation of this doctrine.[232] In cases like this the boundary between symbol and reality often becomes difficult to define.

From an historical point of view, Kāṇha's mention of the Kāpālikas is important since it is the earliest reference to these ascetics in Bengal. Kāṇha's date is uncertain but it seems probable that he and the other authors of the Sahajiyā *dohās* and *caryāpadas* flourished during the eighth to twelfth centuries under the Pālas.[233] If Kāṇha is the same as the Siddha Kānu-pā, as seems quite possible, he must have lived sometime after the tenth century.[234]

---

of the Sanskrit *Kṛṣṇa*. Kānu-pā's *guru* was named Jālandharī-pā. In song no. 36 Kāṇha mentions a Jālandharī-pā as his, or at least a former, teacher. Dasgupta is disinclined to accept these identifications (*Obscure* . . ., pp. 392–94), but to us this seems rather stubborn-minded.

[232]See below, pp. 76–77.

[233]Dasgupta, *Obscure* . . ., p. 9.

[234]Ibid., pp. 386–93.

CHAPTER III

KĀPĀLIKA CULT AND DOCTRINE

The Mahāvrata

One of the most puzzling problems about the Kāpālikas, and to some extent the Kālāmukhas as well, is their association with penance or vow called the *Mahāvrata* (Great Vow). Since there is reason to believe that the Kāpālika and Kālāmukha Mahāvratas were different vows, we will discuss them separately beginning with the former.

A large number of sources connect the Kāpālikas with the Mahāvrata. Jagaddhara, a commentator on *Mālatī-Mādhava,* explains *Kāpālika-vrata* or *Kapāla-vrata* as Mahāvrata.[1] Similarly, Caṇḍapāla, a commentator on Trivikrama-bhaṭṭa's *Nalacampū* (p. 164), equates Kāpālikas and Mahāvratikas. A Śaivite ascetic in Somadeva's *Kathāsaritsāgara* v. 2. 81 is called a Kapālin Mahāvratin. Kṣīrasvāmin (eleventh century), in his commentary on the *Amarakośa,* lists together Kāpālin, Mahāvratin, Somasiddhāntin, and Tāntrika.[2] A Mahāvrata-Kāpālika named Mahāvrata, who follows the 'heretical *Mahāvrata-siddhānta,*' appears in Gokulanātha's *Amṛtodaya* (*c.* 1700).[3] As we have seen,[4] some of the Purāṇas and a few other sources contain lists of sects in which the Kāpālikas (or Kālāmukhas) are replaced by Mahāvrata-dharas or Mahāvratins. In one or two of these sources, however, Mahāvratins are listed as distinct from both Kāpālikas and Kālāmukhas. In two plays, *Mattavilāsa* and *Caṇḍakauśika,* a Kāpālika character refers to Śiva's performance of this vow.[5] In the latter work the Kāpālika himself is called a Mahāvrata-cārin as well.[6] We have already discussed the seventh century Cālukya grant from Nasik District, which registers a donation to the Mahāvratin priests of a Kāpāleś-

---

[1]Ed. R.G. Bhandarkar, text p. 33.

[2]Quoted in Śrīharṣa, p. 640.

[3]Ed. Śivadatta and K.P. Parab, pp. 41–42.

[4]See above, pp. 7–11.

[5]Mahendravarman, *Mattavilāsa,* ed. T.G. Śāstrī, vs. 17 and Kṣemīśvara, *Caṇḍakauśika,* Act IV, vss. 26–27.

[6]Act IV, after vs. 29.

vara temple, and the eleventh century grant from Baroda District, which compares its priestly donee to Kapālin Śaṃkara.

What was this Mahāvrata? The best known rite by this name takes place during the last day but one in a *sattra* and is described in the *Jaiminīya Brāhmaṇa* and a few other early works. It is associated with the mysterious brotherhood, the *Vrātyas,* whom Hauer saw as precursors of the yogins,[7] and it incorporates a number of features which seem appropriate for a Kāpālika ceremony, such as ritual reviling, obscene dialogue and sexual intercourse.[8] There is little likelihood, however, that this ritual would have been resurrected several hundred years after it had to all intents and purposes died out and after its original religious and social context had disappeared. Furthermore, there is another Mahāvrata which may be identified with some certainty as the Great Vow of the Kāpālikas. This is the chief penance prescribed for the removal of the sin of (accidently) killing a Brāhmaṇa.

The rules for this penance, with several variations, are found in most of the major law books, but it is called the Mahāvrata in only one of them, the *Viṣṇu-smṛti*. This work says :

> 1. Let a man make a hut of leaves in a forest and dwell in it;
> 2. And let him bathe (and perform his prayers) three times a day;
> 3. And let him collect alms, going from one village to another, and proclaiming his own deed;
> 4. And let him sleep upon grass :
> 5. This is called a [the] Mahāvrata (great observance).
> 6. He who has killed a Brāhmaṇa (unintentionally) must perform it for twelve years.
>
> . . . . . .
>
> 15. He who is performing any of those penances must carry (on his stick) the skull of the person slain, like a flag.[9]

---

[7]J.W. Hauer, *Der Vrātya*. J.C. Heesterman has recently taken issue with the views of Hauer and others in his article 'Vrātya and Sacrifice' (*IIJ*, VI [1962–63], 1–37). Heesterman sees them as 'authentic Vedic Aryas' whose rituals 'are the crude predecessors of the śrauta ritual' (p. 36).

[8]See Hauer, pp. 246ff.; Eliade, pp. 103–105; and Kane, *HDS*, II, 1243–45.

[9]Trans. J. Jolly, 1. 1–6, 15. Ed. V. Krishnamacharya. Compare *Manu-smṛti*, trans. G. Bühler, xi. 73; *Yājñavalkya-smṛti*, ed. N.R. Acharya, iii. 243; *Gautama Dharmaśāstra*, trans. G. Bühler, xxii. 4–6; *Baudhāyana Dharmaśāstra*, trans. G. Bühler, ii. 1. 2–3; *Āpastambīya Dharmasūtra*, trans. G. Bühler, i. 24. 11–20; ibid., i. 28. 21 to i. 29. 1; and *Kūrma Purāṇa*, ii. 30.

We have quoted above the version of this penance prescribed in the *Yājñavalkya-smṛti* iii. 243.[10] There the performer is called a *kapālin,* but only in the sense of 'one who carries a skull.' Yajñavalkya implies that the penitent should carry a skull in his hand as well as on his staff. The commentators disagree about whether or not he should use the skull in his hand as a begging bowl.[11] In the *Āpastambīya Dharmasūtra,* however, a person who has killed a learned Brāhmaṇa *(Bhrūṇahan)* is required to 'take a human skull for his drinking-vessel.'[12] One who kills an ordinary Brāhmaṇa, on the other hand, is merely instructed to carry a shallow metal or clay vessel.[13] Several works require the penitent to carry a skull on his staff, and this skull is generally identified as the skull of the person slain.[14] Some works also require the carrying of a *khaṭvāṅga,*[15] the staff most often associated with the Kāpālikas. In his comments on *Āpastambīya Dharmasūtra* i. 29. 1, Haradatta (*c.* twelfth century) in fact says : 'the word *khaṭvāṅga* is well known in the *Kāpālika-tantra.*'[16] Literally, *khaṭvāṅga* means 'limb of a bedstead,' apparently on account of its shape. Vijñāneśvara's *Mitākṣara* on *Yājñavalkya* iii. 243 describes it as a 'banner made of a skull mounted on a stick *(daṇḍa).*'

A few of the law books specify the clothes the penitent must wear. Āpastamba says that a Bhrūṇahan 'shall put on the skin of a dog or of an ass, with the hair turned outside.'[17] Baudhāyana (ii. 1. 3) prescribes the hide of an ass alone. For an ordinary Brahmahan Āpastamba (i. 24. 11) requires a plain hempen loincloth reaching from the navel to the knees.

Because he is polluted by his crime, the sinner must live in a hut in the forest and avoid entering a village except to beg. According

---

10See above, p. 13.

11See Kane, *HDS,* IV, 89. Kane discusses in some detail this and other penances for the crime (ibid., pp. 87–96).

12Trans. Bühler, i. 28. 21. See also *Baudhāyana* ii. 1. 3 and *Gautama* xxii. 4.

13*Āpastambīya* i. 24. 14.

14*Manu* xi. 73 and *Āpastambīya* i. 24. 11. Vijñāneśvara's *Mitākṣara* (ed. N.R. Acharya) on *Yājñavalkya* iii. 243 quotes Śātātapa as saying that the guilty person should visit the *tīrthas* taking with him the skull of the Brāhmana he has killed. Vijñāneśvara adds that if the head of the person slain is not available, the head of another Brāhmaṇa should be used.

15*Āpastambīya* i. 29. 1 (penance for a *Bhrūṇahan*); *Gautama* xxii. 4; and *Baudhāyana* ii. 1.3.

16Ed. M. Śāstrī and K. Raṅgāchārya.

17Trans. Bühler, i. 28. 21.

to Baudhāyana (ii. 1. 3) a Bhrūṇahan should build his hut in a burial ground. Āpastamba (i. 29. 1) suggests that he should live in an empty house or under a tree.

Apart from begging, the Brahmahan's daily duties are not much discussed. The *Viṣṇu-smṛti* 1. 2 instructs him to perform the usual *trisaṃdhya* ablutions. Āpastamba (i. 24. 11 and 18) requires him to tend cows and restrain his speech. Gautama (xxii. 4) says he should remain chaste.

The Brahmahan must obtain all his food by begging. Āpastamba specifies that he should visit only seven houses on one day. At each he should cry : 'Who will give to an Abhiśasta [guilty one]?'[18] A Bhrūṇahan, says Āpastamba, should cry : 'Who (gives) alms for a Bhrūṇahan?' According to Baudhāyana the Bhrūṇahan should also follow the seven house rule.[19] It is generally agreed that the penance for both the Brahmahan and the Bhrūṇahan should be performed for twelve years, but Āpastamba (i.29.1) says that the Bhrūṇahan must maintain the vow until death.

Several law books list additional penances for the crime of killing a Brāhmaṇa.[20] The commentators assign these different penances according to the education and wisdom of the victim and the presence or absence of intention in the slayer. Some of these alternative penances end in almost certain death and others merely require the spending of large amounts of money for Vedic sacrifices. One of them, the chief penance prescribed for a Bhrūṇahan in the *Vāsiṣṭha Dharmasūtra,* seems to have tantric overtones. The guilty person is instructed to build a fire and offer in it eight oblations cut from his own body : hair, skin, blood, flesh, sinews, fat, bones, and marrow. The successive oblations are offered to Death with the words 'I offer my hair to Death, I feed Death with my hair' and so forth.[21] At the least, this penance requires self-mutilation, and excessive diligence could easily cause death. The rite is reminiscent both of the grisly oblations that the Kāpālika in the *Prabodhacandrodaya* claims to offer to Bhairava and of the sale of flesh cut from their own bodies by the Mahāvratikas of the Caṇḍamārī temple in Somadeva's *Yaśastilaka.*[22]

The Mahāvrata penance of the *Viṣṇu-smṛti* and other law books

---

[18]Trans. Bühler, i. 24. 15.

[19]Trans. Bühler, ii. 1. 3.

[20]See Kane, *HDS,* IV, 87–96.

[21]Trans. J. Jolly, xx. 26.

[22]See above, pp. 17 and 60.

bears an unmistakable resemblance to the observance of the Kāpālikas. These ascetics lived in the forest, wore loincloths or animal skins, carried a *khaṭvāṅga* and a skull bowl, obtained their food by begging, and polluted those with whom they came into contact. Given the pervasive tantric motif of the identity or conjunction of opposites,[23] the relation between the penance of the law books and the vow of the Kāpālikas is not inexplicable. The Kāpālikas, we suggest, adopted this vow precisely because it was the penance for the most heinous of all crimes, the killing of a Brāhmaṇa. They were at the same time the holiest of all ascetics and the lowest of all criminals. As in the case of the *ḍombī* (and the Kāpālin) of Kāṇhapāda's songs, that which is lowest in the realm of appearance becomes a symbol for the highest in the realm of the spirit. Furthermore, if the Kāpālikas were in reality already guiltless, the performance of this penance would result in an unprecedented accumulation of religious merit and hence of magical power *(siddhi)*.

The paradoxical identity of Kāpālika saint and Brahmahan sinner finds its divine archetype in the curious myth of the beheading of the god Brahmā by Śiva. This also introduces the essential ingredient of Śaivism which is lacking in the law book penance. The myth occurs in a number of the major Purāṇas, but their accounts vary considerably. We will summarise the *Matsya Purāṇa* version since it seems to preserve most of the basic features of the story.[24] One day Śiva is asked by Pārvatī why he never leaves the Avimukta *kṣetra* in Varanasi, where the Kapālamocana (Setting Free of the Skull) *tīrtha* is located. Śiva replies (clxxxiii. 84–87) :

> Formerly, O Varārohā, there was an excellent fifth head of Brahmā. It arose, O Śuśroṇī, having the same lustre as gold. When that flaming fifth head of the great-souled one was produced, O Devī, he said (to me) : 'I know (the circumstances of) your birth.' Then, filled with anger and my eyes inflamed, I cut off his (fifth) head with the tip of the nail of my left thumb. Brahmā (then) said : 'When you cut off the head of me who is guiltless, you will become a Kapālin endowed with a curse. Having become burdened

[23]See above, pp. 70–71.

[24]Ānandāśrama edition, clxxxiii. 83–108.

> with the (sin of) *Brahmahatyā* you should visit the *tīrthas* on earth.'

By cutting off the head of Brahmā, Śiva himself becomes guilty of the crime of killing a Brāhmaṇa and must undergo the prescribed penance. The head magically attaches itself to his body, and he travels with it to the Himalayas to ask Nārāyaṇa (Viṣṇu) for alms. Nārāyaṇa lacerates his own side with the tip of his nail. A great flood of blood streams out and spreads over fifty *yojanas*. This great flood flows for a thousand divine years, but it cannot fill the skull. Nārāyaṇa asks Śiva about the origin of this amazing skull, and Śiva tells him the story of the beheading and its aftermath. Śiva is then instructed to go to 'his own place' where the skull 'will establish itself.' Śiva travels to many famous *tīrthas* but the skull does not 'establish itself' until he visits 'the great resting place Avimukta' and there his curse finally departs. Śiva concludes his tale :

> Through the grace of Viṣṇu, O Suśroṇī, the skull was there broken in thousands (of pieces). As many pieces were produced as riches are obtained in a dream. This sacred field *(kṣetra)* I made the *tīrtha* which removes (the sin of) *Brahmahatyā*. It is renowned on earth, O Devī, as the Kapālamocana of the gods . . . Whoever abandons his body while abiding there will merge with me.

Every ritual has a divine model or archetype, and the penance Śiva performs is the model of the Mahāvrata penance for the killing of a Brāhmaṇa. The Kāpālika in the *Mattavilāsa* makes this identification explicit :

> By strict observance of this holy course [Mahāvrata]
> Our Lord whose crest-gem is the crescent moon

[25]Ibid., 100–101, 104. For summaries of the other purāṇic versions of this myth, see T.A.G. Rao, *Elements of Hindu Iconography*, II, Part I, 295–300; M.A.D. Rangaswamy, *The Religion and Philosophy of Tēvāram*, Book I, pp. 372–76; and S. Das Gupta's introduction to her edition of Kṣemīśvara's *Caṇḍakauśika*, p. lxx. See also *Vāmana Purāṇa* ii. 17 to iv. 1; *Kūrma Purāṇa* ii. 30 and 31; and *Canna-Basava Purāṇa*, trans. G. Wurth, chaps. xviii–xx. Rao identifies Śiva's penance with the Bhrūṇahan vow in the *Āpastambīya Dharmasūtra*. Another version of the myth is found in *Kathāsaritsāgara* ii. 13.

Was freed from guilt that sprang from cutting off
The Grandsire's head . . .[26]

Although the myth is *religiously* prior to the legal prescription, the historical precedence is uncertain. The law books are in general much older than the Purāṇas, but both classes of works are based on earlier sources which are now lost. The killing of a Brāhmaṇa *(Brahmahatyā)* is already regarded as the worst of all sins in the Brāhmaṇas,[27] but these works do not refer to the expiatory penance. The essential features of the Śiva-Brahmā myth are found, however, in the story of Rāma Rāghava and the sage Mahodara from the *Śalyaparvan* of the *Mahābhārata*.[28] According to this story Rāma once fought and beheaded a wicked Rākṣasa. The demon's head attached itself to the thigh of the sage Mahodara. The sage wandered from *tīrtha* to *tīrtha* trying to rid himself of this burden, but he had no success until he bathed at the Auśanasa *tīrtha* on the Sarasvatī River. This place, named after the sage Uśanas or Śukrācārya, washed away the skull and thereafter became known as Kapālamocana.[29]

There can be little doubt that the two myths are related. Even the name, if not the location, of the sacred *tīrtha* is the same. The *Mahābhārata* legend, however, contains no suggestion of Brahmahatyā. The Rākṣasa's skull attaches itself to Mahodara because it is itself demonic, not because of the guilt of beheading. We suggest the following historical development. The Rāma-Mahodara story, or some similar prototype,[30] was borrowed to provide the basis of the myth of the beheading of Brahmā, and this myth was then used to give divine sanction or precedent to the already existing legal prescription against killing a Brāhmaṇa.

The relative priority of the Śaivite myth and the Kāpālika

---

[26]Trans. Barnett, *BSOS*, V, 713. Ed. Śāstrī, vs. 17. The *Kūrma Purāṇa* (ii. 30–31) also says that Śiva had to perform the penance of a Brahmahan but does not call it the Mahāvrata.

[27]See Kane, *HDS*, IV, 10–12.

[28]Ed. R.C. Dandekar, xxxviii. 1–20. Another version of this myth, in which the sage is called Rahodara, appears in the *Vāmana Purāṇa* xxxix. 1–14.

[29]This Kapālamocana is probably identical with a tank of this name on the Sarsutī or Sarasvatī River ten miles south-east of Sadhaura. See A. Cunningham, *Report of a Tour in the Punjab in* 1878–79, pp. 75–78.

[30]The Vedic myth of Indra's destruction of Vṛtra, the demon son of Tvaṣṭṛ, is similar insofar as the sin of killing a Brāhmaṇa was thought to attach to Indra's deed.

ascetics themselves is also uncertain. Did the Kāpālikas invent the myth in order to provide a divine model for their ascetic observance, or did they model the observance on the myth? The evidence is inconclusive. The sources in which the myth first appears, the Purāṇas, also mention human Kāpālikas, and there are no references to the ascetics significantly earlier than these works. In some respects this question is a needless one. Since both the penance for killing a Brāhmaṇa and the association of Śiva, the god of death and destruction, with skulls undoubtedly antedated the Śiva-Kapālin myth, Śaivite ascetics who observed the Mahāvrata might also have antedated it. Whether or not such ascetics existed and whether or not they themselves invented this myth, it is certain that the later Kāpālikas adopted it as their divine archetype.

The ultimate aim of the Kāpālika observance was a mystical identification or communion with Śiva. Through their imitative repetition of Śiva's performance of the Mahāvrata, the ascetics became ritually 'homologised' with the god and partook of, or were granted, some of his divine attributes, especially the eight magical powers *(siddhis)*.[31]

An important aspect of this ritual communion with Śiva-Kapālin seems to have been the identification of the devotee's begging skull with the skull of Brahmā. As their name indicates, this skull bowl was the Kāpālika's trademark. In the *Prabodhacandrodaya* (act III, vss. 12–13), the Kāpālika describes himself as one who 'eats from a human skull' and says that 'the conclusion of our fast (is accomplished) by drinking liquor distributed in the skull of a Brahman *(Brahma-kapāla)*.' The Kāpālika in Yaśaḥpāla's *Moharājaparājaya* (act IV, vs. 23) states : 'Nara-kāpālin declares that he who invariably eats human flesh in the skull of a noble man *(uttama-puruṣa)* obtains the position of Śiva *(Śiva-sthāna)*.' Ugra-Bhairava, the Kāpālika opponent of Śaṃkarācārya, claims that Giriśa (Śiva) had told him that he would attain the ultimate goal of men if he would 'sacrifice in the sacrificial fire either the head of an ominscient sage or the head of a king.'[32] In the *Mattavilāsa,* the Kapālin's wench laments that their lost skull 'was as splendid as the skull of the Lotus-throned God,' another allusion to the Śiva-Brahmā myth.[33] We have noted that some of the law books specify

[31]The psychology of this type of ritual identification with gods and heroes is well analyzed by M. Eliade in his *Cosmos and History* (chaps. i and ii).

[32]Mādhavācārya, *Śaṃkara-digvijaya* xi. 11.

[33]Trans. Barnett, *BSOS,* V, 712–13. In Rājaśekhara's *Karpūramañjarī* the tantric

that the Mahāvratin should carry the skull of the Brāhmaṇa he has slain as his alms bowl. This is what Śiva does with the skull of Brahmā. It is unnecessary and unlikely that the Kāpālika Mahāvratin first killed a Brāhmaṇa in order to obtain a skull bowl, but not any old skull, it seems, would suffice. It had to be the skull of a noble man *(uttama-puruṣa-kapāla)* or the skull of a Brahman *(Brahma-kapāla)*. If our hypothesis about the ascetics' identification with Śiva-Kapālin is correct, the term *Brahma-kapāla* would equally imply the skull of the god Brahmā.

There remains one other Mahāvrata we have yet to discuss. According to Patañjali's *Yogasūtra* ii. 30–31, when the five *yamas* (restraints) of *ahiṃsā* (non-injury), *satya* (truthfulness), *asteya* (non-theft), *brahmacarya* (chastity and restraint of the senses), and *aparigraha* (non-acceptance of more than is necessary for bodily subsistence) are practised without exception being made for status, place, time, or occasion, the observance is known as the Mahāvrata.[34] Its performance is incumbent on yogins at all stages.[35] This Mahāvrata, we believe, is the Mahāvrata of the Kālāmukhas. Although the evidence to support this contention is rather slim, there is virtually no reason to connect the Kālāmukhas with the Mahāvrata of the Brāhmaṇas or the Mahāvrata of the *Viṣṇu-smṛti*.[36] On the other hand, the Kālāmukhas of the Kōḍiya-maṭha in Belagāve (Shimoga District, Mysore) are said to study the *Pātañjala* and other *Yogaśāstras*,[37] and most Kālāmukha inscriptions stress the yogic attainments and virtues of these ascetics. Furthermore, the texts of the Pāśupatas, the sect most closely related to the Kālāmukhas, lay particular emphasis on the performance of the five *yamas*. Kauṇḍinya's commentary on the *Pāśupata-sūtra* attributed to the Pāśupata-Kālāmukha saint Lakulīśa devotes no less than nineteen pages to praise of

ascetic Bhairavānanda, who might be a Kāpālika (see above, p. 49), praises the goddess Kālī, who drinks the blood of demons 'from a goblet made of the skull of Parameṣṭhin [Brahmā].' (Trans. Lanman, Act IV, vs. 19).

[34]'ahiṃsā-satyāsteya-brahmacaryāparigraha yamāḥ/ jāti-deśa-kāla-samayānavacchinnāḥ sārvabhaumāḥ Mahāvratam//' Ed. J. Ballantyne.

[35]See Kane, *HDS*, V, Part II, 1420.

[36]If one does not accept the identification of the Kāpālika Mahāvrata with the penance of the Brahmahan, one could argue that the *Yogasūtra* Mahāvrata was also the vow of the Kāpālikas. The insistence of the *Yogasūtra* on absolute *ahiṃsā* and *brahmacarya*, however, makes this doubly unlikely.

[37]See below, p. 104.

the five *yamas* and five *niyamas*.[38] In the absence of other alternatives, it is best to assume that the Mahāvrata of the Kālāmukhas was the same as the Mahāvrata of Patañjali's *Yogasūtra*.

Somasiddhānta

In a number of sources the doctrine of the Kāpālikas is called Somasiddhānta.[39] Śrīharṣa's *Naiṣadhacarita* contains a lengthy description of the goddess Sarasvatī in which the various parts of her body are said to be formed from different philosophical doctrines. Her face is Somasiddhānta.[40] The commentator Cāṇḍūpaṇḍita explains this as *Kāpālika-darśana-śāstra*.[41] The Kāpālika characters in Kṛṣṇamiśra's *Prabodhacandrodaya* and Ānandarāya's *Vidyāpariṇayana* are both named Somasiddhānta. Gokulanātha's *Amṛtodaya* (act II, after vs. 25) claims that Vardhamāna, the commentator on Udayana's *Nyāyakusumāñjali,* fought and killed Somasiddhānta, also called Somatantra. When Somasiddhānta fell, his comrades Kāpālika, Nīlalohita, Mahābhairava, Bhūtaḍāmara, and Umāmaheśvara all fled the field. As we have noted, Kṣīrasvāmin, a commentator on *Amarakośa,* identifies Mahāvratin, Kapālin, Somasiddhāntin, and Tāntrika.[42] We have also seen that a few Purāṇas and other sources contain sect lists which seem to replace Kāpālika by Soma, Sauma or Saumya.[43] Raghūttama's commentary on Vātsyāyana's *Nyāya-bhāṣya* includes Sauma in a list of six heretical doctrines *(ṣaḍ bahyāḥ siddhāntāḥ)*. The six are Cārvāka, Sauma, Saugata, Jina, Ārhata, and Digambara.[44] Somasiddhānta-vādins are also mentioned in the *Akulavīratantra*.[45] G. Tucci has found allusions to a philosophical school called *na ya siu mo* in the Chinese translations of Harivarman's *Tattvasiddhiśāstra* (fourth century A.D.) and Asaṅga's *Madhyāntānugamaśāstra*. This school, Tucci believes, should be transcribed in Sanskrit as *Nyāyasauma* or *Nayasaumya* and is the same as Somasiddhānta.[46]

---

[38]Ed. R.A. Sastri, pp. 15–34.

[39]Most of the Sanskrit references to Somasiddhānta have been collected by Handiqui in the notes to his translation of Śrīharṣa's *Naiṣadhacarita,* pp. 640–44.

[40]Ibid., x. 87 (p. 149).

[41]Cited ibid., p. 427.

[42]See ibid., p. 640.

[43]See above, pp. 7–11.

[44]Cited by G. Tucci, *JRASB,* n.s. XXVI, 130.

[45]Cited ibid.

[46]Ibid., pp. 129–30.

None of the sources which refer to Somasiddhānta say much about the term apart from identifying it as the name of the Kāpālika doctrine. Several commentaries on the *Prabodhacandrodaya* derive the word *Soma* from the compound *sa-Umā* (with Umā, i.e. Pārvatī).[47] Although this etymology is not historically correct, by the time of Kṛṣṇamiśra Soma or Someśvara was a common name for Śiva. The sexual implications of the derivation *sa-Umā* are particularly suitable for the god of the Kāpālikas.

A few inscriptions briefly mention the Somasiddhānta doctrine but do not contain any significant information about it. A priest entitled Caturānana-paṇḍita, who headed the Tiruvoṟṟiyūr *maṭha* (Chingleput District, Madras) in A.D. 1171–72, is described as a contemporary of a Somasiddhāntin named Vāgīśa Bhaṭṭa.[49] The priests of the Tiruvoṟṟiyūr *maṭha* were Mahāvratins.[49] Another allusion to the Somasiddhānta doctrine is found in an inscription from Mēvuṇḍi in Dharwar District dated A.D. 897.[50] As we have seen,[51] Somakhaḍḍuka ascetics of the congregation of Muṇḍa-śṛṅkhalika Pāśupatācārya are named as donees in a seventh century grant from Nepal.

Kāpālika Bhakti

While we possess no actual Kāpālika text, we can attempt to reconstruct the basic doctrines and attitudes of the sect from the many references we have cited. The keystone of the Kāpālika faith was *bhakti,* personal devotion to a personal god. This god was usually identified as Śiva in his terrific Bhairava incarnation. The rituals into which the Kāpālika's *bhakti* was channeled were either propitiatory, imitative or a combination of both. The aim of these rituals was a mystical communion of the worshipper and his god. The rewards of this communion were twofold. On the mundane plain the devotee gained suprahuman magical powers *(siddhis)* while on the eschatological plain he attained final liberation from transmigratory existence *(mukti)* and dwelt in a heaven of perpetual sexual bliss.

The statements of Bodholbaṇa-nityānanda and his Kāpālika followers in Ānandagiri's *Śaṃkara-vijaya* form the *locus classicus,*

---

[47]See ibid., p. 131. See also V. Paṇśīkar's edition of the play, pp. 111, 113–14.

[48]See V. Raghavan, *EI,* XXVII, 297.

[49]See ibid., p. 300 and text vs. 3.

[50]C.R. Krishnamacharlu (ed.), *SII,* XI, Part I, no. 22, line 48.

[51]See above, p. 30.

as it were, of Kāpālika *bhakti*. When Śaṃkara asks them to describe the observances *(ācāra)* and precepts *(vidhi)* of their *kula,* they reply :

> O Svāmin, our observance, which is free from *karman,* causes satisfaction to all beings since it is said : 'There is no salvation with (or by means of) *karman.*' I should worship Bhairava alone, the creator of the world, who afterwards becomes the (cause of) destruction. He who is the cause of destruction is also the cause of preservation and creation . . . All the gods, each endowed with a particular authority, are merely portions of him. They carry the command of Bhairava on their heads, and their powers, which attend on his word, are each directed to a particular duty.[52]

Parts of this passage are ambiguous but its general purport is clear. The word *Karman,* for instance, may imply either 'religious ritual and good works' or 'the effects of past good and bad deeds', although the latter interpretation is clearly the more plausible one. The chief object of the passage is to proclaim Bhairava to be the creator, preserver, and destroyer of the universe and lord of all the gods. The epithet 'world-creator' *(jagat-kartṛ)* suggests the dualistic distinction between the material and instrumental causes of the universe which Rāmānuja and other *Brahma-sūtra* commentators attribute to the Kāpālikas and other worshippers of Paśupati. The demotion of the many gods of the Hindu pantheon to the position of portions *(aṃśas)* of one primary god is a concept frequently found in *bhakti* literature, particularly the Purāṇas, and is a form of what has been called henotheism, a kind of halfway house between polytheism and monotheism.

Bodholbaṇa-nityānanda and his followers continue with an elaboration of their doctrine. Bhairava, they claim, has eight major forms : Asitāṅga, Ruru, Caṇḍa, Krodha, Unmatta, Kāpālin, Bhīṣaṇa, and Saṃhāra. The first seven of these forms they identify

---

[52]'Svāminn asmad-ācāraḥ sarvva-prāṇi-santoṣa-karaḥ karma-hīnaḥ, karmaṇā na muktir iti vacanāt/ mad-upāsyo Bhairava eka eva jagat-karttā/ tataḥ pralayo bhavatīti yo vā pralaya-karttā sa eva sthity-utpattyor apīti/. . . tad-aṃśā eva sarvve devāḥ tat-tad-adhikāra-sampannāḥ śrīmad-Bhairavājñāṃ śirasā dhṛtvā tad-ukti-pratyāsanna-śaktayaḥ tat-tat-kāryya-parāḥ babhūvuḥ/.' Ed. J. Tarkapanchanana, chap. xxiii.

with the gods Viṣṇu, Brahmā, Sūrya, Rudra, Indra, Candra,[53] and Yama respectively. The eighth, Saṃhāra-Bhairava, is Bhairava himself. The remaining gods are merely his 'portions' and are further distinguished as creation-makers *(sṛṣṭikartṛs)*, preservation-makers *(sthitikartṛs)* and destruction-makers *(saṃhārakartṛs)*. Taken all together, the creation-makers are his Rudra (*sic* for Ruru-Brahmā) portions, the preservation-makers his Asitāṅga (Viṣṇu) portions, and the destruction-makers his Krodha (Rudra) portions. The Kāpālikas conclude: 'Thus having caused the creation of the world etc., and afterwards the dissolution, he makes a contraction of seven of his forms and one eternal Saṃhāra-Bhairava remains who is the *paramātman*.'[54]

This omnipotent deity demands both propitiation and imitation from his devotees. In this respect the Kāpālika faith differs from other theistic religions only in the procedures adopted. Ritual propitiation is sacrifice. Externally this usually takes the form of human or animal sacrifice. To be acceptable to the deity, the victim must be of auspicious color and size, unpolluted, and, in the case of humans, morally pure. At the same time, however, he is normally regarded as a scapegoat, the repository of the transgressions of the sacrificers. The Kāpālikas, if their critics are to be believed, specialised in human sacrifice.

As we have seen, allusions to Kāpālikas performing human sacrifices, making offerings of human flesh, or doing *pūjā* with the aid of corpses are numerous. In *Mālatī-Mādhava* (act V, vs. 25) the faultless heroine is led forward wearing the marks of a sacrificial victim. The heartless Kāpālika Aghoraghaṇṭa raises his weapon and invokes Cāmuṇḍā: 'O divine Cāmuṇḍā, the offering *(pūjā)* placed before you was promised at the beginning of the performance of incantations. May you (now) receive it.' More often the god the Kāpālikas invoke is Bhairava. At the end of our fast, says the Kāpālika in *Prabodhacandrodaya* (act III, vs. 13): 'Mahābhairava should be worshipped with offerings of awe-inspiring human sacrifices from whose severed throats blood flows in torrents.' To this god, he adds, we offer oblations of 'human flesh mixed with brains, entrails, and marrow.' Śaṃkarācārya's Kāpālika opponent Krakaca puts the matter more forcefully: 'If he (Kāpālin-

[53]Another word for Candra (the moon) is Soma. The equation of Kāpālin-Bhairava and Candra might have something to do with Somasiddhānta.

[54]Ānandagiri, chap. xxiii.

Śiva) does not receive Bhairava worship with liquor and blood-smeared lotuses which are human heads, how can he attain joy when his body is embraced by the lotus eyed Umā . . . ?'[55] Here Bhairava seems to be not only gratified by head-offerings but in some sense dependent upon them.

Although little reliance can be placed on the specific details of these statements—the authors were all opponents of the Kāpālikas—it is difficult to doubt that the Kāpālikas practised human sacrifice. The purpose of the rite was to appease and gratify a wrathful and blood-thirsty deity. The idea of the victim as a scapegoat is less explicit but is inherent, in any case, in the very concept of sacrificial propitiation.

Human sacrifice existed in India, as in most parts of the ancient world, from a very early date. According to a legend which first appears in the *Aitareya Brāhmaṇa,* the Īkṣvāku king Hariścandra volunteered to sacrifice his first-born son to the god Varuṇa.[56] The *puruṣamedha* (man-sacrifice) is described in a number of Brāhmaṇas but had become merely symbolic by the time of the *Śatapatha Brāhmaṇa.*[57] Human sacrifices were given a new lease on life, as it were, with the emergence of tantric cults in the early mediaeval period. In some regions, particularly Bengal and Assam, the practice became fairly common. The sixteenth century Koch king, Nar Nārāyaṇ, is said to have sacrificed about 150 men at a single ceremony.[58] A combination of British suppression and Hindu reform virtually eliminated the practice by the early nineteenth century, but cases of alleged human sacrifice are still reported sporadically.[59]

The important Śākta work, the *Kālikā-Purāṇa,* devotes an entire

---

[55]Mādhavācārya, xi. 11.

[56]vii. 13–18, cited by E.A. Gait, 'Human Sacrifice (Indian),' *ERE,* VI, 849–53. See also P.B. Joshi, 'On the Rite of Human Sacrifice in Ancient, Mediaeval and Modern India and Other Countries,' *JAnSB,* III (1893), 275–300; and R. Mitra, 'On Human Sacrifices in Ancient India,' *JRASB,* XLV (1876), 76–118.

[57]See Joshi, *JAnSB,* III, 280.

[58]Gait, *ERE,* VI, 850.

[59]*The Indian Express,* August 15, 1966, reports a case from Medak District in Andhra Pradesh. *The Milwaukee Journal,* Sept. 15, 1968, reports that Prime Minister Gandhi sent 1,000 rupees to the family of a twelve year old boy sacrificed 'at the laying of the foundation stone for an irrigation project' in Rajasthan. The same paper, Oct. 31, 1968, contains an account of the beheading of another twelve year old boy at a town 200 miles southeast of New Delhi. The boy was sacrificed to Śiva.

chapter to animal and human sacrifice.[60] It justifies the rite with arguments similar to those attributed to the Kāpālikas :

> By a human sacrifice attended by the rites laid down, Devī . . . remains gratified for a thousand years; and by the sacrifice of three men, one hundred thousand years. By human flesh the goddess Kāmākhyā's consort Bhairava . . . remains pleased three thousand years. Blood consecrated immediately becomes abrosia and since the head and flesh are gratifying, therefore should the head and flesh be offered at the worship of the goddess. The wise should add the flesh free from hair, among food offerings.[61]

Before executing his victim, the sacrificer says to him: 'Thou, by gratifying Caṇḍikā, destroyest all evil incidents to the giver. Thou, a victim who appearest as a sacrifice meet for the Vaiṣṇavī, hast my salutations.'[62] The scapegoat aspect of the sacrificial propitiation of Bhairava and Durgā is here made more explicit.

The personal counterpart to animal and human sacrifice is self-sacrifice. This concept subsumes a wide range of activities from self-immolation or suicide to self-mutilation and from physical penances to simple exercises of mental discipline. The chief penance performed by the Kāpālikas was, of course, the Mahāvrata. There is also some evidence that they occasionally practised various forms of self-mutilation such as cutting flesh from their own bodies for sacrificial oblations.[63] The Kāpālika Ugra-Bhairava claims to have gratified Ugra (Śiva) 'with arduous and severe penances for a full one-hundred years.'[64] The Kāpālika in *Caṇḍakauśika* (act IV, vs. 26) claims to subsist on unrequested alms and to have control over the five senses. The king greets him as a Mahāvratin who has undertaken a vow of lifelong chastity (act IV, after vs. 29). In *Prabodhacandrodaya* (act III, vs. 13) Somasiddhānta claims to see 'through eyes made clear by the

---

[60]This chapter was translated at the end of the eighteenth century by W.C. Blaquiere in *Asiatic Researches,* V (1797), 371–391. We have not found an edition or more recent translation although H. Zimmer paraphrases parts of the Purāṇa in his *The King and the Corpse.*

[61]Passage translated by Gait, *ERE,* VI, 850.

[62]Ibid.

[63]See above, pp. 17 and 76.

[64]Mādhavācārya, xi. 10.

ointment Yoga' and to conclude his fast *(pāraṇā)* by drinking liquor. Several references, albeit sarcastic ones, to Kapālin *tapas* also appear in *Mattavilāsa*.[65] Although the above allusions to Kāpālika asceticism and Yoga are few and not very detailed, it is evident that the authors were aware that the Kāpālikas were not simple hedonists.

In addition to propitiating Bhairava through various kinds of sacrifice, the Kāpālikas imitated the god by ritual reenactment of his mythological exploits. To a large extent the paths of propitiation and imitation overlap. The Mahāvrata, for instance, is both a propitiatory penance and a reenactment of the penance of Śiva. In some rituals, however, the idea of propitiation is absent or insignificant. Most of these are communion rituals in which the worshipper is united with divinity through food, drink, sex, or mental ecstasy. These rituals are normally preceded by propitiatory ones which give the devotee preparatory purification. The Kāpālika in *Prabodhacandrodaya* does not drink until he has fasted; Ugra-Bhairava gratifies Ugra with severe penances for one-hundred years 'in order to go to Kailāsa with this body to sport with Īśa.'

Kāpālika rituals of food and drink are referred to in a number of sources.[66] In Yaśaḥpāla's *Moharājaparājaya* the Kāpālika says that one obtains *Śiva-sthāna* by eating human flesh in the skull of a noble man. The lost skull bowl of Mahendravarman's Kapālin was full of roast meat. Guṇaratna and the *Bārhaspati-sūtra* claim that the Kāpālikas are sybaritic Nāstika materialists addicted to wine, meat and illicit intercourse. Śaṃkara's opponent Krakaca fills his skull bowl with *surā* through his power of meditation. After drinking half of it, he invokes the god Bhairava. Unmatta-Bhairava, another of Śaṃkara's Kāpālika opponents, proudly declares that his father and gradfather were liquor makers and espouses a thoroughly hedonistic code of conduct. In *Mattavilāsa* the Kapālin similarly advocates wine and women as the road to salvation recommended by Śiva, and the Kāpālika in *Prabodha-candrodaya* describes wine as the 'remedy against (transmigratory) existence prescribed by Bhairava.' In Ānandarāyamakhin's *Vidyā-pariṇayana* (act IV, after vs. 32) the Kāpālika Somasiddhānta almost apologetically defends his use of wine and meat by maintaining that they are prescribed in the *Bhairavāgamas*: 'We are

---

[65]Mahendravarman, after vss. 6 and 10 and vs. 21.

[66]See above, chap. ii.

counted among heretics through divergence from the Veda by addiction to wine *(madhu)*, meat *(māṃsa)*, etc., which are prohibited in the Vedas, (but in fact we hold) the doctrine of the authoritativeness of the Veda with compliance to the *Bhairavāgamas*.'

Since the Kāpālikas were a tantric Śaivite sect, their addiction to meat and wine, as well as sex, should be associated with the five Ma-sounds *(pañcamakāra)* of tantric tradition and not with hedonistic materialism. The passage from *Vidyāpariṇayana* mentioning *madhu* and *māṃsa* tends to confirm this association. In Ānandagiri's *Śaṃkara-vijaya* the Kāpālika Bodholbaṇa declares (chap. xxiii) that true and fearless sages are 'all always dependent on knowledge *(bodha)* produced from substances *(dravya)*.' These 'substances' probably represent the five Ma-sounds since the terms *pañcadravya* and *pañcamakāra* (also *pañcatattva)* are synonymous in tantric texts. The context of Bodholbaṇa's statement also tends to support this interpretation.

In tantric practice the partaking of wine and meat has both a hedonistic and eucharistic aspect but is in no way connected with materialism. Hedonistically, the first four of the five Ma-sounds —wine, meat, fish, and grain *(mudrā)*—are regarded as aphrodisiac *(uttejaka)* preparatives to the final *maithuna* or sexual union between the initiated adept and his female partner. These four ingredients do not in fact possess aphrodisiac qualities although wine, of course, may help to release inhibitions. A. Bharati points out that the only substance used in tantric *sādhanā* which has any such qualities is *vijayā* or Indian hemp *(Cannabis Indica)*.[67] This is taken about an hour and a half before the five Ma-sounds.

The eucharistic significance of the four preliminary ingredients is variously explained in tantric sources. *Kulārṇava-tantra* v. 79–80 says: 'Wine *(surā)* is Śakti; the meat is Śiva; the enjoyer of those is Bhairava himself. The bliss sprung from the union of those two (? =Śiva and Śakti) is called *mokṣa*. This bliss, which is the form *(rūpa)* of Brahman, is established in the body (of the worshipper). The wine makes it manifest. For that reason the yogins drink.' The reformist *Mahānirvāṇa-tantra* states: 'Wine [*surā*] is Tārā Herself in liquid form, Who is the Saviour of beings, the Mother of Enjoyment and Liberation.'[68] In the *Kaulāvalinirṇaya* the goddess is worshipped as the *surā* which was churned from the milk-

---

[67] *The Tantric Tradition*, p. 252.

[68] Trans. Woodroffe, xi. 105.

ocean and emerged from the *kula*-nectar : 'Having eighteen arms, lotus-eyed, born on the summit of bliss, (and thence also originated) bliss as Maheśvara. From their union come forth Brahmā, Viṣṇu, and Śiva. Therefore I drink thee with my total personality, o goddess of liquor.'[69] Bharati's tantric informants variously interpreted the term *kula*-nectar *(kulāmṛta)* as 'the spiritual essence of the five *makāras* . . ., the cosmic residuum caused by Śiva's and Śakti's eternal copulation'; 'the liquid which emerges from the contact of Śiva and Śakti'; and the *rajas* (menstrual blood) of the goddess.[70] *Śaktisaṅgama-tantra* ii. 32. 25 says that the wine 'is produced from the *rasa* of Śakti.' This statement seems to have similar sexual implications although it appears in the context of a list of substitutes *(pratinidhi)* suitable for *dakṣiṇācāra* worship.

All of the symbolic equations just cited clearly indicate the presence of an element of totemic communion in the ritual consumption of the first four Ma-sounds. This alimentary communion is based on the archaic maxim that we are what we eat—*man ist was er isst*. The identification of the ritual foods with the body or body products of Śiva and Śakti confers on the communicant consubstantiality with them. He *becomes* the god and shares various divine attributes such as immortality and magical powers. Before discussing these supernatural benefits, however, we must examine the central ritual of tantric communion, sexual intercourse.

Since some of our sources for the Kāpālikas are quite explicit about the significance of this ritual, it is not necessary to rely on tantric works except for confirmation. The archetypal basis of the ritual is delineated most succinctly in the traditional etymology for the term Somasiddhānta—the doctrine of Soma (Śiva) united with Umā *(Umayā sahitaḥ Somas tasya siddhāntaḥ)*.[71] The human participants of the ritual mentally identify themselves with Śiva and Śakti respectively. In the bliss of sexual union the human pair realize the divine bliss of Śiva and Śakti. Final salvation *(mukti)*, on this view, is perpetual orgasm, not merely extinction of the cycle of rebirth.

When asked about his conception of *mokṣa*, the Kāpālika in *Prabodhacandrodaya* replies (act III, vs. 16) :

---

[69]Trans. by Bharati in *The Tantric Tradition*, p. 259.

[70]Ibid., pp. 259–60.

[71]*Prakāśaṭīkā* to Kṛṣṇamiśra's *Prabodhacandrodaya*, ed. Paṇśīkar, p. 114. See also *Candrikāvyākhyā*, ibid., p. 111, and G. Tucci, *JRASB*, n.s. XXVI, 131.

> Thus spoke the Lord of Mṛdānī (Śiva): 'Bliss is not found anywhere without sense objects. How (can) *mukti* be desired (when) the condition of the soul *(jiva)* is the condition of a stone, devoid of the awakening of bliss. One who has the appearance *(vapus)* of the Moon-crested (Śiva) and amuses himself in the embrace of his wife, the image of Pārvatī, is (truly) liberated.'

A similar view is put forward by the Kāpālika Unmatta-Bhairava in the commentary to Mādhava's *Śaṃkara-digvijaya* xv. 28: 'The bliss which becomes manifest through sexual union is the (true) form of Bhairava. The attainment of that (bliss) at death is *mokṣa*. This is the ultimate truth.'[72]

The Kāpālika Bodholbaṇa-nityānanda praises the fearless sages who are 'always dependent on the knowledge produced from substances *(dravya)*, whose hearts are gratified by the embrace of Kāpālika *śaktis,* who are addicted to drinking the excellent nectar arising from sexual union, ... and who (declare that) Bhairava is the abode *(pada)* in death.'[73] The drinking of the nectar of sexual union is probably a reference to the yogic exercise of reabsorbing with the penis the seminal fluid discharged in coitus. The rationale for this practice, called the *vajrolimudrā,* is explained in the *Haṭhayogapradīpikā*: 'Having drawn up his own discharged *bindu* [the Yogī] can preserve (it) ... By the loss of *bindu* (comes) death, from its retention, life.'[74] The same idea lies behind the allied practice of *coitus reservatus* recommended especially in Buddhist Vajrayāṇa texts. Breath *(prāṇa),* thought *(citta),* and semen *(bindu)*—the three jewels—must be simultaneously 'immobilised' in an act which yields the perfect state of oneness in duality.[75] The belief that the loss of semen causes the destruction of mental and spiritual as well as physical potency is widespread even in modern industrial societies. In India the association of celibacy and religious or magical power has been stressed since early times. To cite just one example, a legend about the *ṛṣi* Dadhīca in the *Śalyaparvan* (chap. 1) of the *Mahābhārata* tells how the gods became imperilled by the sage's growing ascetic

[72]Dhanapatisūri, *Ḍiṇḍima* commentary, vs. 22.

[73]Ānandagiri, chap. xxiii.

[74]Trans. Briggs in *Gorakhnāth* ..., p. 334.

[75]See Eliade, *Yoga* ..., pp. 248–49, 253–54 and Bharati, p. 265.

power *(tapas)* and sent a beautiful Apsaras to earth to tempt him. When Dadhīca spied the celestial nymph, he lost his semen, and consequently his sacred power, in the Sarasvatī River. The Sanskrit word for religious novice, *brahmacārin,* quite early came to refer mainly to sexual continence although its original etymological meaning was 'moving in Brahman,' one whose mind is fixed on the absolute.[76]

The Kāpālika in *Caṇḍakauśika* (act IV, vs. 34) implies a sexual—or at least a sensual—conception of *mokṣa* when he praises the immoral world where the Siddhas frolic on the peaks of Meru. In Rāmānuja's *Śrībhāṣya* ii. 2. 35–37, the Kāpālas declare that 'he who meditates on the Self as seated in the female vulva attains *nirvāṇa.*' This statement may reflect a partial spiritualisation or sublimation of overt sexual ritual.

Vāmamārg, a modern tantric manual in Hindi and Sanskrit by V.S. Vaidyarāj, describes the climax of *pañcamakāra-sādhanā* in terms similar to those attributed to the Kāpālikas: 'Viewing the Śakti as Gaurī (i.e. the spouse of Śiva) and himself as Śiva, he [the *sādhaka*] should pronounce the root-*mantra* of his chosen deity and should offer that father-face into the mother-face.'[77] During the sexual act the *sādhaka* should mentally recite a *mantra* verse to the goddess. By this means 'he creates the attitude of the oneness of Śiva and Śakti.'[78] As he 'abandons his semen' he should recite the following *mantra*: '*Oṃ* with light and ether as my two hands, I, the exulting one, relying on the ladle, I, who take *dharma* and non-*dharma* as his sacrificial ingredients, offer (this oblation) lovingly into the fire, *svāhā.*'[79] Here orgasm is both communion and sacrifice!

The aim of the Kāpālika's religious endeavours is not simply the attainment of a state of divine bliss. On a more mundane or practical level, he seeks magical yogic powers *(siddhis).* These may be won either through the achievement of consubstantiality with Śiva in rituals of communion or, more directly, as a gift

[76]See A. Bharati, *The Ochre Robe,* p. 99. The psychiatrist-anthropologist G.M. Carstairs found that a preoccupation with the involuntary discharge of semen, the source of bodily and spiritual strength, forms 'the commonest expression of anxiety neurosis among the Hindu communities of Rajasthan, and perhaps elsewhere as well' (*The Twice Born,* p. 87).

[77]Trans. Bharati in *The Tantric Tradition,* p. 264.

[78]Trans. ibid., p. 265.

[79]Trans. ibid.

from the deity earned by penance or sacrifice.

The priest-magician existed in India, as elsewhere, from earliest times. His penances, spells, and magic rituals gave him the power to perform supernatural deeds with or without the assistance of the gods. The development of the doctrine and practices of Yoga led to a systematic cultivation and enumeration of the priest-magician's magical powers.[80] In the *Yogasūtra* of Patañjali, generally dated sometime between 200 B.C. and A.D. 300,[81] a considerable number of magical powers are said to stem from the practice of *saṃyama*.[82] The powers include the ability to know present, past and future, to become invisible, to become strong as an elephant, to enter another's body, to walk on water or thorns, to hear inaudible sounds, and to fly through the air. Elsewhere in the *Yogasūtra* Patañjali states that the *siddhis* may be obtained by any of five methods: birth, drugs, *mantras,* penance, and *samādhi. Yājñavalkya-smṛti* iii. 202–203, a work slightly later than or contemporary with the *Yogasūtra,* says that supra-normal powers of hearing, seeing, remembering, becoming invisible, abandoning one's body, and entering another's body are the mark of *Yoga-siddhi.* The *Rājamārtaṇḍa* commentary on Patañjali by King Bhoja (early eleventh century) contains a list of eight great *siddhis (mahāsiddhis)* which can be won by Yoga: (1) *aṇiman,* the power of becoming small; (2) *laghiman,* the power of levitation; (3) *gariman,* the power of becoming heavy; (4) *mahiman,* the power of becoming limitlessly large; (5) *īśitva,* control over body and mind; (6) *prākāmya,* irresistible will; (7) *vaśitva,* control over the five elements; and (8) *kāmāvasāyitva,* fulfilment of desires.[83] Similar lists are found in the *Yogabhāṣya* of Vyāsa (seventh to eighth centuries), the tantric *Prapañcasāra,* and other works.[84]

In spite of the abundant textual references to various *siddhis* in classical Yoga texts, many modern Indian scholars, and like-minded western ones as well, have seized on a single *sūtra* of Patañjali (iii. 37) to prove that magical powers were regarded as

---

[80]Perhaps the oldest mention of the *siddhis* is in the *Āpastambīya Dharmasūtra* ii. 9. 23. 6–7.

[81]See Kane, *HDS,* V, Part II, 1395–99 and Eliade, *Yoga* . . ., pp. 370–72.

[82]*Yogasūtra* iii. 16–50. The term *saṃyama* refers to the last, and highest, three 'limbs of Yoga': concentration *(dhāraṇā),* meditation *(dhyāna)* and *samādhi.*

[83]Commentary on *Yogasūtra* iii. 44, cited by Eliade, *Yoga* . . ., p. 88. Most of the English equivalents given are based on Eliade's renderings.

[84]See, Kane, *HDS,* V, Part II, 1112–13.

subsidiary, and even hindrances, to final liberation and consequently not worthy of concentrated pursuit.[85] This attitude may have been operative in Vedāntic and Buddhist circles and is now popular among practitioners imbued with the spirit of the Hindu Renaissance, but it was not the view of Patañjali and certainly not the view of mediaeval exponents of Haṭha Yoga. Arthur Koestler has pointed out that the *sūtra* in question seems clearly to refer back only to the powers mentioned in the previous one or two *sūtras* and not to the many powers mentioned afterwards.[86] He concludes that 'all disclaimers notwithstanding, the siddhis are an integral part of Yoga,' a statement that has the explicit support of no less a scholar than P.V. Kane.[87]

Most tantric sects were well-infused with the doctrines and practices of Haṭha Yoga, and it is unlikely that the Kāpālikas were an exception. Our sources suggest that they were especially preoccupied with magic and the *siddhis*. The Kāpālika Ugra-Bhairava laments to Śaṃkara that 'the skull of an anointed king or a lord of *munis* is the prerequisite for my *siddhi*.'[88] Śaṃkara's enemy Krakaca fills a skull bowl with wine through the power of meditation.[89] In *Caṇḍakauśika* (act IV, vss. 31–32) the Kāpālika offers King Hariścandra a large collection of magical skills and equipment as well as a great treasure of immortality-bestowing *siddharasa* (?=a mercurial drug). Other references to the magical powers of Kāpālika ascetics appear in the *Kathāsaritsāgara* stories of Madanamañjarī, Candrasvāmin, Devadatta, and the Kāpālika spy.[90] In Jambhaladatta's *Vetālapañcaviṃśati* (pp. 10–11) the Kāpālika mutters a great incantation *(mahāmantra)* in order to obtain *siddhi*. The Kāpālin-Pāśupata Aśvapāda in Kalhaṇa's *Rājataraṅgiṇī* displays the ability to remember his past lives and to magically transport his disciple to Kashmir.[91]

Kṛṣṇamiśra's *Prabodhacandrodaya* (act III, vs. 22) contains a particularly interesting allusion to the *siddhis* of the Kāpālikas.

---

[85] Even as objective a writer as Eliade partially succumbs to this view (*Yoga* . . ., pp. 88–90). He and other scholars also ignore the mention of drugs among the means of obtaining *siddhis*, perhaps for similar reasons.

[86] *The Lotus and the Robot*, pp. 110–11.

[87] *HDS*, V, Part II, 1451–52.

[88] Mādhavācārya, xi. 14.

[89] Ibid., xv. 23–24.

[90] See above, pp. 62–64.

[91] See above, pp. 66–67.

Somasiddhānta here claims that in his doctrine the devotee gains the eight *mahāsiddhis* without renouncing the pleasures of the senses. In other doctrines, he says, even the ordinary *siddhis (prākṛtasiddhis)* of subjecting *(vaśya)*, attracting *(ākarṣa)*, bewildering *(vimohana)*, stupefying *(praśamana)*, agitating *(prakṣobhana)*, and removing *(uccāṭana)* are no more than obstacles for the learned. This list seems to be unique, but the idea that certain *siddhis* may be obstacles probably alludes to *Yogasūtra* iii. 37.

The fifth act of Bhavabhūti's *Mālatī-Mādhava* begins with the entrance by an aerial path of Kapālakuṇḍalā, the female disciple of the Kāpālika Aghoraghaṇṭa. In her opening invocation to Śiva she asserts that the god's '*ātman* is situated in the midst of the ten *nāḍīs* and six *cakras*' and that he 'gives *siddhis* to those who know (him).' The theory of the six *cakras* and ten *nāḍīs* forms the core of the mystical physiology of Haṭha Yoga. Since this theory is well-known[92] we need only note here its association with the Kāpālikas. Kapālakuṇḍalā then tells how she flies through the sky, clearing the clouds in front as she goes. She claims to perceive the *ātman* manifested in the lotus of the heart as the form of Śiva through her power of yogic absorption *(laya-vaśāt)* and to fix it in the six *cakras* by the practice of *nyāsa*.[93] Then she causes the drawing off of the five elements from the body by means of the swelling of the *nāḍīs* (with the breath restrained by *prāṇāyāma*) and flies up into the air.

---

[92]See Eliade, *Yoga* . . ., pp. 236–45, and the *Ṣaṭ-cakra-nirūpaṇa*, ed. and trans. J. Woodroffe, *The Serpent Power*.

[93]The Haṭha Yoga and tantric meditation called *nyāsa* 'ritually projects' various divinities into different parts of the body by touch and *mantra* recitation.

CHAPTER IV

KĀLĀMUKHAS OF THE ŚAKTI-PARIṢAD

Preliminary

The Kālāmukha sect of Śaivite ascetics inhabited the Karṇāṭaka region mainly during the eleventh, twelfth and early thirteenth centuries. The name Kālāmukha, sometimes spelt Kālamukha, may refer to a practice of marking their foreheads with a black streak.[1] Judging from the large number of epigraphs recording donations to Kālāmukha temples and *maṭhas,* these ascetics must have wielded considerable influence in the region. Unfortunately few indications of their beliefs and ritual survive apart from the information which can be gleaned from these epigraphs. They reveal the existence of at least two major divisions of the Kālāmukha order—the *Śakti-pariṣad* and the *Siṃha-pariṣad.* Records of the latter division have been found over a wide area including various parts of Andhra Pradesh and Mysore. The former division seems to have been limited mostly to the Dharwar and Shimoga Districts of Mysore. Nonetheless, the number of extant Śakti-pariṣad epigraphs is greater and they have been found at a larger number of sites. Moreover, they are generally of greater length and contain more religious information. Barring historical accident, it must be assumed that the Śakti-pariṣad was the more important of the two groups.

Approximately sixty-five inscriptions from eighteen Śakti-pariṣad temples have been found and published. Its control over two of the temples is doubtful, however, and a few of the inscriptions, though found in Kālāmukha temples, date from a period either before or after Kālāmukha occupation. Four separate subdivisions of the Śakti-pariṣad are distinguished, and it may be assumed that others existed whose names have not survived. The most prominent division was centred in the Kedāreśvara temple at Belagāve in Shimoga District.[2] The ascetics styled themselves as

---

[1]T.A.G. Rao, *Elements of Hindu Iconography,* II, Part I, 25.

[2]Most of the records found at this temple have been edited and translated by B.L. Rice in *EC,* Vol. VII. This line of ascetics has been discussed at some length by J.F. Fleet ('Inscriptions at Ablur,' *EI,* V [1898–99], 213–65) and by A. Venkata

members of the *Mūvara-kōṇeya-saṃtati* (or *-santāna*) of the *Parvatāvaḷi* (or *Parvatāmnāya*) of the *Śakti-parṣe* (or *-pariṣad*). No less than fifty of the sixty-five epigraphs refer to this line of ascetics. About twenty-two of the records are located at the Kedāreśvara temple itself. The rest are at five other temples in the region. The same ascetics seem to have been in charge of all six temples. At two of them, however, the connection with the Śakti-pariṣad is based merely on the correspondence of ascetics' names and dates.

The records are slightly inconsistent about the hierarchy of the three parts of the organisation. The Kedāreśvara epigraphs of 1094 and 1103[3] and the duplicate Ablūr epigraph of 1101–4[4] refer to the Mūvara-kōṇeya-saṃtati of the Parvatāvaḷi of the Śakti-parṣe, but the Kedāreśvara record of 1113[5] seems to refer to the Śakti-parṣe of the Mūvara-kōṇeya-santāna of the Parvatāmnāya. The 1129 and 1156 Kedāreśvara records[6] mention only the Mūvara-kōṇeya-saṃtati of the Parvatāvaḷi, while the Ablūr record of 1144 and the Kedāreśvara one of 1164[7] only mention the Mūvara-kōṇeya-saṃtati. The Kedāreśvara record of 1193[8] refers to the Parvatāvaḷi alone. This confusion is easily resolved by comparing the names used by the other subdivisions of the Śakti-pariṣad. An inscription from Hoṃbaḷ in Dharwar District praises some ascetics belonging to the Parvatāvali and *Beḷḷeya-santāna*.[9] Another from Gogga in Shimoga District mentions the ascetics of the Śakti-*paridhi* of the Parvatāvali and *A*. .*ka-santati*.[10] One from Maṭṭikoṭe in Shimoga District eulogises ascetics of the Śakti-parṣe of the *Bhujaṅgāvaḷi* of the *Iṭṭige-saṃtati*.[11] If all these terms are collated only one order of precedence is possible—*saṃtati* of *āvaḷi* of *pariṣad*.

Subbiah ('A Twelfth Century University in Mysore,' *Quarterly Journal of the Mythic Society* [Bangalore], VII [1917], 157–96). The architecture and sculpture of this and many other of the Kālāmukha temples are described by H. Cousens *(The Chālukyan Architecture of the Kanarese Districts)* and in *Mysore Gazetteer* (ed. C. Hayavadana Rao, Vols. II and V).

[3]Ed. and trans. Rice, *EC*, VII, Sk. 94 and 98.

[4]Ed. and trans. Fleet, *EI*, V, Nos. A and B.

[5]Ed. and trans. Rice, *EC*, VII, Sk. 99.

[6]Ibid., Sk. 100 and 104.

[7]Ed. and trans. Fleet, *EI*, V, No. C and Rice, *EC*, VII, Sk. 108 respectively.

[8]Ed. and trans. Rice, *EC*, VII, Sk. 105.

[9]Ed. P.B. Desai, *SII*, XV, no. 73.

[10]Ed. and trans. Rice, *EC*, VII, Sk. 316.

[11]Ed. and trans. Rice, *EC*, VII, Sk. 292.

These various terms clearly denote organisational divisions, although they may have encompassed some doctrinal differences as well. A few of the terms derive from Kannada, the language of most of the inscriptions, while the others derive from Sanskrit. *Parṣe* is a Kannada variant of *pariṣad* (group, assembly, council). *Āvaḷi* (row, line, lineage, dynasty), *āmnāya* (sacred tradition or texts, instruction), and *saṃtati* or *santāna* (continuation, lineage, offspring) are common Sanskrit words, but their use in this context is rare. We may translate the Śakti-pariṣad as the Assembly-of-the-Goddess and the Parvatāvali as the Mountain-Lineage. The latter term probably refers to the sacred mountain Śrīparvata or Śrīśaila in Kurnool District. A priest of the Parvatāvali named Rāmeśvara was presiding over the *Mallikārjuna-śilā-maṭha* at this site in A.D. 1090.[12] Srīparvata was an important pilgrimage center for the Kālāmukhas and is frequently mentioned in their epigraphs. *Parvata* might also refer to the holy Himalayan mountain Kedāranāth commemorated in the name of the Belagāve temple or to the goddess Pārvatī, who was herself of the lineage of the Mountain. The Bhujaṅgāvali or Serpent Lineage may be an allusion to the association of Śiva with the cobra. The Kannada term *Mūvara-kōṇeya* is obscure. J.F. Fleet notes (*EI*, V, 219) :

> *Mūvara* must be the genitive of *mūvaru,* 'three persons', unless it can be connected with *mū,* = *mudu*, 'advanced age'. For *kōṇe,* of which *kōṇeya* is the genitive, the dictionary only gives the meanings of 'a pitcher; an inner apartment or chamber, a room'.

Beḷḷeya seems to be the genitive of *beḷḷi,* a Kannada word meaning 'silver.' *Iṭṭige,* 'a brick,' is still current in Kannada. It is derived from the Sanskrit *iṣṭakā* or *iṣṭikā.*

The Mūvara-kōṇeya-saṃtati

The Mūvara-koṇeya-saṃtati of the Parvatāvali had its headquarters at Belagāve, but its control extended to about five additional sites in the surrounding region. These are the Brahmeśvara temple

[12]See the inscription ed. and trans. by P. Sreenivasachar, *HAS,* XIII, Part II, no. 7. Sreenivasachar mistakenly read 'Appaparv(v)atv=Aḷiya Rāmēśvara-paṃḍitarg(ge)' for 'Appaparv(v)atāvaḷiya Rāmēśvara-paṃḍitarg(g)e.' The correction was made by N. Venkata Ramanayya in G. Yazdani (ed.), *The Early History of the Deccan,* II, 705.

at Ablūr, the Mallikārjuna temple at Haḷe-Niḍnēgila, the Trikūṭeśvara temple at Gadag, and the Nagareśvara temple in Sūḍi—all in Dharwar District—and the Koṭīśvara temple at Devasthāna-Hakkalu near Kuppaṭūr in Shimoga District. The last two sites, however, cannot with certainty be said to belong to this line. The earliest inscription at the Kedāreśvara temple in Belagāve is dated by Rice at *c.* A.D. 1078.[13] It is a grant made to the priest Vālmīki-muni, the second in descent from Kedāraśakti-munipati. Another priest second in descent from Kedāraśakti was Someśvara-paṇḍita-deva. He is the donee in four grants : three dated A.D. 1094, 1103 and 1113 from the Kedāreśvara temple and one dated 1101 from Ablūr.[14] Subtracting about twenty-five years for each priest, Kedāraśakti must have headed the monastery between about 1025 and 1050. If the Belagāve-Ablūr Someśvara is identical with the ascetic by that name teaching at Sūḍi as early as 1060,[15] Kedāraśakti may be placed slightly earlier. The name Kedāraśakti suggests that he may have been the founder of the Kedāraśvara temple and priesthood. The latest inscription of this priesthood found at the temple is dated 1215[16] although a collateral line at Gadag has left a record dated 1225.[17] If we can identify the priesthood at Devasthāna-Hakkalu as another collateral line, the period may be extended up to the twelfth year of Rāmacandra-rāya of the Seunas, or 1280.[18] This is one of the latest dates of all Kālāmukha epigraphs. The majority of the Mūvara-kōṇeya-saṃtati records are dated in the second half of the twelfth century. The diagram of the genealogy of this priesthood is on next page.

The full name of the form of Śiva who presided over the Belagāve temple was Dakṣiṇa-Kedāreśvara, Lord of the Southern Kedāra. This implies a comparison with the northern Kedāraśvara, the god of the famous and holy Kedāra Mountain in the Himalayas. The Belagāve temple was built in the southern portion of the town

[13]Ed. and trans., *EC,* VII, Sk. 107.

[14]Ibid., Sk. 94, 98, 99, and Fleet, *EI,* V, No. A–B respectively.

[15]See L.D. Barnett, 'Inscriptions of Sūdi,' *EI,* XV (1919–20), 73–112 (No. F). A.V. Subbiah (*QJMS,* VII, 184) claims that the Kedāreśvara temple did not yet exist in A.D. 1054. This statement is based on the absence of any mention of the temple in a record dated in this year (ed. and trans. Rice, *EC,* VII, Sk. 118), which lists most of the other temples in Belagāve, but not the Kedāreśvara. The portion of the record in which this list appears, however, seems to date from about a century later.

[16]Ed. and trans. Rice, *EC,* VII, Sk. 95.

[17]Ed. Desai, *SII,* XV, no. 609.

[18]Ed. and trans. Rice, *EC,* VIII, Sb. 275.

- KEDĀRAŚAKTI-munipati
  - RUDRABHARAṆA
    - VALMĪKI-muni (*c.* 1078)
  - ŚRĪKAṆṬHA-paṇḍita I
    - SOMEŚVARA-paṇḍita-deva (1094, 1103, 1113) (1101–4 Ablūr)
      - VIDYĀBHARAṆA (1129)
        - VĀMAŚAKTI-munīśvara I (*Ibid.* 1129)
        - GAUTAMA-muni (*Ibid.* 1129, 1139, 1149)
          - VĀMAŚAKTI-paṇḍita-deva II (1156, 1159, *c.* 1160, 1162, 1164, 1168, 1171, ?1181, 1181, 1193) (1165 Haḷe-Niḍnēgila)
            - JÑĀNAŚAKTI-deva II (?1181)
              - ŚRĪKANTHA-deva II
                - VĀMAŚAKTI-deva III (1215)
        - JÑĀNAŚAKTI I (1130, 1144 Ablūr)
        - CANDRABHŪṢAṆA paṇḍita-deva (1191, 1192, 1199 Gadag)
          - KRIYĀŚAKTI-paṇḍita (1213, 1225 Gadag)

on the bank of a tank called Tāvaregeṟe or Tāvareyakeṟe, 'the tank of the water lilies.'[19] The priests of the temple also controlled another temple or shrine at this site dedicated to the god Nakhareśvara or Nagareśvara.[20] In A.D. 1139 a third shrine was constructed at the site by two sculptors who set up an image of the god Kusuveśvara and presented the 'temple of the god ... as attached to the god Kedāreśvara.'[21]

The inscription of *c.* 1078 contains the following genealogy :

> In the world-renowned Śakti-parṣe, in the Mūvara-kōṇeya-santati (? of the Parvvatāvaḷi), shone Kedāraśakti-munipati. His disciple, an ornament to the Lākula-samaya, was Rudrābharaṇa. His disciple was Vālmīki-muni (his praise, including)? a hand to Lākula.[22]

The remainder of the inscription is damaged. It records a gift to a temple, presumably the Kedāreśvara. This line of ascetics seems to have died out with Vālmīki-muni since both he and his predecessor, Rudrābharaṇa, are mentioned only in this record. The term *Lākula-samaya,* 'doctrine of Lakula,' and other references to this Śaivite saint frequently appear in Kālāmukha epigraphs and will be discussed below. The special significance, if any, of the phrase 'a hand to Lākula' is not known.

The main line of Kedāreśvara pontiffs passed from Kedāraśakti through Śrīkaṇṭha-paṇḍita to Someśvara-paṇḍita-deva. Ignoring some minor variation, the four grants written during Someśvara's reign describe Kedāraśakti as follows :

> In the line named Parvatāvaḷi, which was esteemed to be greatly (*i.e.* undoubtedly) the leading *(division)* of the sect, celebrated in the world named Śakti-parṣe, there became famous the eminent ascetic Kedāraśakti, an ornament to the succession named Mūvara-kōṇeya-saṃtati.[23]

The grant of A.D. 1113 adds the important information that this priest and his disciples were included 'among the Kāḷamukhas,

[19] Fleet, *EI,* V, 221.
[20] Ibid.
[21] Ed. and trans. Rice, *EC,* VII, Sk. 112.
[22] Ibid., Sk. 107.
[23] Ed. and trans. Fleet, *EI,* V, 219.

who . . . had caused themselves to be spoken of as the very burst of the rainy season for the *cātaka*-birds that are disciples.'[24] Someśvara is called a 'Kāḷamukhācārya' in the Gadag record of 1192 and his disciple's disciple Siddhānti-candrabhūṣaṇa is said to have 'sprung from the lineage of Kālamukha ācāryas.'[25] Several inscriptions of other branches of the Śakti-pariṣad establish the connection between it and the Kālāmukha order beyond any doubt.

The *maṭha* (cloister or college) of these priests is called the *Kōḍiya-maṭha* in the Kannada grants and the *Kōṭi-maṭha* in a Sanskrit passage from the record of 1215.[26] It is also referred to as the *Kedāra-maṭha* and the *Kedāra-sthāna*. On the basis of the inscription of 1159 Fleet suggested that the *maṭha* was built by the *hergaḍe* Veṇṇamarasa,[27] but the passage which he translates as 'the Kōḍiya-maṭha of the *Hergaḍe* Veṇṇamarasa' is ambiguous. Rice in fact connects this Veṇṇamarasa with the Tripurāntaka temple in Belagāve, not the Kōḍiya-maṭha.[28] More plausible is Fleet's suggestion that the *maṭha* was so named because 'it stood somewhere near the *kōḍi* or outlet of the Tāvaregeṟe tank.'[29]

Among the several descriptions of the Kedāreśvara temple and maṭha, the following from the record of A.D. 1162 is the most striking :

> There is the Kōḍiya-maṭha, which has become the abode of the god Kedāra of the South,—a very field charming with a crop which is the standing erect of the hairs of the body that is induced by doing worship to the *liṅga* of Śiva, —a place devoted to the observances of Śaiva saints leading perpetually the life of celibate religious students,—a place for the quiet study of the four Vedas, the *Ṛc, Yajus, Sāman,* and *Atharvan,* together with their auxiliary works,—a place where commentaries are composed on the *Kaumāra, Pāṇinīya, Śākaṭāyana, Śabdānuśāsana,* and other grammatical works,—a place where commentaries are composed

[24]Ibid., 221.

[25]Ed. H. Lüders, 'Gadag Inscription of Vira-Ballala II,' *EI,* VI (1900), 96–97.

[26]Ed. and trans. Rice, *EC,* VII, Sk. 95. See Fleet, *EI,* V, 221–22.

[27]*EI,* V, 221–22.

[28]Ed. and trans. Rice, *EC,* VII, Sk. 123. The text reads: 'Śrī-Tripurāntakad ācāryya Jñānaśakti-paṇḍita-dēvara mattam alliya herggaḍe Veṇṇamarasa Śrī-Kōḍiya-maṭhad ācāryya Vāmaśakti-paṇḍita-dēvara . . .'

[29]*EI,* V, 222.

> on the six systems of philosophy, namely the *Nyāya, Vaiśeṣika, Mīmāṃsā, Sāṃkhya, Bauddha, etc.,*—a place where commentaries are composed on the *Lākuḷa-siddhānta,* and the *Pātañjala* and other *Yogaśāstras,*—a place for *(studying)* the eighteen *Purāṇas,* the law books, and all the poetical compositions, the dramas, the light comedies, and the other various kinds of learning,—a place where food is always given to the poor, the helpless, the lame, the blind, the deaf, and to professional story-tellers, singers, musicians, bards, players, and minstrels whose duty it is to awaken their masters with music and songs, and to the naked and the crippled [*nagna-bhagna*], and to *(Jain and Buddhist)* mendicants [*kṣapaṇakas*], to *(Brāhmaṇa)* mendicants who carry a single staff [*ekadaṇḍins*] and also those who carry a triple staff [*tridaṇḍins*], to *haṃsa* and *paramahaṃsa* ascetics, and to all other beggars from many countries [*nānā-deśa-bhikṣuka-jana*],—a place where many helpless sick people are harboured and treated,—a place of assurance of safety for all living creatures.[30]

The description continues with an elaborate and uninspired series of metaphors and similes which compare the temple and its maṭha to various mythological places and personages. These metaphors and similes also appear in the records of 1129 and 1156.[31] The 1129 record adds an attractive comparison of the temple and the Himalayan mountain Kedāra :

> Moreover the course of the sacred bathing streams there at the temple is like that of the Ganges at Kedāra, the lofty tower of the Śiva temple piercing the sky rises up like the peak of Kedāra, and the holy ascetics performing penance there are like holy ascetics at Kedāra whose minds are bent on the performance of the most difficult penances,—thus this is a new Kedāra, the standing crops of its fertile fields resembling the horripilation arising from the Śiva-liṅga worship, its temple the abode of Parameśvara.
>
> The god Kedāra therein, who, thinking with supreme benevolence on his faithful worshippers,—afraid of the

[30] Ed. and trans. Fleet, ibid.

[31] Ed. and trans. Rice, *EC,* Sk. 100 and 104.

cold and unable to make the distant pilgrimage (to Kedāra) —frees them from all sins (here) . . . —may he protect you, the wearer of the crescent moon.

These descriptions are remarkably different from what one would have expected on the basis of the statements of Yāmunācārya and Rāmānuja. Certainly these Kālāmukhas do not seem to uphold a doctrine 'in conflict with the Vedas *(Veda-virodha),*' unless by this Rāmānuja merely means in conflict with his own Vedic exegesis. The list of subjects studied at the maṭha includes nearly the whole of traditional Sanskrit learning with the addition of two slightly less orthodox subjects, *Lākula-siddhānta* and *Pātañjala Yogaśāstra*. The eclecticism in the choice of alms recipients is astonishing and testifies to the charity and tolerance of the directors of the maṭha. The sectarian affiliations of all the various classes of ascetics given alms cannot be determined exactly, but the list probably includes Jains, Buddhists, Śaivas, Vaiṣṇavas, and perhaps even Ājīvikas. The term *kṣapaṇaka* usually refers to naked Jain ascetics although it occasionally refers also to Buddhists. *Haṃsa* and *paramahaṃsa* ascetics may be either Vaiṣṇava or Śaivite since these terms seem to denote levels of spiritual advancement rather than sectarian affiliation.[32] There is some confusion regarding the titles *ekadaṇḍin* and *tridaṇḍin*. G.S. Ghurye believes that the former are Śaivite and the latter Vaiṣṇava while A.L. Basham seems to suggest the opposite.[33] K.K. Handiqui has clearly shown that the original sources themselves are ambiguous or contradictory.[34] Basham further suggests that the compound *nagna-bhagna,* 'naked and crippled,' may refer to a class of ascetics, possibly the Ājīvikas, who were 'naked and crippled' owing to ritual austerity and initiatory mutilations.[35]

The comparison of the Southern-Kedāra with the original Himalayan mountain points to some connection between these ascetics and the North-west. Several Kālāmukha priests in Mysore bore the name Kāśmīra-paṇḍita, and this fact led A.V. Subbiah to assert that the Kālāmukha sect originated in Kashmir.[36] This

[32]See G.S. Ghurye, *Indian Sadhus,* pp. 72–78, and A.L. Basham, *History and Doctrines of the Ājīvikas,* p. 114.

[33]Ghurye, pp. 71–72, and Basham, *History* . . ., p. 105.

[34]See Śrīharṣa, pp. 586–88.

[35]*History* . . ., p. 105.

[36]*QJMS,* VII, 176.

is too sweeping a generalisation, but evidence has since been discovered which explicitly confirms that at least some of these ascetics did migrate from the Kashmir region. This will be discussed below.

The successor of Kedāraśakti in the main line of Kedāreśvara pontiffs was Śrīkaṇṭha. In the 1094 grant he is called Kedāraśakti's 'chief disciple . . . of whom what more can be said than that he was himself Lākuḷīśa in the world, and farther, shone as the equal of omniscience.'[37] The Kedāreśvara grant of 1103 and the duplicate grant of 1101–04 from the Brahmeśvara temple at Ablūr contain the following additional verses in praise of Śrīkaṇṭha (with some minor variation) :

> Of that great ascetic Kedāra, the disciple praised indeed throughout the world, was Śrīkaṇṭha, abounding in extremely pure virtues, of spotless behavior, a very cuckoo (or ring-dove) in the grove of mango-trees that are learned men. Amidst great applause, Śrīkaṇṭhadeva, abounding in great virtue, an ornament of great saints, a forehead-ornament of learned people, a very ocean of the science of logic [*tarkka-vidyā*], firmly fixed his thoughts on the water-lilies that are the feet of the god Hara (Śiva), and made the beauty of the goddess of eloquence abide in the charming water-lily that was his mouth, and maintained purity in all his behaviour, and established to the ends of all the points of the compass a brilliant fame like that of (Airāvata) the elephant of *(the east which is)* the quarter of Indra.[38]

In the Kedāreśvara grant of 1113, as we have noted, Śrīkaṇṭha is included 'among the Kāḷamukhas.' The record continues :

> Praised by the learned, the son of Kedāraśakti, ever cherishing Śrīkaṇṭha (Śiva) in the lotus of his heart, his holy throat *(śrīkaṇṭha)* retained the blessed words uttered by the *munipati*. Understanding the *paramātmāgama*, skilled in overpowering eloquence, like the purest gold if it had acquired perfume, having placed the lotus feet of Īśvara

[37]Ed. and trans. Rice, *EC*, VII, Sk. 94.

[38]Ed. and trans. Fleet, *EI*, V, 219, This is the Ablūr version.

on his head, self-chosen husband of the wife severe penance, distinguished by all the *ācārya* qualities, was Śrīkaṇṭha-yogīśvara.[39]

The Kedāreśvara grant to Gautama dated 1129 asserts that Śrīkaṇṭha was 'like a pearl necklace to the throat of Sarasvatī, a touchstone for testing the gold of learning, reverenced by the world.'[40]

Although these descriptions, like those of the Kōḍiya-maṭha, tend to run counter to some of the accusations made against the Kālāmukhas by Rāmānuja, there are also several points of agreement between his account and the epigraphs. First, both the Kālāmukhas of Rāmānuja and the priests of the Kedāreśvara temple are worshippers of Śiva. Furthermore, however great the learning of the Kōḍiya-maṭha priests, the essential feature of their faith seems to be personal devotion or *bhakti* to Śiva rather than metaphysical speculation or a religion of sacrifice and ritual observance. In this respect these priests bear resemblance to their famous opponent who at this time was preaching his *bhakti-yoga* at Śrīraṅgam some 250 miles to the south-east.

Rāmānuja identifies the Kāpālas, Kālāmukhas, Pāśupatas, and Śaivas as the four Śaivite orders which follow the doctrine of Pāśupati. The association of the Kālāmukhas with the Pāśupatas is well-documented. Many Kālāmukha teachers, including Śrīkaṇṭha, are identified with Lakulīśa, the famous Pāśupata saint to whom the *Pāśupata-sūtra* is traditionally ascribed. *Lākulasiddhānta*, the Doctrine of Lakula, is one of the chief subjects studied at the Kōḍiya-maṭha, and most of Śrīkaṇṭha's successors are either identified with Lakula or said to follow the *Lākulasiddhānta* or *Lākulāgama*. Other South Indian inscriptions attest to the importance of Lakulīśa to the Kālāmukhas and consequently to the close relation between the Kālāmukhas and Pāśupatas. A nearly identical verse contained in two records from Belgaum District—one from Sirasangi dated A.D. 1148 and one from Nesargi dated 1219–20[41]—seems to identify the Kālāmukhas as Mahāvratins and Mahāpāśupatas. The names Jñānaśakti and Kriyāśakti,

---

[39]Ed. and trans. Rice, *EC*, VII, Sk. 99.

[40]Ibid., Sk. 100.

[41]Ed. Panchamukhi, *Karnatak Inscriptions*, I, no. 24 of 1939–49, and ed. and trans. J.F. Fleet, *JBBRAS*, X, 167–298 (No. VI).

which are frequently adopted by Kālāmukha ascetics, are also technical terms for various mystic powers in Pāśupata texts.[42]

There are a number of post-Gupta statues from northern India which have been identified as representations of Lakulīśa. These usually portray him as a naked yogin with a staff *(lakuṭa)* in his left hand and a citron in his right, with his penis erect, and either standing or seated in the *padmāsana*. At about the beginning of the eleventh century, however, the Lakulīśa cult seems to have shifted its activities to southern India, especially to the Mysore region. The number of statues in northern India declines and the name Lakulīśa suddenly appears in a large number of Kannada epigraphs. Some of the donees in these epigraphs are identified as Kālāmukhas and others as Pāśupatas. It is likely that there was an actual migration of Lakulīśa devotees to the Karṇāṭaka region from various parts of north-western India.

As we have noted, V. Subbiah suggested that the Kālāmukhas originated in Kashmir. In support of this theory, however, he could cite only a few inscriptions which mentioned Kālāmukha ascetics named Kāśmīra-paṇḍita. A recently edited inscription from Muttagi in Bijāpur District dated A.D. 1147 helps to give the theory some added weight.[43] The record eulogises a line of Śaivite priests who had migrated from Kashmir and had settled at Bijāpur. This priesthood is positively identified as a Kālāmukha one in a grant of A.D. 1074–75 from Bijāpur itself.[44] It appears, in fact, that the priests belonged to the Bhujaṅgāvali, another branch of the Śakti-pariṣad. One of them was named Kāśmīra and another Lakulīśvara.

The reason or reasons for the migration from the North of Lakulīśa devotees are uncertain. Missionary zeal, loss of patronage, unsettled political conditions, and famine are all possible factors. Several Kālāmukha ascetics are known to have been peripatetic teachers, but missionary activity in the South cannot explain why the Lakulīśa cult seems to have lost its power in the North. Famine or loss of patronage by one or more royal dynasties are quite strong possibilities but virtually impossible to confirm. Many parts of north-western India were being rocked by the incursions of Mahmūd of Ghaznī at about this time and this may also have

---

[42]The date and teachings of Lakulīśa are discussed in detail below, chap. vi.

[43]Ed. Desai, *SII,* XV, no. 32.

[44]Ed. and trans. J.F. Fleet, 'Sanskrit and Old-Canarese Inscriptions,' *IA,* X (1881), 126–31.

been a factor in the move to the South. Two northern sites connected with the worship of Lakulīśa and attacked by Mahmūd were Mathurā and Somnāth. In A.D. 380 the former city was the home of the group of ascetics who traced their descent from Kuśika, a disciple of Lakulīśa. In A.D. 1287 Somnāth was the home of a line of Pāśupatas who traced their descent from Gārgya or Garga, another of Lakulīśa's disciples. Kashmir itself, however, was not conquered by Mahmūd although he plundered the Kashmir valley in A.D. 1014 and again attacked the place, this time without success, in the following year. In about A.D. 1030 the great Muslim scholar Al-Bīrūnī noted that 'Hindu sciences have retired far away from those parts of the country conquered by us, and have fled to places which our hand cannot yet reach, to Kashmīr, Benares, and other places.'[45] If many Hindu scholars had fled to Kashmir, many of the more prudent Kashmiri scholars must have decided that the time was ripe to move elsewhere. Among them may have been the Kashmiri Kālāmukhas who travelled to the South where some of their co-religionists had established themselves as early as the end of the eighth century.

Several interesting similarities exist between the Somnāth Pāśupatas and the Belagāve Kālāmukhas in addition to their association with Lakulīśa. The Cintra *praśasti* of 1287 records the consecration of five *liṅga* temples in Somnāth.[46] The Pañcaliṅga temple in Belagāve belonged to the Kālāmukhas. The five *liṅgas* at Somnāth were consecrated by a priest named Tripurāntaka. One of the Kālāmukha temples in Belagāve was dedicated to the god Tripurāntaka. The Somnāth Tripurāntaka's preceptor was Vālmīki-rāśi, a name also found among the early priests of the Mūvara-kōṇeya-saṃtati. The Somnāth record describes a pilgrimage undertaken by Tripurāntaka during which he visited two sites with important Kālāmukha associations—Kedāra in the Himalayas and Śrīparvata in Kurnool District. These similarities show that the Pāśupatas and Kālāmukhas continued to share a large body of common traditions in addition to having a common base in the teachings of Lakulīśa.

A third point of agreement between the statements of Rāmānuja and the Kālāmukha epigraphs is their references to the *āgamas*. Rāmānuja seems to state that the doctrines of the Śaivas and other

---

[45]Trans. E.C. Sachau, *Alberuni's India*, I, 22.

[46]Ed. and trans. G. Bühler, *EI*, I, 271–87.

worshippers of Paśupati are 'set forth in the *Śaivāgamas.*' Many Kālāmukha epigraphs refer to the *Lākulāgama.* The Mūvarakōṇeya-saṃtati priest Vāmaśakti II, for instance, is called 'an ornament of *Lākulāgama,*' and the earlier priest Śrīkaṇṭha is said to understand the *Paramātmāgama.*[47] The *Śaivāgamas* seem to have originated mainly in South India. Tradition enumerates twenty-eight of these texts, but the actual number is much larger. They are usually associated with the doctrine of the Śaiva sect proper, *Śaiva-siddhānta,* but other Śaivite schools developed their own *āgamas.* Most of these are now lost although there are several extant *āgamas* of the Vīraśaiva or Liṅgāyat sect. The term *āgama* is sometimes used simply as a generic term for Śaivite religious texts or for the Tantras.

A fourth point of agreement is the connection with Yoga. Śrīkaṇṭha is called a 'Lord among Yogins *(Yogīśvara),*' while Rāmānuja's Kālāmukhas practise various Yoga type rituals. The emphais on Yoga is better exemplified by some of the epithets of Śrīkaṇṭha's successors, but nowhere do the inscriptions suggest quite such unusual measures as those listed by Rāmānuja. We have noted above the description of a Kālāmukha priest as a typical Śaivite ascetic in the 1252–53 record from Munavaḷḷi.[48]

One additional feature to emerge from the descriptions of Śrīkaṇṭha is their emphasis on his knowledge of the science of logic, or *tarka-vidyā.* This emphasis becomes more explicit in the epithets of some of his successors who are called Naiyāyikas and Vaiśeṣikas. The Nyāya-Vaiśeṣika system of philosophy is preeminently the science of logic and is closely associated with the Pāśupatas.[49] We might also compare the predilection for logical, or rather casuistical, argument of the Kāpālika in Mahendravarman's *Mattavilāsa.*

Someśvara-paṇḍita-deva, the third in the main line of Kedāreśvara pontiffs, is the reigning pontiff in three records from Belagāve and in two identical records from Ablūr, all dated between 1094 and 1113.[50] He may also be identical with the Someśvara who

---

[47]Ed. and trans. Rice, *EC,* VII, Sk. 123.

[48]See above, p. 6.

[49]This association of Nyāya-Vaiśeṣika philosophy with Pāśupata Śaivism has been convincingly documented by R.G. Bhandarkar, p. 117, and by S.N. Dasgupta in his *A History of Indian Philosophy,* V, 143–45.

[50]Ed. and trans. Rice, *EC,* VII, Sk. 94, 98 and 99; Ed. and trans. Fleet, *EI,* V, no. A–B.

was presiding over the Nagareśvara temple in nearby Sūḍi between 1060 and 1084.[51] The inclusion of verses eulogising him in many records of his successors indicates that he was an important member of this priesthood.

The inscription of A.D. 1094 is the earliest of the dated records from the Kedāreśvara temple.[52] It records a grant made by the whole town of Belagāve to Someśvara-paṇḍita-deva, 'the *ācārya* of the god Nakhareśvara of Tāvaregeṟe in the southern quarter' of the town, 'for the service and decorations of the god, for repairs to the temple, for gifts of food to the students and ascetics there.' Someśvara is called the pupil of Śrīkaṇṭha and the possessor of the yogic virtues of *yama* (restraints), *niyama* (disciplines), *svādhyāya* (repetition of the scriptures to one's self), *prāṇāyāma* (control of respiration), *pratyāhāra* (ability to free sense activity from the domination of external objects), *dhyāna* (meditation), *dhāraṇā* (concentration), *maunānuṣṭhāna* (constant silence), *japa* (incantation or murmured prayer), and *samādhi* (yogic ecstasy).[53] These are more or less standard yogic virtues and exercises, and the list is similar to that given in Patañjali's *Yogasūtra* ii. 29.[54] We have seen that Patañjali's *sūtras* and other *Yogaśāstras* were included in the curriculum of the Kōḍiya-maṭha. The present record further claims Someśvara proficient in *siddhānta* (doctrine), *tarka* (logic), *vyākaraṇa* (grammer), *kāvya* (poetry), *nāṭaka* (drama), *Bharata* (?=music), and 'many other branches of literature and learning.' The term *siddhānta* may refer simply to philosophy in general; to Śaiva-siddhānta, the doctrine of the Śaiva sect; or, most likely, to the Lākula-siddhānta taught at the Kōḍiya-maṭha.

The duplicate inscription of A.D. 1101–04 found at the Basaveśvara temple at Ablūr reveals that the original name of the temple was Brahmeśvara, after the name of the official who built it.[55] According to this record, the village of Muriganahaḷḷi was given to the temple by the *daṇḍanāyaka* Govindarasa in the year 1101. On this occasion Govinda washed the feet of Someśvara, the disciple of Śrīkaṇṭha

[51]Ed. and trans. Barnett, *EI,* XV, nos. F–I.

[52]Ed. and trans. Rice, *EC,* VII, Sk. 94.

[53]Most of these terms are analyzed in detail by M. Eliade in his *Yoga* . . ., pp. 47–100. We have used his translations for some of the terms.

[54]He lists *yama, niyama, āsana, prāṇāyāma, pratyāhāra, dhāraṇā, dhyāna,* and *samādhi.*

[55]Ed. and trans. Fleet, *EI,* V, no. A–B.

who was the disciple of Kedāraśakti. Someśvara is described as follows :

> Some people are learned in logic [*tarka*], and some can impart the knowledge of well-chosen speech; some are acquainted with the dramas, some are conversant with good poetry, and some know grammar [*vyākaraṇa*] : there are none (others) who know all of these; but the learned Someśvara, indeed, the sinless one, the leader of the Naiyāyikas, knows them all.
>
> A very season of Caitra (*i.e.* a very month of spring) to *(develop the fruit of)* the mango-tree that is Akalaṅka,—a very cool-rayed moon to *(bring the full tide to)* the ocean that is the Lokāyatas,—a very guardian elephant of that quarter of the region which is the *Sāṃkhya*-doctrine,—a very pearl-ornament glittering on the white throat of the woman who is the *Mīmāṃsā*,—a very hot-rayed sun to *(close)* the water-lilies *(blooming at night)* that are the Buddhists,—the logician [*tārkika*], the learned Someśvara, the leader of the Naiyāyikas, attained greatness.[56]

These two verses are repeated in reverse order and with some minor variation in the Kedāreśvara temple record of A.D. 1103.[57] The references to Akalaṅka (probably the famous Jain logician by that name), the Lokāyatas, the *Sāṃkhya*-doctrine, and *Mīmāṃsā*, as Fleet notes, are confusing since Someśvara would be expected to oppose rather than to support them. Fleet thinks there may be 'some hidden second meanings,' but we feel they are probably correct as rendered. If they are correct, then the reference to the Buddhists must also be a positive one. The water-lilies *(nīrējāta)* of this passage are, in fact, probably day-blooming, not night-blooming. Someśvara would then be the sun that *opens* the water-lilies that are the Buddhists. The object of the whole passage is to announce Someśvara's mastery of all philosophical doctrines. We have noted that commentaries to the 'six systems of philosophy' including the Bauddha system were said to have been composed at the Kōḍiya-maṭha. Vācaspati Miśra provides a precedent for this. He wrote treatises on each of the orthodox systems of philosophy

---

[56]Ibid., pp. 219–20.
[57]Ibid., p. 219.

with the exception of the Vaiśeṣika. Similarly, Sāyaṇa-Mādhava, in his *Sarvadarśana-saṃgraha,* temporarily adopts the views of his opponents for the purpose of explication.

This rather lengthy eulogy to Someśvara continues with a series of rhyming-compound epithets which also appear in the Belagāve record of A.D. 1103. The first of these epithets merely repeats the yogic virtues mentioned in the 1094 grant with the exception of *prāṇāyāma* and *pratyāhāra*. His praise continues :

> He who is gracious to learned men; he who is a very sun to *(open)* the great cluster of water-lilies *(blooming in the daytime)* that is the *Nyāyaśāstra,* and who is a very autumn-moon to bring to full tide the ocean of the Vaiśeṣikas; he who is a very ruby-ornament of those who are versed in the *Sāṃkhyāgama,* and who is a very bee on the water-lilies that are the feet of his teacher; he who is a very spring to the grove of mango-trees that is the *Śabdaśāstra,* and who has given new life to the *Lākulasiddhānta* by the development of his wisdom; he who is a very stream of the river of the gods in unequalled reasoning, and who has made the assembly of his disciples to prosper by the favour of the counsel given by him; he who is a very ocean to *(receive)* the stream of the great river that is the *Sāhityavidyā,* and who has quite satisfied the god Parameśvara (Śiva) with the unbroken flow of his devotion; he who is the sole abode of the virtues of blameless and spotless penance, and who has delighted the whole circuit of the earth with the moonlight that is his fame.[58]

The Belagāve record of 1103 is a grant to the temple of Dakṣiṇa-Kedāreśvara made by the same *daṇḍanāyaka* Govindarasa for incense, lights and offerings to the god while washing the feet of Someśvara.[59] In addition to the above epithets, he is also called 'the *ācārya* of the temple of the southern Kedāreśvara of the Tāvaregeṟe of Baḷḷigāve.' Thus it appears that Someśvara was at the same time the *ācārya* of the Nagareśvara temple, the Brahmeśvara temple, and the Daksina-Kedaresvara temple (unless he had by this time given up the former positions).

---

[58]Ed. and trans. Fleet, *EI,* V, 220.

[59]Ed. and trans. Rice, *EC,* VII, Sk. 98.

In A.D. 1113 Govinda made another grant to the temple of Dakṣiṇa-Kedāreśvara for 'sandal, flowers, incense, lights, offerings and all manner of services, and for the food of the ascetics and others there.'[60] The inscription opens with an invocation to Śiva as Lakulīśa, who is 'the heart of Brahma shining as a stone on which is inscribed the *śāsana* of the Vedas which extol the abode of Viśvanātha.' This inscription, as we have mentioned, identifies the ascetics Kedāraśakti, Śrīkaṇṭha and Someśvara as 'Kāḷamukhas.' Someśvara is called not merely the disciple, but the son of Śrīkaṇṭha, and is extolled in another series of rhyming compounds which includes one or two epithets found in the earlier records.

Most of the epithets are of little interest save one, listed twice, which identifies him as a 'distinguished Sārasvata.' In all likelihood the term Sārasvata designates the caste of Someśvara although the generic sense, 'a learned man,' may also be implied. The Sārasvatas were and are a Brāhmaṇa caste resident chiefly in Punjab and Sind but also prominent in both Kashmir and Mysore. The identification of a Kālāmukha priest as a member of this caste shows that at least some, and probably most, of the Kālāmukha priests claimed Brāhmaṇa status and also tends to confirm the connection of the Kālāmukhas with the Northwest and Kashmir. It seems probable that a good number of the present day Sārasvatas of Mysore are descended from northern migrants including the Kālāmukhas. A famous member of the Sārasvatas, the poet Bilhaṇa, migrated from Kashmir to the court of Vikramāditya VI, a patron of the Kālāmukhas, in the second half of the eleventh century.[61] It is not inconceivable that Bilhaṇa himself was in some way allied with the Kālāmukhas.

An ascetic bearing the name Someśvara was attached to the gods Nagareśvara and Acaleśvara in Sūḍi, a village in Dharwar District not too far from Belagāve, at about this time. He is mentioned in grants dated A.D. 1060, 1069–70, 1075, and 1084.[62] He may plausibly be identified with the Mūvara-kōṇeya-saṃtati priest, but this identification cannot be confirmed since none of the Sūḍi records mention any of his preceptors or the Śakti-pariṣad. The Nagareśvara temple is known to have contained Kālāmukhas, however, from this unusual statement from the record of 1060 :

---

[60]Ibid., Sk. 99.

[61]See V.S. Pathak, *Ancient Historians of India,* pp. 56–57.

[62]Ed. and trans. Barnett, *EI,* XV, nos. F–I.

> If the Goravas [Śaivite ascetics of the monastery] who are Kālāmukhas should not be devout, if they should be so neglectful that the company of fair women [*vara-kāntā-saṃkulam*] should not come for three days for enjoyment, or if all the students should fail to study actively always, the worthy superintendents must never allow them to stay.[63]

Here its seems that the Kālāmukhas were responsible for the upkeep and management of the temple under the overall supervision of some sort of board of directors who were perhaps government officials. The company of fair women must be the 'public women' (*sūḷeyar,* i.e. *devadāsīs),* who figure prominently among the donees in this grant.

The Sūḍi records praise the ascetic called Someśvara in terms which closely mirror the praises of the Ablūr and Belagāve inscriptions. The record of 1060 says :

> 'O thou whose lotus-feet are scarred by the rubbing of the crest-jewels of all monarchs, crest-jewel of Vaiśeṣikas, sun to the lilies of Naiyāyikas, excellent in mastery of Sāṃkhya, a Brahman in grammatical science, who is peer to thee?' On this account the great ascetic Sōmēsvara, a worthy *Gotra-trāsi* [family- or mountain-shaker = Indra] to Mīmāṃsakas, has become renowned on earth.[64]

The record of 1075 adds :

> A primal Buddha to the Buddhist, a primal Jina to an Akalaṅka, an Akṣapāda (Gōtama) to the student of logic [*pramāṇa-mārga*], a Kaṇāda skilled in discrimination of all meanings to the student of (the science of) the soul, and likewise a Jaimini indeed to the student of (scriptural) texts, a Bṛhaspati to the student in the realm of grammar: thus was the master of (the temple of) Nagareśvara renowned.[65]

He is further said to practise the yogic virtues of *yama, niyama, svādhyāya, dhyāna, dhāraṇā, maunānuṣṭhāna, japa,* and *samādhi*

---

[63]Ibid., p. 93.
[64]Ibid., p. 92.
[65]Ibid., p. 99.

and to favor the *Lākulāgama*. He was 'a royal swan in the lake of Sāṃkhya doctrine, an ear-jewel of the lady of Nyāya doctrine, a crest-jewel of Vaiśeṣika doctrine.' The similarities between this description and that in the 1101–04 grant from Ablūr are too many to be ignored, especially his characterisation as the master of all the rival religious doctrines. We are inclined, therefore, to accept his identity with the Someśvara at Ablūr and Belagāve.

Someśvara is further praised in several records of his successors. The A.D. 1129 Kedāreśvara epigraph lists the entire line of ascetics from Kedāraśakti to Gautama but claims that 'the fortune of the Kedāra temple was planted, as if a tree of plenty for the world, through Someśvarārya.'[66] The 1156 epigraph of Vāmaśakti II, disciple of Gautama, contains a nearly identical statement.[67] The much defaced grant of *c.* 1164 mentions Someśvara as a disciple of Śrīkaṇṭha.[68] Someśvara-deva begins the list of *ācāryas* in the Trikūṭeśvara temple inscriptions from Gadag of the years 1191 and 1192.[69] The inscription of 1192, as mentioned above, adds the significant title 'Kāḷamukha-ācārya' to his name.

The main line of the successors of Someśvara seems to have passed from Vidyābharaṇa, also called Vādividyābharaṇa, to Vāmaśakti I and Gautama-muni. These three as well as their three predecessors all appear in the 1129 Kedāreśvara inscription. The description of Vidyābharaṇa makes clear what must have been the true attitude of these ascetics to the rival creeds of Buddhism, Mīmāṃsā, and Syādvāda or Jain scepticism :

> After that, the equal of the celebrated Bhārabhūti [unidentified], was celebrated that fortunate *munipa's* [Someśvara's] younger brother, Vidyābharaṇa, a faultless ornament of learning, an ornament of the lady fame. A thunderbolt in splitting the great boulders the Bauddhas, a lion in tearing open the frontal lobes of the elephant the Mīmāṃsā creed, a sun to the cluster of water-lilies the Syādvāda,— shines

[66]Ed. and trans. Rice, *EC,* VII, Sk. 100.

[67]Ibid., Sk. 104.

[68]Ibid., Sk. 108.

[69]Ed. F. Kielhorn, 'Gadag Inscription of the Yadava Bhillama,' *EI,* III (1894–95), 217–220, and ed. H. Lüders, *EI,* VI, 89–97. The second inscription was earlier edited and translated by J.F. Fleet, 'Notes on Inscriptions at Gaddak in the Ḍambaḷ Tālukā of the Dhārwāḍ District,' *IA,* II (1873), 296–303.

> Vidyābharaṇa, a true ornament and *muni* of the Naiyyāyikas.[70]

The record then states that Vidyābharaṇa 'made over the business of the *maṭha'* to his senior disciple Vāmaśakti-munīśvara in order to devote all of his time to the cultivation of learning. Nonetheless, it was to Vidyābharaṇa that the Cālukya king Someśvara III came to make a grant to the temple in 1129. After the details of the grant—a gift of the village of Tadavaṇale for repairs to the temple and for worship of the god—the inscription continues with an unusual passage which relates how 'Vidyābharaṇa, despising it [the gift] as being a cause for the destruction of the various pleasures of learning and the happy state of *yoga,* made it over to his own world-renowned senior disciple Gautama-muni, with the headship of the maṭha.' The section closes telling how the tree which is the Kedāreśvara temple was planted by Someśvara, 'threw out branches, was filled with sprouts, blossomed and spread into all the world' under Vāmaśakti I and bore fruit through the great Gautamācārya. Vidyābharaṇa is not mentioned. The invocation, however, declares that Vidyābharaṇa has commanded the god Kedāreśvara to protect Gautama, 'a present manifestation of the ancient Gautama-muni.'

Evidently something unusual must have happened in the succession of the maṭha at about this time. Fleet (*EI*, V, 224) notes that there is nothing in the inscription to explain why both Vāmaśakti and Gautama are called the chief disciples of Vidyābharaṇa and nothing to explain 'why Vidyābharaṇa "censured" or came to regret the happiness of having devoted himself to the various delights of learning because it had proved "destructive of stability," and on that account, appointed Gautama to the office of Maṭhapati.' The former question is a bit puzzling, but the latter one, at least in the terms given by Fleet, is based on an inaccurate transcription of the text. It is not happiness which is destructive of stability, but the gift which is destructive of Vidyābharaṇa's happiness. The main problem seems to be why Vāmaśakti was passed over in favor of Gautama when it came to choosing the successor of Vidyābharaṇa. Vidyābharaṇa, it should be emphasised, only transferred the 'business of the maṭha' to Vāmaśakti. The record does not state that Vāmaśakti ever received the actual

[70]Ed. and trans. Rice, *EC,* VII, Sk. 100.

title of *maṭha-pati*. Vidyābharaṇa seems to have kept this honour for himself, since it is to him that Someśvara III of the Cālukyas went in 1129 to make the grant. Vāmaśakti was probably appointed only executive director of the monastery and may have either died before the final appointment of Gautama or else simply have been passed over for some unknown reason. Fleet thinks that the inscription was drawn up at some time considerably after 1129 but we cannot see any significant reason why this should be the case.

In the 1149 Kedāreśvara grant, Gautama is called the disciple of Vādividyābharaṇa-paṇḍita-deva.[71] Vidyābharaṇa is given the same expanded title in a grant from the Brahmeśvara temple at Ablūr dated A.D. 1130 and 1144.[72] This grant introduces us to a new member of this priesthood named Jñānaśakti-paṇḍita-deva who was 'the disciple of Vādividyābharaṇa-paṇḍita-deva of the Mūvara-kōṇeya-saṃtati.' The inscription records how a certain Bammagāvuṇḍa was reminded that the shrine of Brahmeśvara at Ablūr had prospered under the protection of his father and grandfather and that he too should make donations to this temple. Bammagāvuṇḍa accordingly became 'inflamed more than ever with a desire for union with the passionate woman that is devotion to the god Śiva.' He then mounted a horse and promised to donate as much land as the horse could cover while running at top speed. After this unusual miniature *aśvamedha* he washed the feet of Jñānaśakti and presented the land he had promised. This was in 1130. In 1144 a *daṇḍanāyaka* named Mallibhāvarasa made another grant to the Brahmeśvara temple. Both grants were 'preserved' by Bammagāvuṇḍa and the great saint Jñānaśaktideva. A Jñānaśakti is named as the priest of the Tripurāntaka temple in Belagāve in two grants dated *c.* 1150 and 1159, but it is unlikely that he is the same person.[73]

Gautama again appears in the 1139 Kedāreśvara temple inscription.[74] This grant records the establishment of an image of the god Kusuveśvara and the donation of its temple, 'as attached to the god Kedāreśvara,' to Gautama-deva by two sculptors named Bāvaṇa and Rāvaṇa 'in order to clear an aspersion on their own race of the sculptors.' What this aspersion or fault of their guild

[71] Ed. and trans. Rice, *EC,* VII, Sk. 103.
[72] Ed. and trans. Fleet, *EI,* V, no. C.
[73] Ed. and trans. Rice, *EC,* VII, Sk. 118 and 123.
[74] Ibid., Sk. 112.

was the record does not say. The two sculptors claim that 'Gautamārya, reverenced by a multitude of *munis*, and the others who were *ācāryas* of the Kōḍi-maṭha were their religious teachers.' In response to this gift, Gautama is said to have himself allotted some land for this temple.

The Kedāreśvara inscription of 1149 announces the arrival in Belagāve of a Sāntara feudatory of the Cālukya Jagadekamalla for the purpose of granting the village of Kundūr in the Koḍanād Thirty of the Sāntalige Thousand for the Kedāresvara temple. The feudatory made the grant while washing the feet of 'Vādividyābharaṇa-paṇḍita-deva's disciple Gautama-paṇḍita-deva :

> To describe the qualities of the great ācārya of that Kedārasthāna,—Gautamārya :—Like bright lamps many munīndras, abodes of the highest good qualities, illumined that maṭha; after whom the muni Gautama, a pure jewel lamp like a young bud, ever shone in it with world-wide fame, while all the world, folding their hands, addressed him as Jīya.[75]

Gautama is also mentioned in a few of the numerous grants of his successor Vāmaśakti II, namely the Kedāreśvara grants of 1156, 1162, 1168, 1179, and 1193,[76] but these grants add nothing of importance, except those of 1179 and 1193 which call Vāmaśakti the son rather than the disciple of Gautama. It is not clear whether this means spiritual or actual son.

Before discussing Vāmaśakti II we must refer to another important disciple of Vidyābharaṇa named Siddhānti-candrabhūṣana-paṇḍita-deva, alias Satyavākya. This priest is the donee in three late 12th century grants found in the Trikūṭeśvara temple at Gadag in the Dharwar District. These record donations to this temple by the Yādava king Bhillama in A.D. 1191, by the Hoysala king Vīra-Ballāla II in 1192, and again by the latter king in 1199.[77] The inscriptions of 1191 and 1192 are of considerable importance for the political history of the area since they show that Vīra-Ballāla II defeated Bhillama and his general Jaitrasiṃha sometime between these two dates. The 1191 inscription of Bhillama is the only

[75]Ibid., Sk. 103.

[76]Ibid., Sk. 104, 102, 92, 123, and 105.

[77]Ed. Kielhorn, *EI*, III, 217–220; Lüders, *EI*, 89–97; and Desai, *SII*, XV, no. 214.

extant reference to his support of these ascetics, but at least one inscription from Belagāve issued during the reign of Ballāla records a donation to the Kedāreśvara temple. These two grants from Gadag and another dated A.D. 1213[78] are the only Śakti-pariṣad records written mainly in Sanskrit.

One of the most remarkable features of these Gadag grants is their location so far from Belagāve. Gadag is situated some seventy-five miles north-north-east of Belagāve. Ablūr and Sūḍi are only about fifteen to twenty miles from Belagāve. This long distance raises the possibility that Candrabhūṣana of Gadag was not in fact a member of the Belagāve line. His rather late dates also suggest this. In the 1129 Kedāreśvara grant Vidyābharaṇa must already have been quite old since he had seemingly turned over management of the maṭha to first one and then a second senior disciple. If Candrabhūṣaṇa was still alive in about 1199 and was, say, about eighty years old, he would have been only ten years old in 1129. In addition, the Gadag inscriptions mention neither the Śakti-pariṣad, the Mūvara-kōṇeya-saṃtati, nor the Parvatāvali. Nonetheless, the evidence in favor of Candrabhūṣaṇa belonging to the Belagāve line is too strong to be dismissed. Most important is the designation of his teacher and teacher's teacher as Vidyābharaṇa-deva and Someśvara-deva respectively. The odds against these two being persons other than the Kedāreśvara ascetics are high on the basis of the identity of the names alone. Siddhānti-candra-bhūṣaṇa-paṇḍita-deva's name, particularly the ending 'paṇḍita-deva,' and the explicit mention of his belonging to the Kālāmukha lineage render the identification nearly certain. Although Ablūr and Sūḍi are much nearer than Gadag to Belagāve, they provide a precedent for the extension of the priesthood to other temples. The large gap in years between the 1129 inscription of Vidyābharaṇa and the 1199 inscription of his disciple Candrabhūṣaṇa is rather difficult to account for, but it is not impossibly large if Vidyābharaṇa lived until about 1140 or 1150. The fact that he is given the expanded title Vādividyābharaṇa-paṇḍita-deva in the 1144 grant to his Ablūr disciple Jñānasakti and in the 1149 grant to his Belagāve disciple Gautama suggests that he acquired the title sometime after 1129. This could have happened any time up to 1144 and he may have been alive even after this date.

Vīra-Ballāla's grant of A.D. 1192 includes several Sanskrit verses

---

[78]Ed. Desai, *SII*, XV, no. 159.

in praise of Candrabhūṣaṇa, one of which calls this priest a *jaṃgama*, a term later used for the Liṅgāyat priesthood :

There is in the village named Kratuka ([Gadag] the god) Svayambhū called Trikūṭeśvara. (He is) Śiva whose pleasing seat is decorated with the radiance of the crest-jewels of all kings.

The *ācārya* of the *sthāna* of that (god) is the *muni* named Siddhānti-candrabhūṣaṇa-paṇḍita-deva born in the lineage of Kālāmukha *ācāryas*.

(People) regard that same god, (who is known as) Trikūṭeśvara on account of his three stationary (or mountain) *liṅgas* (i.e. Kāleśvara, Śrīśaila and Bhīmeśvara), as Catuṣkūṭeśvara on account of that *jaṃgama* (priest or moving liṅga).

(That priest) today becomes indifferent to women and appears as if a *brahmacārin* like Śiva, owing to his close union with Gaurī who eternally occupies half of his body.

Even when the *kula*-mountains tremble and the rivers overflow their banks, he whose second name is Satyavākya does not abandon the truth.

There is no equal of him not only in (the knowledge of) *kāvya, nāṭaka,* Vātsyāyana, Bharata, *rājaniti,* etc., but also in all the *kathā-siddhāntas.*

At some time there might be seen the cessation of the waves in the ocean but never (a cessation) in offerings being given to those who eat them because of (his great) share of compassion.

There is no limit of men whom he continually gratifies not only with food but with gold, medicines, water, cloth, etc.

In that *sthāna* he renovated everything which was ruined and built a new and pleasing *pura.* To the vicinity of the (temple of the) god he brought a street of public women *(veśyā-vīthī)* which had been situated elsewhere (formerly).

(He then) built a lotus pool filled with water which resembles nectar and a grove of trees which resembles Nandana (the garden of Indra) covered with various flowers and creepers.

But why tell more? Whatever was already full here

> outside the rampart's stony wall has been rendered perfect. (It is all) his work.[79]

The grant proceeds to register Vīra-Ballāla's donation of the village of Hoṃbālalu in the Beḷvola Three Hundred to the temple. The above passage is written in a pleasing *kāvya* style and contains several points of interest. First, the priest is said to command the support and respect of royalty. Although he does not claim the rank of *rājaguru* like other Kālāmukha priests, the list of his intellectual attainments, particularly the inclusion of *rājanīti* or polity, is well-suited for a royal advisor. The term *Vātsyāyana* might refer to the famous fourth century commentator on the *Nyāya-sūtra,* but the context favors an identification with the author of the *Kāma-sūtra*. Second, Candrabhūṣaṇa seems to have carried on the tradition of his Belagāve preceptors in acts of charity and munificence and to have instituted much building and expansion of the temple and the area about it. Third, he is shown to have supported the practice of temple prostitution. This settles any doubts about whether or not *devadāsīs* were employed at Kālāmukha temples. They obviously were, and this practice may have been partially responsible for Rāmānuja's dislike of the Kālāmukhas.

Several other epigraphs have been found at the Trikūṭesvara temple in Gadag, but most are fragmentary or contain little information about the priesthood. The earliest, dated A.D. 1002, registers a land grant to the temple of Svayambhū in Gadag.[80] The gift was entrusted to the priest Kāḷajñāni-vakkhāṇi-jīya, the disciple of Koppina-vakkhāṇi-deva, a disciple of Pūliya-paṇḍita. Although there were no priests by these names at the Kedāreśvara temple in Belagāve, the Svayambhū temple is evidently the same as the temple of Svayambhū Trikūṭeśvara. A later Koppina-vakkhāṇa-deva appears in a genealogy of Parvatāvali ascetics at Rōṇ, also in Dharwar District.[81] Another priest unknown to the Belagāve records, Kriyāśakti-paṇḍita, was the head of the maṭha of Svayambhū Trikūṭeśvara in A.D. 1102 when a feudatory of the Cālukya king Vikramāditya VI made a grant to the temple.[82] This priest

[79]Ed. Lüders, *EI,* VI, 96–97. My translation.

[80]Ed. N.L. Rao, *SII,* XI, Part I, no. 48.

[81]Ed. and trans. L.D. Barnett, 'Two Inscriptions from Ron, of Saka 944 and 1102,' *EI,* XIX, 222–236.

[82]Ed. N.L. Rao, *SII,* XI, Part II, no. 15.

must also have belonged to the Mūvara-kōṇeya-saṃtati. The Belagāve priests evidently never took direct control over the Gadag temple, probably because its distant location made this impracticable. A fragmentary grant to the Trikūṭeśvara temple made in 1184–85 contains the name Vidyābharaṇa but must have been made to his disciple Candrabhūṣaṇa.[83] Candrabhūṣaṇa's own disciple Kriyāśakti-paṇḍita is the donee in a grant to the temple made in A.D. 1213.[84] The grant is badly damaged and fragmentary. In 1225 two golden banners were given to the temple by Caṇḍauvve, the 'daughter,' i.e. disciple, of Siddhānti-Kriyāśakti-paṇḍita.[85] This must have been the same priest with an expanded title like that of his preceptor.

The prestige of the Belagāve maṭha probably was greatest during the reign of Gautama's main line successor Vāmaśakti (II) who claims the exalted rank of *rājaguru* in seven grants dated between 1159 and 1193[86] during the reigns of the Kalacuris Bijjala, Someśvara Deva, and Āhavamalla Deva, and of the Hoysala Vīra-Ballāla II. That Vāmaśakti should have held such a post is not inherently unlikely, since there are several other examples of Kālāmukhas assuming this title. Rudraśakti-deva claims it is a grant made in 1249 to the Koṭīśvara temple at Kuppaṭūr in the Shimoga District.[87] An earlier priest from this temple named Sarveśvaraśakti-deva is called *rājaguru* in a grant dated 1070.[88] Another Kālāmukha priest named Sarveśvara-deva takes the title in the 1252 grant from Munavaḷḷi in Belgaum District.[89] It is by no means certain if any of these priests were ever *rājaguru* to a more exalted official than local feudatory rulers and officials.

Vāmaśakti II first appears in a grant to the Kedāra-maṭha dated A.D. 1156 during the reign of the Cālukya Taila III.[90] It was issued by a minister of Taila III's feudatory, the Kalacuri Bijjala-devarasa, at the request of 'learned men and attendants' to provide for offerings to the god, for food for the temple ascetics, and for

---

[83]Ed. Desai, *SII,* XV, no. 547.

[84]Ibid., no. 159.

[85]Ibid., no. 609.

[86]Ed. and trans. Rice, *EC,* VII, Sk. 123 (A.D. 1159), 92 (1168), 150 (1171), 96 (1181), 101(?1181), 97 (1186–87), and 105 (1193).

[87]Ed. and trans. Rice, *EC,* VIII, Sb. 270.

[88]Ibid., Sb. 276.

[89]Ed. Panchamukhi, I, no. 31 of 1939–40.

[90]Ed. and trans. Rice, *EC,* VII, Sk. 104.

repairs to the temple buildings. Following the previously quoted description of the maṭha, it tells how the fortune of the *Kalpa* vine which was the Kedāra-*sthāna* was raised on the soil of Someśvarāryya's penance and :

> well nourished and covered with branches and blossoms through Gautamārya, till its fame has spread over all the world through Vāmaśakti-munīndra. His face a pleasure-house for Vāṇī [Sarasvatī], his true heart a pure jewelled house for the Destroyer of Madana [Śiva], of worldwide fame was Vāmaśakti-paṇḍita-deva.

He had acquired the ascetic virtues—*yama, niyama, svādhyāya, dhyāna, dhāraṇā, maunānuṣṭhāna, japa* and *samādhi*—and was the '*ācārya* of the temple of the god Dakṣiṇa-Kedāreśvara of the royal city Balipura.'

In A.D. 1159 Bijjala's feudatory or officer Keśirāja-daṇḍādhīśa, Kēsimayya, or Keśava-deva, constructed a temple to Keśava 'in the southern quarter of Balipura' on land obtained from Sarveśvara, priest of the Pañcaliṅga temple.[91] He also established a 'quarter' *(pura* or *Brahmapura)* of the town named *Vīra-keśava-pura* and donated it to a band of Brahmans. In trust to these brahmans and others in the town of Belagāve he gave :

> to the god Jagadēkamallēśvara, 2 shares; to the Pañca-Liṅga god, 2 shares; to the god Kēdāra, 2 shares; to the Brahmans, 38 shares; to the *pūjari,* 1 share; to the garland maker, 1 share; —altogether 46 shares, in the village of Belvaṇi.

This eclectic gift was made in the presence of the officials and prominent people of the 'royal city' Balipura or Belagāve, including Vāmaśakti-paṇḍita-deva and the heads of other temples in the town. All of these priests appear to have been Śaivite. One of them named Dharmaśiva-deva, however, is said to be the head priest of the five maṭhas or Pañca-maṭha, which, according to the record of A.D. 1129, comprised the temples of Hari, Hara, Kamalāsana (Brahmā), Vītarāga (Jina) and Bauddha. It seems probable then that not only were rival creeds tolerated in Belagāve, but that their monasteries were administered by a Śaivite priest. Although the

[91]Ibid., Sk. 123.

Kōḍiya-maṭha does not appear to have been one of the 'five maṭhas,' we have noted above the highly syncretic character of the knowledge attributed to the Kōḍiya-maṭha pontiff Someśvara. Not all of the Kedāreśvara inscriptions display such tolerance, however, and it is impossible to determine what exactly were the relations between the Mūvara-kōṇeya-saṃtati priests and their rivals. Perhaps they constantly altered in accordance with the personalities of the reigning priests.

Bijjala's 'great minister Kēsimayya-daṇḍanāyaka' had established and endowed a temple and a *Brahmapuri* dedicated to Keśava-Viṣṇu. One would naturally suppose him to be a staunch Vaiṣṇava. The inscription of 1159 claims, to the contrary, that none other than Vāmaśakti, priest of the Kedāreśvara temple, was his *ārādhya* or family priest and that it was to him that the superintendence of the new temple and *Brahmapuri* was entrusted :

> Washing the feet of his *ārādhya* possessed of . . . [the ascetic virtues *yama, niyama, etc.*], kind to the learned, patron of the assemblies of good poets, delighting in gifts of food, gold, virgins, cows, lands, shelter, medicine and many other gifts, an ornament of the *Lākuḷāgama,* skilful in his investigation of all the *śāstras* and *āgamas,* son of Gautama-muni, worshipper of the lotus feet of the god Dakṣiṇa-Kēdārēśvara of Balipura,—the *rājaguru* Vāmaśakti-deva, [Kēsimayya] gave to him that place and the superintendence of the *Brahmapuris.*[92]

This again suggests a degree of syncretism in the religion professed by the priests of the Kōḍiya-maṭha. Otherwise this passage adds no new information. The title *ārādhya* is interesting, however, since it was also attributed to the legendary founders of the Vīraśaiva sect.

In 1162 A.D., according to another Kedāreśvara inscription,[93] Bijjala came to 'Baḷḷigāve' in order to subdue the southern region. His feudatory Kasapayya-nāyaka then petitioned him to make a donation to the Kedāreśvara temple and its chief priest, Vāmaśakti II, who is compared to a tree of plenty *(kalpa-vṛkṣa)* and said to restrain the actions of Desire (Kāma) in the world through the

---

[92]Ibid., Sk. 123.
[93]Ibid., Sk. 102.

severity of his penance. In a verse identical to one describing Gautama in the record of 1149, it is claimed that the whole world addressed Vāmaśakti as Jīya. A supplementary grant appended to the same record states that Bijjala donated the revenue of several villages 'for the decorations of the gods Dakṣiṇa-Kēdārēśvara of the Kōḍiya-maṭha, Sōmanātha, and Brahmēśvara of Abbalūr . . .' As we have seen, the Brahmēśvara temple at Ablūr was staffed by ascetics of the Kōḍiya-maṭha. The Somanātha temple cannot be identified, although it too must have belonged to this maṭha.

A much defaced grant to Vāmaśakti which Rice dates *c.* 1164 A.D.[94] briefly mentions Vāmaśakti and the earlier priests Kedāraśakti, Śrīkaṇṭha, and Someśvara as well as two unidentified ascetics named Kedāraśaktīśvara and Devavrata. The donor was Mahādeva-daṇḍanāyaka, a feudatory or officer of Bijjala and ruler of the Banavāsi province. One day, the record states, 'the famous muni Kedāraśakti delivered a discourse on *dharma,* his text was this,— "Whoso sets up but one *liṅga,* obtains a myriad-fold all the merit described in the *āgamas*".' Mahādeva-daṇḍanāyaka then washed the ascetic's feet and set up an image of the god (? Ma) lapeśvara, presumably in the form of a *liṅga*. The emphasis on *liṅga* worship has already been met in some of the earlier Mūvara-kōṇeya-saṃtati epigraphs. It connects these Kālāmukhas both with their ancestors, the Lakulīśa-Pāśupatas, and their successors, the Vīraśaivas.

In 1168 A.D. the feudatory or officer Kēśava-daṇḍanāyaka was administering 'all the countries attached to the treasury of the south' under the new Kalacuri king Rāyamurāri-Sōvi-Dēva or Someśvara. An inscription in the Kedāreśvara temple states that on this date Keśava made a visit to Belagāve and was impressed by the temple and its chief priest :

> [He approached] the *ācārya* of the temple, the *rājaguru-deva;* he noted for a long time his pre-eminence in all learning. In grammar, Pāṇini paṇḍit; in polity and discernment, Śrībhūṣaṇācārya; in drama and the science of music, Bharata-muni; in poetry Subandhu himself; in *siddhānta* Lakulīśvara; in Śiva devotion Skanda;—thus in the world is he truly styled the *rājaguru,* the *yati* Vāmaśakti.[95]

---

[94]Ibid., Sk. 108.
[95]Ibid., Sk. 92.

Keśava then petitioned the king and obtained from him a copper *śāsana* donating a village for the temple. A nearly identical passage appears in an 1181 A.D. grant to the temple by the Kalacuri king Saṅkama-Deva.

Vāmaśakti must have already been a fairly old man by 1171 A.D. since a warrior memorial in Belagāve dated in that year mentions an attack by some robbers on 'the *rājaguru* Vāmaśakti-deva's grandson.'[96] He was still alive in 1193, however, after nearly fifty years as head of the Kōḍiya-maṭha. The reference to his grandson shows that not all the ascetics of the monastery were celibate.

In about 1181 A.D. Vāmaśakti and his disciple Jñānaśakti-deva (II) undertook to maintain some land, money and three houses in Belagāve, all of which had been granted 'to the dancing girl . . . Mallave and the drummer Mādiga as a temple endowment.'[97] Temple dancers and musicians are mentioned in other grants to this and other Kālāmukha temples. Together with the *devadāsīs* they apparently provided entertainment for the lay supporters of the order. Vāmaśakti's disciple Jñānaśakti appears only in this record.

The *rājaguru* Vāmaśakti was still head of the maṭha in 1193 A.D. when a feudatory of the Hoysala king Vīra-Ballāla II donated land to the god Dakṣiṇa-Kedāreśvara.[98] The grant includes a lengthy eulogy of this priest from which the following excerpt is taken :

> The glory of the penance of the priest of that temple, the *rājaguru* Vāmaśakti-deva,—that great one's possession of all the ascetic virtues . . . [*yama, niyama, etc.*], his being surrounded with disciples devoted to the *aṣṭāṅga-yoga* which he expounded to them; his lotus feet covered with clusters of bees the large sapphires set in the crowns of friendly kings bowing before him . . . ; a portable tree of plenty for giving joy to poets, declaimers, orators, conversationalists and other manner of learned men; able in giving decisions on the meaning of the *vedānta, siddhānta, āgama,* the six systems of logic, all branches of grammar, pure *dharmaśāstra,* and all other sciences; skilled in

[96]Ibid., Sk. 150.
[97]Ibid., Sk. 101.
[98]Ibid., Sk. 105.

> splitting, as with a thunderbolt, the *pēṭana* of the mountains opponent speakers; ... devoted to gifts of food, gold, virgins, cows, lands, and gifts of freedom from fear, of medicine, and all other benefactions; ... worshipper of the holy lotus feet of the god Dakṣiṇa-Kedāreśvara of the immemorial city, the royal city *(rājadhāni)* Balipura; master of all kinds of spells [*visiṣṭa-nāna-mantra-sādhakar*]; ... His commands on the heads of kings, his fame in the dwellings of the learned, his mind at the feet of the lord of the life of Pārvatī, ...—long may he live, the world-renowned *bhratīndra* [*sic*] Vāmaśakti. A mountain for the rising sun of logic, an ocean for the jewels good poems, clever in investigating the principles of grammar, foremost in formulating prosody, an only treasure to those who desire instruction in such learning, an expounder of principles ... With those who with cheeks puffed out play all manner of tunes on the flute, with singing women who give forth enchanting songs with clear modulation of the seven notes, and with those who play sweet sounds on drums? bound to their waists,—is he the most skilled in the world in daily performing pleasant dances,—Vāmaśakti-bhratīndra. One man composes the aphorisms of a science, another analyses the words, and yet another makes the commentary; but the marvel here is that Vāmaśakti occupies himself alone in both composing, analysing, commenting, and even instructing those who do not understand.

This verbose recitation adds little to our knowledge of Vāmaśakti and the other priests of the Mūvara-kōṇeya-saṃtati, but it does forcefully underline the main themes of the earlier epigraphs; the priest's possession of the usual yogic or ascetic virtues; his formidable learning in a vast array of subjects, particularly philosophy, logic, poetry, and grammar; his influence over kings; his debating and teaching skill; his charity; and his devotion to Śiva. The reference to him as a master of various *mantras* suggests tantric influence. The unusual term *aṣṭāṅga-yoga,* may refer to the eight 'ascetic virtues' or to eight parts of the body. It is highly unlikely that Vāmaśakti himself was 'most skilled in the world in daily performing pleasant dances,' since he must have been an exceedingly old man by this date. Some sort of ritual dancing may have been practised by the priests of this temple, however, since Sāyaṇa-Mādhava includes song *(gīta)* and dance *(nṛtya)* among the six oblations *(ṣaḍaṅgopahāra)* to be performed by the followers of Nakulīśa,[99] but it is somewhat difficult to reconcile this with the frequent inscriptional emphasis on penance and asceticism. This statement apart, the record gives an attractive picture of the singing and dancing at the temple.

Vāmaśakti's name appears in one other epigraph, a grant from the village Haḷe-Niḍnēgila in Dharwar District dated 1165 A.D. during the reign of the Kalacuri king Bijjala.[100] On this date a Sinda *mahāmaṇḍaleśvara* feudatory of this king made a gift to the Mallikārjuna temple in the village after washing the feet of Vāmaśakti-paṇḍita-deva, the temple priest of the god Dakṣiṇa-Kedāreśvara of the town 'Balipura.' The name of the effective head of the Mallikārjuna temple is not given but it seems certain that he was another member of the Mūvara-kōṇeya-saṃtati. Vāmaśakti is not called a *rājaguru* in this record, a fact which supports the theory that he was never royal advisor to a higher official than the local rulers of the region about Belagāve.

After 1193 A.D. nothing more is heard of Vāmaśakti or his shadowy disciple Jñānaśakti II. The last record of the Mūvara-kōṇeya-saṃtati at Belagāve is dated 1215 A.D. during the reign of Siṃhaṇa-Deva of the Devagiri Yādavas. On this date a grant was made to the Kedāreśvara temple by an official named Hemayya-Nāyaka and his wife Ruppabāyi, and was given in trust to the temple *ācārya,* 'Śrīkaṇṭha-deva's disciple, the *mahābrati* Vāmaśakti-deva (III).'[101] We have discussed above the possible implications of the term *Mahāvratin.*[102]

There remains one other site which may have been connected with the Mūvara-kōṇeya-saṃtati. This is the Koṭīśvara temple at Devasthāna-Hakkalu near or in Kuppaṭūr in the Shimoga District. About nine inscriptions have been found in this place which belong to the period of Kālāmukha occupation. They range from 1070 A.D. to 1280 A.D. In the year 1231 A.D. an official and a general of the Yādava king Siṅghana-Deva, on orders from their sovereign, donated two villages to the temple in care of the Kālāmukha priests Rudraśakti-deva and his younger brother

---

[99]Ed. U S. Sharma, p. 311.
[100]Ed. A.M. Annigeri, *Karnatak Inscriptions,* IV, no. 13.
[101]Ed. and trans. Rice, *EC,* VII, Sk. 95.
[102]See above, pp. 73–82.

Sarveśvara-śakti-deva.[103] At this time several temples were attached to the Koṭīśvara temple including the Siddhanātha temple of Kabbina-Sirivūr, the Svayambhū temple of Mulugunda, the Rāmanātha temple of Kiruvaḍe, the Grāmeśvara temple of Abbalūr (Ablūr), the Mūlasthāna Vosavanteśvara of Tiḷuvaḷḷi, the Caitrāpura of Devaṅgiri, Mūlasthāna of Hānuṅgal, and the Rāmanātha temple of Kuppaṭūr. If Grāmeśvara is a scribal error for Brahmeśvara, the Ablūr temple of the Mūvara-kōṇeya-saṃtati, then we might assume that all these temples belonged to this organization. Although there does not appear to be any record of a Grāmeśvara temple at Ablūr, this hypothesis is a dubious one. It is best to assume that the Kuppaṭūr temple of Koṭīśvara and its subsidiaries formed a separate complex. The arrangement into a central archdiocese with various parishes in the surrounding region may well have been a regular feature of the Kālāmukha church. The efficiency of this type of organisation may help to explain the sect's rapid rise to prominence in the region. Similar tactics were successfully employed by Śaṃkarācārya as well as by the Christian church.

Other Divisions of the Parvatāvaḷi

The most important of these was the Beḷḷeya-santāna. Inscriptions of this group have been found at Hoṃbaḷ and Lakshmēśvar in Dharwar District. The latter town, under its ancient name of Puligeṟe or Huligeṟe, was the capital *(rājadhāni)* of the province known as the Puligeṟe Three-Hundred. In A.D. 1118 an officer of the Kalyāṇa Cālukya king Vikramāditya VI made a gift of income from certain taxes to Sāmavedi-paṇḍita, the *ācārya* of the Rāmeśvara-deva temple in this town. Sāmavedi-paṇḍita is said to belong to the 'Beḷḷeya-dēvara-santāna.'[104] In 1123 another feudatory or officer of the same king gave some land to Agastya-paṇḍita-deva who was teaching *Kaumāra-vyākaraṇa* to the students of the maṭha attached to this temple. Agastya-paṇḍita-deva was the disciple of Sāmavedi-paṇḍita-deva of the 'Beḷḷeya-saṃtāna.'[105] The temple no longer stands. Another epigraph from the same place states that in 1161 during the reign of Bijjala of the Kalacuris, Devarāśi-paṇḍita, disciple of Amṛtarāśi-paṇḍita and *ācārya* of the temple of 'Rāmaidēva' or 'Rāmaiya-dēva,' bought some land and donated

---

[103]Ed. and trans. Rice, *EC*, VIII, Sb. 275.

[104]Ed. G.S. Gai, *SII*, XX, no. 78.

[105]Ibid., no. 83.

it for worship of the god Muttinakeyya-Indreśvara.[106] Devarāśi is said to have belonged to the Kālāmukha-*samaya,* but it is not certain whether this is the same temple or same line of ascetics.

The *Grammar of Kumāra (Kaumāra-vyākaraṇa)* taught by Agastya-paṇḍita-deva was also part of the curriculum at the Kōḍiya-maṭha in Belagāve. The name Sāmavedi-paṇḍita undoubtedly indicates that this priest was especially devoted to that Veda, but this fact does not seem to be unduly significant.

A single record from Hombaḷ in the Gadag Taluk of Dharwar District contains a good deal more religious information than the laconic grants from Lakshmēśvar.[107] It introduces a famous teacher named Bonteyamuni and two generations of his disciples. Bonteyamuni is called a 'Kāḷamukha-munīśvara' and a member of the Beḷḷeya-santāna and Parvatāvali. His chief immediate disciple was Avadhūta who had the following junior colleagues: Kēdāraśakti, Mallikārjuna, Mūrujāvi, Nirvāṇayōgi, Vāmadēva or Vāmaśakti, Siddhēśakti, Rudraśakti, and Kriyāśakti. Vāmaśakti had three disciples: Bonteyaguru, Mallikārjuna, and Rudraśakti. In 1189 A.D. this last-named priest purchased some land from the local officials of Hombaḷ for the temple of the god Kumāra-Bontēśvara which he had built in memory of his teacher Vāmaśakti. Other gifts were made to the god by local artists and merchants on the same occasion. The most important feature of this lengthy record is the following unique recitation of a series of miracles performed by Bonteyamuni:

> Of the powers of Bonteyamuni, the outstanding were: In summer, when the burning heat was attacking him from all the four directions, he stood unperturbed on a slab of *Sūryaśiḷā* in Śrīgiri with his uplifted pleasant face and hands: seeing this the Sun granted him omniscience and told him 'Preach *Kartṛvāda* to whomsoever you meet whether they be *dēvas, manuṣyas, yakṣas* or *rakṣasas.*' Having received this favour from the sun, Bonteya, full of all powers and dedicated to *Śivadharma,* returned from the mountain and performed a *liṅga-pratiṣṭhāpana* during which there was a *hōma* whose fires burned in the skies, and he made many scholarly Brahmans fold their hands in respect.

---

[106] Ibid., no. 137.

[107] Ed. Desai, *SII,* XV, no. 73.

Moreover, as he was (once) coming to Karahaḍa begging alms, an arrogant man on the way drew his dagger out and waved it in front of him saying 'Receive the alms!' and acted as if he was going to stab him. The dagger melted and collected like water in his bowl. He drank it and went on his way as everyone was amazed at his great powers.

Further, taking a round in Kaṭaka he came to the emperor Jayasiṃha's house and stood in front of him. At that time famous and well-versed logicians of other systems of philosophy were there and questioned him how the *Kartṛ* he defended could be formless. He stood invisible (became formless) amidst the hundred logicians for a while and made them speechless (answerless), and expounded the philosophy of *Īsvara-kartṛvāda*. Thus, by his negation of the other schools of philosophy, he got the title *Kartṛvāda-cakravarti*.

Furthermore, (once) as Bonteya was coming on a round in the capital, he was seen by a man who was riding an (intoxicated) elephant in rut and who said: 'Hey! Did you see a *bonte* (a jumble bundle—a pun on the name of Bonteyamuni)?' Hearing that the sage threw it (the *bonte*) on the ground. The elephant came and lifted it up and collapsed to the ground. [This section is obscure].

Further, as he was going round different countries for pilgrimage, one day he was begging alms in Kollāpura and a *jōgini* (sorceress) offered him molten metal as alms and he received it without evading it and drank it; the *jōgini* was in flames.

Further, once when he was attacked by fever, as if to illustrate the moral that even great ones get rid of the effects of their past deeds, he placed the fever apart in a bag and was busily engaged in the meditation of God.[108]

Several of the places visited by this peripatetic teacher can be identified. Śrīgiri is probably the same as Śrīśaila or Śrīparvata, the famous pilgrim center in Kurnool District. At about this time the *Mallikārjuna-śilā-maṭha* of Śrīparvata was headed by a Kālāmukha priest of the Parvatāvali named Rāmeśvara-paṇḍita.[109]

[108]Ibid., 11. 16–26. We thank Professor H.S. Biligiri of Deccan College, Poona, for this translation.

[109]Ed. and trans. Sreenivasachar, *HAS,* XIII, Part II, no. 7.

Karahaḍa must be the same as Karahāṭa, the modern Karāḍ or Karhāḍ on the river Krishṇā in the southern part of Sātāra District in Maharashtra. During this period Karahāṭa was the capital of the province known as the Karahāṭa Four (or Ten) Thousand. It is not clear whether *Kaṭaka* is to be taken as a proper noun. The word generally means simply 'royal camp' and in this sense might refer to a number of places. If a proper name is meant, the most likely possibilities are Cuttack (Kaṭaka) in Orissa and Dhānyakaṭaka, sometimes called simply Kaḍaka and better known as Amarāvatī in Andhra Pradesh. The latter site is a better choice since it is known to have contained a Kālāmukha temple in the 10th century [110] and is not very far from Śrīparvata. Nonetheless, there was no king named Jayasiṃha ruling over either town at this time. Jayasiṃha seems certain to be the younger brother of the Kalyāṇa Cālukya Vikramāditya VI. As early as 25 June 1077 he was the *de facto* ruler of the regions known as the Belvola Three Hundred and the Puligeṟe Three Hundred under the nominal overlordship of his older brother. He rapidly extended his control to the Kandur One Thousand, the Banavāsi Twelve Thousand and the Santalige One Thousand. His name disappears from inscriptions after A.D. 1083. Bilhaṇa's *Vikramāṅkadeva-carita* tells of a quarrel between the two brothers the consequence of which was the defeat of Jayasiṃha. This must have taken place in about 1083.[111] Jayasiṃha's *kaṭaka* or royal camp was probably located in this region, which roughly corresponds to the present day Shimoga and Dharwar Districts. The 'capital' *(rājadhāni)* mentioned in the next section of the inscription might refer to Kalyāṇa, the main Cālukya capital; to Belagāve, the capital of the Banavāsi Twelve Thousand and Santalige One Thousand; or to any one of several regional capitals in the Cālukya empire. Kollāpura is, of course, the same as the modern city Kolhāpur in southern Maharashtra. Kollāpura was the center of a Śākta cult of Pāśupata *ācāryas* dedicated to the goddess Kollāpura-mahālakṣmī.[112] This may well account for the presence of a *jōgini* there.

The dates of Jayasiṃha's viceroyalty, *c.* 1077–1083, give the best clue to the period of Bonteyamuni's priesthood. This is slightly

---

[110]See B.V. Krishnarao (ed.), 'Tandikonda Grant of Ammaraja II,' *EI*, XXIII (1935–36), 161–70.

[111]See G. Yazdani (ed.), *The Early History of the Deccan*, I, 356–59.

[112]Ibid., pp. 441–42.

earlier than would be expected by calculating backwards from the date of his great-great-disciple Rudraśakti so we may assume that the great debate took place early in Bonteyamuni's career.

The Sun (Sūrya) instructed Bonteyamuni to preach *Kartṛvāda* or *Īśvara-kartṛvādā,* the doctrine of Īśvara as Creator. This is, in essence, the doctrine which Rāmānuja attributed to the Kālāmukhas and other worshippers of Paśupati—the dualistic view of Śiva as the instrumental but not the material cause of the universe. The term *Īśvara-kartṛvādā,* in the form *issarakāranavādi,* first occurs in the *Māhābodhi Jātaka* where an adherent of this doctrine appears as one of the five heretical councillors of King Brahmadatta of Benares.[113] Śaṃkarācārya, in his *Brahma-sūtra-bhāṣya* ii. 2. 37, discusses the views of the *Īśvara-kāraṇins*. These persons are allied to or identical with the Māheśvaras who 'maintain that the five categories, viz. effect [*kārya*], cause [*kāraṇa*], union [*yoga*], ritual [*vidhi*], the end of pain [*duḥkhānta*] were taught by the Lord Paśupati (Śiva) to the end of breaking the bonds of the animal (*i.e.* the soul); Paśupati is, according to them, the Lord, the operative [instrumental] cause.'[114] These Māheśvaras must be Pāśupatas since the same five categories appear in Kauṇḍinya's *bhāṣya* on the Pāśupata *sūtra* and, in a disjointed form, in Sāyaṇa-Mādhava's discussion of the Nakulīśa-Pāśupata system. The extant Pāśupata texts do not make any special effort to give an ontological analysis of the material world, but they do maintain an essentially dualistic world view. In at least one important respect, therefore, the Kālāmukhas appear to have followed the philosophical doctrines of their close spiritual relatives, the Pāśupatas.

Śaṃkarācārya further associates his Māheśvaras with the Vaiśeṣikas, who teach 'that the Lord is somehow the operative cause of the world,' and with the Naiyāyikas.[115] We have noted above the frequent epigraphical references to Kālāmukhas as Naiyāyikas and Vaiśeṣikas. There is other evidence connecting the Pāśupatas with these two closely related philosophical systems. Bhāsarvajña, the author of the well-known *Nyāya-sāra,* also wrote a commentary on the Pāśupata work, the *Gaṇakārikā*. Guṇaratna, the author of a commentary on the *Ṣaḍdarśana-samuccaya* of Haribhadra, describes the adherents of both the Nyāya and

[113]*Jātaka,* ed. V. Fausboll, V, 228, 238 and 241.
[114]Trans. G. Thibaut.
[115]Ibid.

Vaiśeṣika systems as typical Śaivite *yogins* and claims that the Naiyāyikas especially adore the eighteen *avatāras* of Śiva beginning with Nakulīśa. The Naiyāyikas, he says, call themselves Śaivas and the Vaiśeṣikas, Pāśupatas. Rājaśekhara, in his *Ṣaḍdarśana-samuccaya,* speaks of the Nyāya sect of Pāśupatas.[116] In all likelihood the philosophical position of the Kālāmukhas did not differ a great deal from that of these Nyāya-Vaiśeṣika Pāśupatas.

After receiving his commission from the Sun, Bonteyamuni's first act was to set up a *liṅga*. The establishment of *liṅgas* was a characteristic Kālāmukha activity, but the worship of Sūrya was not. Sūrya's command to preach *Kartṛvāda* to gods, men, and demons is best interpreted to mean that the doctrine was to be taught to men irrespective of caste. This also agrees with Rāmānuja's statements and helps to confirm the historical link between the Kālāmukhas and Vīraśaivas.

Bonteyamuni's miracles themselves need little comment. He performed a great penance and a god then rewarded him with divine knowledge and a commission to preach this to the world. He magically turned back attacks by men, animals, witches, and disease. He converted his opponents in a great debate with the aid of a miracle. These are all typical motifs of religious folklore and occur as frequently in western traditions as in eastern although the contexts may differ. These exploits point to a significant 'magical' element in Kālāmukha belief, but this does not necessarily exclude a high degree of philosophic sophistication as a comparison with mediaeval Catholicism easily shows. The curriculum of the Kōḍiya-maṭha could not have been mastered by a group of illiterate witch-doctors.

There is one other Kālāmukha epigraph which may belong to the Beḷḷeya-santāna, a grant found in the Harihareśvara temple at Sātēnahaḷḷi in Dharwar District.[117] It was issued in A.D. 1204 during the reign of the Hoysala king Vīra-Ballāla II. Seṭṭikavve, the chief lady of Kōṇavatti, is introduced along with her spiritual advisor Haraśakti. His genealogy is given as follows : Pinākapāṇi, a Kālāmukha of the Billa-maṭha; his disciple Śivarāśi, a devotee of Hara; his disciple Amṛtarāśi; and his son or disciple Haraśakti-deva, a devotee of Śiva and follower of the doctrine of Lakula. Haraśakti worshipped the god Bhāyilēśvara of the *agrahāra* village Sūrili but also received a grant of land for the temple of

[116] S.N. Dasgupta, *History of Indian Philosophy,* V, 143–45.

[117] Ed. Annigeri, IV, no. 1.

Harihareśvara in Sātēnahaḷḷi. If the Billa-maṭha can be connected with the Beḷḷeya-santāna, these ascetics must also have belonged to this organisation.

One other *saṃtati* of the Parvatāvali is mentioned in a fragmentary grant from Gogga in the Shimoga District dated A.D. 1117. A local official made a grant of land to an unnamed temple after washing the feet of 'Rudraśakti-paṇḍita, disciple of Kriyāśakti-paṇḍita, promoter of the Kālāmukha-samaya, of the Śakti-paridhi of the Parvvatāvali, and A. .ka-santati.'[118] Unfortunately the full name is lost, Rudraśakti is given the usual list of ascetic virtues but no other significant epithets.

Several other epigraphs mention ascetics of the Parvatāvali but omit the name of the *saṃtati* or *santāna*. The most important of these registers the gift of a village in A.D. 1090 to 'Rāmēśvara-paṇḍita of the Appa-Parvatāvaḷi, the head of the famous Mallikārjuna-śilā-maṭha of Śrīparvata, an ascetic of the Kālāmukha (creed), and to the succession of masters, his disciples,' by King Dugga-Tribhuvanamalla, the son of the Kākatīya Bētarasa.[119] Bētarasa was a feudatory of the Cālukya king Vikramāditya VI. As mentioned above, this grant furnishes the best clue to the meaning of the term Parvatāvali and confirms that Śrīparvata was an important Kālāmukha center. It was found on a pillar at Kāzipet in the Warangal District of Andhra Pradesh. Another grant found at Hanam-Koṇḍa or Anamkoṇḍa in the same district seems to mention the same teacher.[120] This states that the father (?) of king Tribhuvanamalla (Bētarasa II) granted Vaijanapali *alias* Śivapura to Rāmeśvara-paṇḍita. The father of Tribhuvanamalla was Prōla I. King Prōla is called 'the best pupil of that Rāmēśvara-paṇḍita.' The teacher is described as follows :

> This Rāmēśvara-paṇḍita, who pervaded the quarters (*i.e.* was well-known) with the moonlight of his fame, who was a *Mēru* mountain for the gems of qualities, the greatest of Śiva's devotees, compassionate, the giver of food to the poor, to the wretched, to the mendicants and to the brahmins, and who was well known for his *tapas,* conducted service at these temples with great interest . . .

---

[118]Ed. and trans. Rice, *EC,* VII, Sk. 316.

[119]Ed. and trans. Sreenivasachar, *HAS,* XIII, Part II, no. 7.

[120]Ibid., no. 12.

> [This priest] knew the nectar of the essence of the great cult of the *Lakulēśvara āgama* and . . . spread its practice in the world.[121]

The record has been provisionally dated at *c.* 1050.

The Śivapura of this last grant appears to have been the name of the settlement at Śrīparvata. A grant from Śivapura dated A.D. 1069 states that king Someśvara II of the Kalyāṇa Cālukyas granted a village to Sureśvara-paṇḍita, disciple of Gaṅgarāśi-bhaṭṭāraka, for the *satra* in the temple of the god Mallikārjuna at Śivapura at the request of his chief queen Kañcaladēvī.[122] These priests are described as residents of Śrīparvata or Śrīśaila, possessors of the usual ascetic virtues, followers of the Kālāmukha-samaya and Lākula-siddhānta, and Naiyyāyikas. At the request of the queen Maiḷaladēvī the king also granted another village to the same priest and to a priest called Devaśakti-paṇḍita.

An earlier grant, dated 1057 and found at a temple near Kottapalle not far from Śivapura, states that Someśvara I, the father of the previous king, came to Śrīśaila with his queen Maiḷaladēvī and an official named Ballavarasa and in the presence of the god Mallikārjuna donated a village for the god Svayambhū-Bhairavadeva at Kolla near the western gate of Śrīśaila after washing the feet of the same Sureśvara-paṇḍita.[123] The wording of the praises of Sureśvara and his preceptor is nearly identical to that in the Śivapura grant. The relation of these priests to Rāmeśvara, 'the head of the famous Mallikārjuna-śilā-maṭha of Śrīparvata,' is not known. If Rāmeśvara's doubtful date of *c.* 1050 is correct, Sureśvara cannot have been his preceptor and may have belonged to a rival or subsidiary maṭha.

A 1075 record found at Kop in the Bijapur District registers the gift of a village to Tatpuruṣa-paṇḍita-deva, disciple of Tribhuvana-śakti-paṇḍita-deva of the Kālāmukha Parvatāvali, for the maintenance of the Svayambhū-Nagareśvara maṭha at Vikramapura.[124] This must be the town of that name used by Vikramāditya VI as an occasional residence, the modern Arasībīḍi in the same district. The donor was Ballavarasa, a feudatory or official of the Cālukya

[121] Ibid., pp. 55–56.
[122] Ed. R.S. Sastry and N.L. Rao, *SII,* IX, Part I, no. 134.
[123] Ibid., no. 119.
[124] Ed. N.L. Rao, *SII,* XI, Part I, no. 116.

Someśvara II. This is probably the person who accompanied Someśvara I to Śrīparvata. A supplementary grant to the god Gōvardhanēśvara of Śivapura is attached, but the place mentioned here is probably not the town at Śrīparvata.

In 1136 during the reign of the Hoysala king Viṣṇuvardhana a priest named Kalyāṇaśakti-paṇḍita, a descendant of Īśānaśakti-paṇḍita-deva of the Kālāmukha Parvatāvali, resided at the Hoysala capital Dorasamudra, the modern Haḷebiḍu in Hassan District.[125] Another Īśānaśakti from the same line is mentioned in a grant provisionally dated *c.* 1185.[126] The priestly genealogies of these two teachers are confused.

In 1179 Vikramāditya, a Sinda feudatory of the Kalacuri Saṅkama II, made a series of gifts to the sanctuaries of Cāmeśvara and Māleśvara at Rōṇ in Dharwar District.[127] The donee was Guru-bhakta-deva, a priest of the Parvatāvali of the Kālāmukhas. He was the pupil of Jñānaśakti-deva, who was the disciple of Rudra-śakti-deva, who was the disciple of Koppina-vakhāṇa-deva. This is the last of the known Parvatāvali sites.

The Bhujaṅgāvaḷi

A record from Maṭṭikoṭe in Shimoga District dated A.D. 1077 registers a gift to Vareśvara-paṇḍita-deva, disciple of Trilocana-paṇḍita-deva, and chief of the Kālāmukhas of the Śakti-parṣe in the Bhujaṅgāvaḷi and Iṭṭige-santati.[128] The grant was issued by some minor officials, while they were visiting Belagāve, to provide for offerings to the god Mallikārjuna whom they had established in Mariyase (? Maṭṭikoṭe).

It is not inappropriate that these officials were visiting Belagāve at the time of issuing this grant. The Kālāmukhas Vareśvara and Trilocana were heads of the Tripurāntaka temple in that town. In A.D. 1096 Sarvadeva, a *daṇḍādhipa* of Vikramāditya VI, donated some land to a temple of Sarveśvara which he had built in Belagāve 'as an ornament to the famous Tripurāntaka.'[129] He had established the temple through the teaching of Vareśvara-munīndra, or Vareś-vara-deva, the disciple of Trilocana-munīndra. Trilocana was

---

[125]Ed. and trans. Rice, *EC,* V, Bl. 117.
[126]Ibid., Bl. 119.
[127]Ed. and trans. L.D. Barnett, *EI,* XIX, 222–36 (no. B).
[128]Ed. and trans. Rice, *EC,* VII, Sk. 292.
[129]Ibid., Sk. 114.

descended 'in the line of the emperor of Kalāmukha [*sic*] munis, the heavenly seer Kāśmīra-deva.' An earlier, undated inscription mentions a land donation to a dancing girl *(sūḷege)* of the Tripurāntaka temple made by the priest Trilocana-paṇḍita, who must be the teacher of Vareśvara.[130]

Of the several temples in Belagāve the Tripurāntaka is artistically inferior only to the Kedāreśvara temple. Both are now protected monuments. Around the base of the Tripurāntaka is a sculptured frieze illustrating scenes from the *Pañcatantra*.[131] Scattered between these scenes are erotic figures similar to those in the frieze around the plinth of the Lakṣmaṇa temple at Khajuraho. Various theories have been propounded to explain the presence of erotic sculpture in Indian temples. One of the most prevalent views is that it reflects the influence of tantric ideas. Despite the testimony of Rāmānuja, however, there is little evidence that Kālāmukha worship was in any sense tantric. The peculiar scorn-producing ascetic practices *(dvāras)* of the Pāśupatas do include a mild form of sexual exhibitionism called *śṛṅgāraṇa*,[132] but this does not seem sufficient to account for the sculpture, especially since the commentator on the *Pāśupata-sūtra* commends celibacy in no uncertain terms.[133] More significant, we feel, is the evidence of temple prostitution at many Kālāmukha temples including, as the donation of Trilocana shows, the Tripurāntaka in Belagāve. In our opinion the erotic sculpture of this temple, and the Khajuraho temples as well, is basically profane in character. Like the *devadāsīs*—for whom it might have been a type of advertisement—the sculpture was simply one of the many semi-secular entertainments formerly provided by the temple. This view does not debase the undoubted beauty of the sculptor's art, it simply puts it in a different light.[134] It would be useful to learn if erotic sculpture is found on other Kālāmukha temples, especially those which are known to have maintained *devadāsīs*. The Hoysala style Mallikārjuna temple at Kalsi in the same district contains similar sculpture and may well have been staffed originally by Kālāmukha priests.[135]

[130]Ed. *ARMAD* 1929, p. 130.

[131]See *Mysore Gazetteer*, V, 1282. We visited the temple in March 1966.

[132]See below, p. 185.

[133]Ed. R.A. Sastri, pp. 19–21.

[134]Much the same evaluation has been persuasively argued by N.C. Chaudhuri, *The Continent of Circe*, pp. 217–20. For a different view see P. Chandra, 'The Kaula-Kāpālika Cults at Khajuraho,' *Lalit Kalā*, Nos. 1–2 (1955–56), pp. 98–107.

[135]Visited by us in March, 1966.

Some of the successors of Vareśvara are mentioned in grants made to other temples in Belagāve. In A.D. 1098 the chief priest of the Tripurāntaka temple was Caturānana-paṇḍita,[136] in 1113 Kriyāśakti-paṇḍita,[137] and between about 1150 and 1180 Jñāna-śakti-paṇḍita-deva.[138]

The founder of this priesthood, Kāśmīra-deva, may be the donee in a grant made by a local chief to the Mallikārjuna temple at Bēgūr-agrahāra in the same district.[139] This chief issued his donation after washing the feet of Kāśmīra-paṇḍita-deva, a supporter of the Kālāmukha-samaya and a member of the Śakti-pariṣe and Bhujaṅga . . . The remainder is defaced.

A 1074–75 inscription from the city of Bijāpur mentions a line of Kālāmukha ascetics founded by one Bhujaṅga-devācārya.[140] His immediate disciple was Trilocana and a later member of the line was called Kāśmīra. These names suggest some relation with the ascetics at Maṭṭikoṭe, Belagāve and Bēgūr-agrahāra, but there is no way to confirm it. This Bijāpur priesthood also appears in two grants from Muttagi, a village in Bijāpur District.[141]

Two eleventh century epigraphs from Dharwar District which mention only the Śakti-parṣe should also be noted here. In 1067 a local official of Āḍūr donated three-hundred palm trees to the Kāḷēśvara temple and its *ācārya* Bāḷacandra-paṇḍita of the Śakti-parṣe.[142] In 1058 Someśvara I's feudatory Indrakēsiyarasa made a gift to the temple of Jōgēśvara at Kuyibāl headed by the priest Lōkābharaṇa-paṇḍita of the Śakti-parṣe.[143] Both ascetics are given the usual ascetic virtues but no other information is provided.

---

[136]Ed. and trans. Rice, *EC,* VII, Sk. 106.

[137]Ibid., Sk. 99.

[138]Ibid., Sk. 118, 123 and 119.

[139]Ibid., Sk. 206.

[140]Ed. and trans. J.F. Fleet, 'Sanskrit and Old-Canarese Inscriptions,' *IA,* X (1881), 126–32.

[141]Ed. Desai, *SII,* XV, nos. 32 and 97.

[142]Ed. Gai, *SII,* XX, no. 285.

[143]Ibid., no. 38.

CHAPTER V

OTHER KĀLĀMUKHA PRIESTHOODS

The Siṃha-pariṣad

The second of the two known *pariṣads* of Kālāmukhas is the *Siṃha-pariṣad* or Lion Assembly. Grants to temples of this *pariṣad* have been found in the Guntūr District of Andhra Pradesh and in the Bellary, Bijāpur and Gulbarga Districts of Mysore. Although the temples are spread over a large area, they are only five in number and contain a total of only eight relevant inscriptions. It is probable, therefore, that this group was less influential than the Śakti-pariṣad, or at least received less royal and official support.

The Siṃha-pariṣad is first mentioned in the undated Tāṇḍikoṇḍa grant of the Eastern Cālukya king Ammarāja II, who ruled over Veṅgī and parts of Kaliṅga between A.D. 946 and 970.[1] The grant is written in Sanskrit and registers the donation, by the king, of Tāṇḍikoṇḍa and three other villages for the god Umāmaheśvara in the temple *(devālaya)* called Samasta-bhuvanāśraya. The temple was located in the city Vijayavāṭī, the modern Vijayawāda or Bezwāda on the Krishna River about sixty miles from the river's mouth. According to the inscription, the temple was originally established by Vijayāditya Narendramṛgarāja, who must be Vijayāditya II (*c.* A.D. 799–847) of the same dynasty. On the occasion of the summer solstice *(uttarāyaṇa)* Ammarāja II made a gift for the increase of his country, lineage, life, health, and supremacy, in order to provide for temple repairs, *bali*, *naivedya*, music *(ātodya)*, and a free feeding house *(satra)*. After delineating the boundaries of the four villages, the inscription praises a line of 'Kālāmukha' priests belonging to the Siṃha-pariṣad. The diagram of their spiritual genealogy is given on next page.[2]

If we calculate twenty years for each generation of teachers, Lakaśipu-Paśupati must have taught over 100 years earlier than

---

[1]Ed. B.V. Krishnarao, *EI,* XXIII, 161–170.

[2]The editor B.V. Krishnarao interprets the genealogy slightly differently. He makes Kālāmukhendra an alias of Paśupati II and identifies Paśupati II and III. The interpretation turns on the meaning of *ādi* in the expression *Kālamukhendrādya-paranāmā.*

- (1) Lakaśipu alias Paśupati I
  - (2) Prabhūtarāśi-paṇḍita I
    - (3) Vidyeśvara I
    - (4) Vāmeśvara
  - (5) Bhuvanarāśi-muni
    - (6) Paśupati II
    - (7) Prabhūtarāśi II alias Kālamukhendra
      - (8) Paśupati III
        - (9) Vidyeśvara II
          - (10) Prabhūtarāśi III

Prabhūtarāśi III, a contemporary of Ammarāja II. This would be about the time of Vijayāditya II, the founder of the Samastabhuvanāśraya temple. It is likely, therefore, that Paśupati I was the first head priest of this temple. This also makes him one of the earliest known Kālāmukha priests and an approximate contemporary of the Kālāmukha priest Īśvaradāsa of Nandi Hill in Kolar District, Mysore, who is mentioned in a grant dated A.D. 810.[3]

According to the text of the inscription, in various ages of the world numerous *munīśvaras* beginning with Śrī-Lakulīśvara appeared, who were self-made forms of Rudra *(svīkṛta-Rudra-mūrtayaḥ)*. They became self-incarnate *(svayambhuvaḥ)* on earth as teachers of the path of *dharma*. In that succession came the 'Kālamukhas,' who were proficient in the Vedas *(śruti-mukhyāḥ)*, Svayambhūs on earth, and worthy of the homage of kings. Today *(iha)*, the record adds, those *munīśvaras* are the beneficent lords of this *sthāna* of the Siṃha-pariṣad. In the lineage *(santati)*[4] of those 'Kālamukhas,' who were residents of many ancient temples such as that of Amaravaṭeśvara, there arose the *munipa* Lakaśipu or Paśupati (I), who was the husband of Śrī and who understood completely all the *āgamas*. He fed his holy body *(dharma-śarīra)* only on water, vegetables, milk, fruits, and roots (text 11. 51–57).

---

[3]See below, pp. 160–61.

[4]This term may be used in a technical sense such as in the term *Mūvara-kōṇeya-santati*. If so, however, the *santati* is not named.

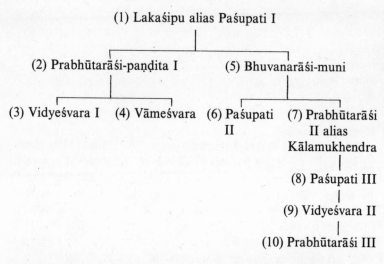

This passage repeats and confirms many of the facts known about the religion of the Śakti-pariṣad. The members of the Siṃha-pariṣad are 'Kālāmukhas'; they trace their descent from Lakulīśa; they worship Śiva; they are proficient both in the Vedas and in the *āgamas*; and they receive the royal homage owed to world-renowned teachers. Their severe asceticism is emphasized in the reference to Lakaśipu's grainless vegetarian diet, resembling the diet of a *vānaprastha* ascetic.

The temple of Amaravaṭeśvara must be the one located at the famous city Amarāvatī which is about twenty-five miles upstream on the Krishna from Vijayavāṭī (Bezwāda). We have noted above that the peripatetic Kālāmukha teacher Bonteyamuni visited a place called Kaṭaka which might be the same as Dhānyakaṭaka, another name for Amarāvatī. Amarāvatī, Bezwāda and Śrīparvata are all located on or near the Krishna River and are natural stopping points for pilgrims, traders and travellers.

The last of Lakaśipu-Paśupati's successors was Prabhūtarāśi III, the heir *(yuvarāja)* to the fame and prosperity of his *guru* Vidyeśvara II and a mighty lord for those who seek refuge *(prabhur āśritānām,* a typical poetic conceit). He is said to have built, in his *guru's* presence, a beautiful stone *devakula* and maṭha of three stories. For this he received from the king three villages and a thousand she-goats. The record ends saying that the king was the donor, the *guru* Vidyeśvara (II) the composer, and Kaṭakanāyaka the executor of the grant (text 11. 61–68). This may imply that Vidyeśvara was the *rajaguru* of Ammarāja II, but we know from other records that this king was not a patron of Śiva alone since he also made donations to some Jain temples in Bezwāda.[5]

Sometime about the end of the tenth century, or possibly earlier, members of the Siṃha-pariṣad established themselves in the Bellary District of Mysore. In A.D. 1045 the Leṅka One Thousand, a military clan led by the *daṇḍanāyaka* Tikaṇṇa, set up *liṅgas* of Nolaṃbeśvara and Leṅkeśvara and won permission from King Someśvara I of the Kalyāṇa Cālukyas to grant some land for worship of the two gods.[6] The gift was made while washing the feet of Someśvara-paṇḍita of the Siṃha-pariṣad, who was in charge of a maṭha in Kōgaḷi, the capital of the Kōgaḷi Five Hundred. The inscription registering the grant was found in the Uddibasa-

---

[5]R.C. Majumdar (ed.), *The Struggle for Empire,* p. 139.

[6]Ed. Sastry and Rao, *SII,* IX, Part I, no. 101.

vaṇṇa temple at Morigeri, a village near Kōgaḷi. In another grant from this temple dated the same year, this clan donated some more land to the god Nolaṃbeśvara while washing the feet of the same teacher in the presence of the god Virūpākṣa (Śiva).[7] Both grants identify Someśvara as the disciple of Jñāneśvara-paṇḍita and disciple's disciple of Maleyāḷa-paṇḍita-deva. These priests are given the usual list of yogic virtues, and in the former grant Maleyāḷa is said to know the true meaning of all the *śāstras* which issued from the lotus-mouth of Śrī-Lakulīśa.[8]

This Maleyāḷa seems to have been an important and well-known religious leader of Siṃha-pariṣad since he begins the priestly genealogies in many grants found at other sites in this region. In A.D. 1093 Gaṅgarasa, a *mahāmaṇḍaleśvara* of the Cālukya king Vikramāditya VI, donated some land for the god Baleśvara in a temple of the god built by Gaṅgarasa's father at the nearby village of Halagondi.[9] The grant was made after washing the feet of the teacher Khaleśvara-paṇḍita. Khaleśvara's teacher was Śāntarāśi-paṇḍita, whose teacher was Someśvara-paṇḍita, whose teacher was Jñāneśvara-paṇḍita, whose teacher was Maleyāḷa-paṇḍita. Maleyāḷa, Jñāneśvara and Someśvara are obviously the same teachers who appear in the two grants from Morigere. The description of Maleyāḷa is in fact copied virtually verbatim from the first Morigere grant. The Halagondi record adds the information that Maleyāḷa was attached to the god Rāmeśvara whose temple was presumably located in Kōgaḷi. Khaleśvara-paṇḍita is given the usual yogic virtues.

Twenty-two years earlier, in A.D. 1071, Vikramāditya VI donated a village to the god Kalideva of Huvina-hadagalli, another village in Bellary District, at the request of the *mahajanas* of the place.[10] The grant was for service to the god and for feeding the students, servants, singers, and ascetics of the maṭha of Lakuleśvara-paṇḍita, a priest who belonged to the lineage *(santati)* of Maleyāḷa-paṇḍita-deva of Rāmeśvara.

This same Maleyāḷa seems to head the priestly genealogies of the donees in two grants found at Yēwūr, a village in Gulbarga

[7]Ibid., no. 104.

[8]Another grant from this temple dated A.D. 1064 (ibid., no. 127) records a gift made to a Śiva temple while washing the feet of '. . . śvara-paṇḍita-deva of Mōṟiṅgere.'

[9]Ibid., no. 163.

[10]Ibid., no. 135.

District of Mysore. On the occasion of a lunar eclipse in A.D. 1077, Ravideva, a Brāhmaṇa minister of Vikramāditya VI, petitioned the king to grant some lands for a temple of Svayambhū which Ravideva had built in Yēwūr.[11] The lands were given in trust 'to the *ācārya* of that place, the fortunate Īśānarāśi-paṇḍita, a disciple's disciple of Cikkadēva of Miriñje, a disciple of Maleyāḷa-paṇḍita-dēva, of a branch-body of the congregation of Eḷemela-Siṃha [*Eḷemela-Siṃha-parṣan-maṇḍaliya*].'[12] The list of items for which the income from these lands was to be used gives a pleasing picture of the daily activities of the temple :

> [These lands are given] for homage with perfumes, incense, lights, oblations, etc.; for the restoration of things broken . . . ; for the set of procession-cloths; for the food and clothing of student-ascetics and scholars reading and hearing [lectures]; for the professors lecturing to them; for the Caitra festival and the festival of the sacred thread, and the entertainment of visitors and other such acts of worship; for the *homa* at the *parva* of a *saṃkrānti*, an eclipse, etc., and for *bali*-sacrifices, etc.; and for the entertainment of poor and destitute Brāhmaṇs and others.[13]

The record closes with some rules advising celibacy for the inhabitants of the monastery : 'Whether they are *ācāryas* of this establishment or ascetics, it is not open to any persons except such as observe strict celibacy to abide in the monastery : the villagers, the burghers, and the king in concert, shall expel those who do not observe celibacy.'[14]

The second record from Yēwūr was issued in A.D. 1179 during the reign of the Kalacuri king Saṅkamadeva II and registers a gift of land to Jñānarāśi, the *ācārya* of the monastery *(sthāna)* of the god Svayambhu-Somanātha in the town, for maintenance of his establishment.[15] Jñānarāśi is said to belong to the spiritual lineage *(saṃtāna)* of Cikkadeva of Miriñje, the disciple of Maleyāḷa-

---

[11]Ed. and trans. L.D. Barnett, 'Inscriptions at Yewur,' *EI*, XII, 268–98 and 329–40 (no. B).

[12]Trans. ibid., p. 290. The name of Īśānarāśi's *guru* is not given.

[13]Trans. ibid., pp. 289–90.

[14]Trans. ibid., p. 290. This may be compared with the rules prescribed for the 'Goravas who are Kālāmukhas' in the A.D. 1060 record from Sūḍi quoted above.

[15]Ed. and trans. ibid., no. G.

deva of the *Srīmad-Eḷemela-śrī-Siṃha-parṣan-maṇḍala*. These can only be the two teachers mentioned in the A.D. 1077 grant.

This Jñānarāśi seems to be again mentioned in an inscription found at Managōḷi in Bijāpur District.[16] This grant, the details of which are lost, was issued during the reign of the Yādava king of Devagiri, Jaitugi I (*c* A.D. 1191–1200). It says that a *munipa* named Gauladeva appeared in a lineage of *ācāryas*. His best disciple was the *vratīśvara* Maleyāḷa-Jñānarāśi, whose son was the *munipa* Dharmarāśi. The name Maleyāḷa-Jñānarāśi should probably be interpreted to mean Jñānarāśi of the lineage of Maleyāḷa.

It is also likely that the same Jñānarāśi is the priest named in a grant dated A.D. 1176 found in a temple of Somanātha at Iṅgalēśwar in the same district.[17] According to this record the Kalacuri king Someśvara donated a village to this temple and entrusted the gift to Jñānarāśi-paṇḍita-deva, the *ācārya* of the god Svayambhu-Kedāreśvara of Vijayāpura (Bijāpur) and a member of the Siṃha-pariṣad. Here again Jñānarāśi traces his descent from Maleyāḷa of the Eḷemēla lineage and the *maṇḍala* of the Siṃha-pariṣad. Apparently Jñānarāśi was in control of the Svayambhū temples at both Yēwūr and Bijāpur.

A collation of all the inscriptions of the Mysore branch of the Siṃha-pariṣad yields the priestly genealogy given on next page.

Other Kālāmukha Inscriptions

In addition to the records left by the Śakti- and Siṃha-pariṣads, there are a large number of Kālāmukha epigraphs which cannot with certainly be said to belong to either organization. These epigraphs are approximately contemporary with and are spread over approximately the same regions as those of the two known *pariṣads*. There are an even greater number of similar inscriptions which mention priests or ascetics, who, by their names or by the doctrines they profess, may also have been Kālāmukhas or at least Lakulīśa-Pāśupatas. It would be impractical to examine all of these records, but we will give a rapid survey, by districts, of those in which the donees are specifically identified as Kālāmukhas.

Shimoga District

Belagāve, headquarters of the Śakti-pariṣad, contained at least

---

[16]Ed. J.F. Fleet, 'Inscriptions at Managoli,' *EI,* V, 9–31 (no. D).

[17]Ed. Desai, *SII,* XV, no. 129.

- Maleyāḷa
  - Jñāneśvara
    - Someśvara (1045 Morigeri)
      - Śāntarāśi
        - Khaleśvara (1093 Halagondi)
  - Lakuleśvara (1071 Huvinahadagalli)
    - Gauladeva
      - Maleyāḷa-Jñānarāśi = ? Jñānarāśi (1179 Yēwūr, 1176 Iṅgalēśwar)
        - Dharmarāśi (*c.* 1195 Managōḷi)
  - Cikkadeva
    - *unnamed*
      - Īśānarāśi (1077 Yēwūr)
        - Jñānarāśi (1179 Yēwūr, 1176 Iṅgalēśwar)

two other Kālāmukha temples besides those dedicated to Tripurāntaka and Dakṣiṇa-Kedāreśvara. An inscription found in the temple of the god now known as Kallēśvara registers two grants to the temple of Kalideveśvara-Svayambhu-deva made during the reigns of the Kalyāṇa Cālukya kings Jayasiṃha II and Vikramāditya VI respectively.[18] In A.D. 1024 the former king donated some land, two shops and a flower garden to the *sthānācārya* of this god, Śivaśakti-paṇḍita, at the request of Kundarāja, the *deśādhipati* of V(B)anavasa. Śivaśakti is called the foremost of the Kālāmukhas and given the usual yogic virtues. The second grant was made by Tambarasa, a governor of Vikramāditya VI. In A.D. 1081 Tambarasa gave some land to the temple in care of Rudraśakti-paṇḍita, the disciple of Śivaśakti-paṇḍita. These seem to be the only records of this priesthood, although a Mūliga-Śivaśakti-paṇḍita of the temple of Mūlasthāna Nandikeśvara is the donee in a grant dated A.D. 1019 found in the town.[19] This priest, who is also given the usual yogic attributes, may well be

---

[18] Ed. and trans. *ARMAD* 1929, pp. 131–140 (no. 65).

[19] Ed. and trans. Rice, *EC,* VII, Sk. 125.

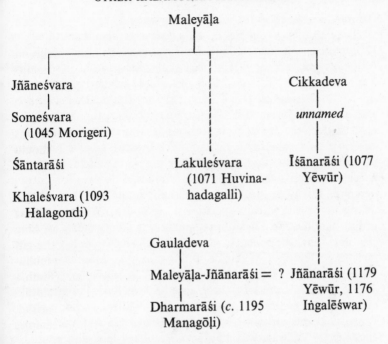

the one mentioned in the Kallēśvara grants.

The Pañcaliṅga temple in Belagāve was also controlled by Kālāmukhas. In A.D. 1036 King Jayasiṃha II of the Kalyāṇa Cālukyas granted some land to Lakulīśvara-paṇḍita, also called Vādi-Rudraguṇa, 'for repairs of the temple of the Pañcaliṅga set up by the Pāṇḍavas, the Kāḷāmukhi [*sic*] Brahmacāri-sthāna of Baḷḷigāve, . . . for sandal, incense and offerings for the god, for food and cloths for the students and ascetics.'[20] This priest is described as a master of logic and other sciences, an able supporter of the Naiyāyikas, and 'a submarine fire to the Bauddha ocean, a thunderbolt to the Mīmāṃsaka mountain, a saw for cutting down the Lokāyata great tree, a great kite to the Sāṃkhya serpent, an axe to the tree Advaita speakers, . . . a noose of Yama to hostile proud paṇḍitas, to Digambara speakers a falling star.' Some of the individual opponents whom he defeated are also named including Tripura Akalaṅka, Vādi-gharaṭṭa, Mādhava-bhaṭṭa, Jñānānanda, Viśvānala, Abhayacandra, Vādībhasiṃha, Vādirāja, and Ayavādi. Several of these can be identified. Vādībhasiṃha must be the Digambara Jain Oḍeyadeva Vādībhasiṃha, pupil of Puṣpasena and author of the *Kṣatracūḍāmaṇi* and the *Gadya-cintāmaṇi*.[21] Vādirāja was another Digambara Jain who wrote his *Pārśvanātha-carita* in A.D. 1025 during the reign of Jayasiṃha II.[22] Abhayacandra might be the Jain author of the *Padmānanda Mahākāvya*.[23] Mādhava-bhaṭṭa might be the Kāvirāja who composed a *śleṣa-kāvya* called *Rāghava-Pāṇḍavıya* under the patronage of Kāmadeva. A.B. Keith identifies this Kāmadeva with a Kadamba king ruling c. A.D. 1182–97 but notes that R.G. Bhandarkar puts him at the beginning of the eleventh century.[24] Vādībhasiṃha, Vādirāja, Abhyacandra, and Mādhava-bhaṭṭa were probably all contemporaries of Lakulīśvara-paṇḍita. Tripura Akalaṅka is either the well-known eighth century Jain logician or some later namesake. The names of many of these theologians, as Handiqui points out (pp. 10–11), reflect the fondness for philosophical debate and polemic which characterised the period.

A few of Lakulīśvara's successors at the Pañcaliṅga temple are

---

[20]Ibid., Sk. 126.

[21]See Handiqui, p. 9, and B.A. Saletore, *Mediaeval Jainism*, pp. 49–54. Saletore attempts to prove that this teacher also bore the names Vādi-gharaṭṭa and Ajitasena.

[22]See Handiqui, p. 9, and Saletore, pp. 43–50.

[23]See R.C. Majumdar (ed.), *The Struggle for Empire*, pp. 301–302.

[24]*A History of Sanskrit Literature*, p. 137.

mentioned in grants to other temples in Belagāve. In A.D. 1098 the Pañcaliṅga was headed by Śrīkaṇṭha-paṇḍita-deva,[25] in 1113 by Kriyāśakti-paṇḍita,[26] between about 1150 and 1159 by Sarveśvara-paṇḍita-deva,[27] and in 1181 by Rudraśakti-deva.[28]

One of the most noteworthy features of the record of Lakulīśvara is a concluding verse in support of Mahādeva (Śiva) and *varṇāśrama-dharma*. Rice translates :

> Mahādeva is god, his feet worthy of worship by all the world. The rule enjoined in the three Vedas for the order of castes and āśramas is *dharma*. Who casts aspersion on these two (statements), on his head will I place my foot in the king's assembly.[29]

It is difficult to estimate the weight to be given to this defence of social orthodoxy. It is fairly certain that most if not all Kālāmukha priests claimed Brāhmaṇa status. This we gather from the 1113 inscription which calls Someśvara of Belagāve a Sārasvata,[30] from a few scattered references to the *gotras* of Kālāmukha priests, and from the common ending to many of their names, '-paṇḍita-deva.' On the whole, however, Kālāmukha inscriptions are remarkably silent on the subjects of caste and class, and in the case of Bonteyamuni of Hoṃbaḷ a Kālāmukha priest is instructed to preach to anyone who would listen.[31] Furthermore, the extant texts of the Pāśupatas, the sect most closely associated with the Kālāmukhas, have virtually nothing to say about the subject, and the Vīraśaivas, the sect which succeeded the Kālāmukhas, were openly hostile to caste consciousness. Without more specific information it is impossible to determine the dominant attitude of the Kālāmukhas to *varṇāśrama-dharma*. In these circumstances the above verse should perhaps be regarded as little more than a stock imprecatory formula.

At least two other religious establishments in Belagāve, the Pañca-maṭha and the Senior- or Hiriya-maṭha, may have belonged

---

[25]Ed. and trans. Rice, *EC,* VII, Sk. 106.

[26]Ibid., Sk. 99. He seems to be different from the Tripurāntaka priest by this name.

[27]Ibid., Sk. 118 and 123.

[28]Ibid., Sk. 119.

[29]Ibid., Sk. 126. Rice says this verse is from Kumārila-bhaṭṭa.

[30]See above, p. 114.

[31]See above, p. 131.

to the Kālāmukha order since the names of their priests end with the titles *deva* and *paṇḍita-deva* in typical Kālāmukha fashion.[32]

One or two other villages in Shimoga District contained Kālāmukha temples which cannot definitely be connected with the Śakti-pariṣad. An inscription found in Belagāve itself registers a grant to the god Siddheśvara of Benakanakoḷa.[33] The donor issued the grant in A.D. 1039 after washing the feet of the Kālāmukha priest Kriyāśakti-paṇḍita-deva. A grant of A.D. 1163 from Bandalike commemorates the construction of a stone tower *(prāsāda)* and a golden pinnacle *(kalaśa)* for the town's Śiva temple by an official named Māceya-nāyaka.[34] This official also set up a *liṅga* named Someśvara—after his feudal overlord, the Kadamba Soma—and donated some land for its temple. Māceya's *guru* was Devaśakti-bratīndra, 'an ornament to the face *(mukha)* of the celebrated Kālāmukhas.' This priest is said to be expert in Vedānta, the eight branches of Yoga, Siddhānta, and the *Śaivāgamas* and to possess the usual yogic virtues. It is also claimed that he received a boon from Aghora, the '*ācārya* of the celebrated Hiriya-maṭha of Bammakūru.' The chief priests of the Brahmacāri-maṭha of the Someśvara temple were named Someśvara-paṇḍita and Bīreya-jīya. About eleven years later, in A.D. 1174, Māceya built another Śiva temple in the town—called Boppeśvara after Kadamba Soma's father Bopparasa—and donated some land to the Mūlasthāna *ācārya,* the Kālāmukha Kalyāṇaśakti-paṇḍita.[35]

Belgaum District

In this district of northern Mysore the ancient town of Pūli, modern Hūli, seems to have been an important Kālāmukha center. A composite inscription found there registers several grants to a temple of Andhāsura (Śiva) which was controlled by a line of Kālāmukha priests.[36] The first grant, dated A.D. 1104, was to the *ācārya* Tatpuruṣa-paṇḍita, a disciple of Jñānaśakti-paṇḍita-deva. Jñānaśakti is praised for his knowledge of logic and grammar and given the second name Ekākṣara. Many monarchs are said to have offered him homage. His spiritual ancestors were the 'eminent

[32]See ibid., Sk. 125, 151, 106, 99, 118, 123, 119, and 168.

[33]Ibid., Sk. 153.

[34]Ibid., Sk. 242.

[35]Ibid., Sk. 236.

[36]Ed. and trans. L.D. Barnett, 'Inscriptions of Huli,' *EI,* XVIII (1925–26), 170–218 (no. E).

saints of the Kāḷāmukha order,' who were noted 'for exalted majesty of learning *(and)* for severe austerities.' They are named as follows: 'Pūliyadeva . . . ; after him, Lakulīśadeva; after him, Vakkhāṇideva excelling in virtues and the great Yogin Vidyeśāna, versed in all arts and sacred tradition [*sarva-kalāgama*]; so after him, the distinguished saint Somadeva.' Apparently Somadeva was the teacher of Jñānaśakti. A second grant, dated A.D. 1162, registers a donation by Jñānaśakti-deva, the *sthānācārya* of the god Andhāsura, for the god's baths and oblations. This may be the same priest or, more probably, a successor. A third grant to the god, made by some leading citizens of Pūli in 1184, does not mention any priest. In 1224 the weavers' guilds of Pūli, worshippers of the god Trikūṭeśvara, made a final gift to Vāmaśakti-deva, the *sthānācārya* of the Andhāsura temple.

An undated record found in Hūli refers to a Jñānaśakti who must be identical with one of the Jñānaśaktis of the previous inscriptions.[37] He is called 'an *ārādhya* adored by bowing monarchs of demons and men,' and 'an excellent mirror of Kālāmukha *(doctrine)*.' His disciple was Nāgarāśi, whose lay disciple Mādi-Gauḍa is mentioned in another record.[38]

This Jñānaśakti and his disciple Nāgarāśi may well be the same as the priests Rirapūli-jñānaśakti and Nata-nāgarāśi included in the genealogy of the Kālāmukha priest Honnayya who taught at Nēsargi in the same district.[39] In A.D. 1219–20 an official of Kārtavīrya IV of the Raṭṭas of Saundatti and Belgaum erected temples of Habbeśvara, Māṇikeśvara and Siddheśvara in Nēsargi. Honnayya was the priest of these temples. His teacher was Vāmaśakti, the elder brother of Nata-nāgarāśi, who was the disciple of Rirapūli-jñānaśakti. Vāmaśakti's own teacher was Rudraśakti, the disciple of Riśīśeṅga. An important verse in praise of Honnayya seems to identify, or at least connect, the Kālāmukhas with Mahāvratins, Mahāpāśupatas and Śrotriyas. It may be translated as follows: 'Among the Mahāvratins who have become famous, among the Mahāpāśupatas who have become famous, among the Śrotriyas —among the unlimited groups (who) have become famous, I cause the most just chief of the Kālāmukha (order) to be praised.'[40]

---

[37]Ibid., no. I. A Jñānasakti is also mentioned in undated record no. K.

[38]Ibid., no. J.

[39]Ed. and trans. Fleet, *JBBRAS*, X, 167–298 (no. VI).

[40]Trans. H. Ullrich in letter to author dated 10 January, 1967. We have discussed some of the implications of this verse on p. 19.

This same verse is found in an earlier grant of A.D. 1148 from nearby Sirasangi, the ancient Riśiriṅgapura or Piriśiṅgi.[41] The Kālāmukha donee of the grant was Rudraśakti-deva, the *ācārya* of the town's Grāmeśvara-deva temple. This priest may be the same as Honnayya's teacher's teacher in the Nēsargi grant. The ancient name of Sirasangi, Riśiśriṅgapura, is very reminiscent of the earliest priest at Nēsargi, Riśīśeṅga.

An inscription from Munavaḷḷi introduces a line of Kālāmukha priests who were in charge of several temples in the surrounding region.[42] The temples included those of Jagadīśvara in Munīndravaḷḷi (Munavaḷḷi) itself, Malleśvara of Śrī-Veḷugrāme (Belgaum), Kalideva of the great *agrahāra* Nēsaṟige, Balleśvara of Gōkāge, Vijayameśvara of Koṭṭumbāgi in the Halasige Twelve Thousand, and Kalideva of Gōḷiyahaḷḷi. In A.D. 1252 several plots of land were given to the priest of the Jagadīśvara temple by various prominent citizens of Munīndravaḷḷi. This priest Sarveśvara, his son Kriyāśakti, and grandson Someśvara are all elaborately extolled. Sarveśvara is said to have gained similarity of form *(sāmya-rūpa)* with the god Śaṃkara and to have 'kept himself apart from passion, anger, pride, wealth, error, fear, and avarice.' He bore the distinguished title of Holy Royal Preceptor *(rāyarājaguru)* and possessed the usual yogic virtues.[43] Furthermore, he was a priest :

> who was intent upon the six duties of offering sacrifices, conducting the sacrifices of others, studying, imparting instruction, giving presents, and receiving gifts; who delighted in all the learning of the *Ṛg-veda,* the *Sāma-veda,* the *Atharva-veda,* the *Yajur-veda,* the Vedānta, the six systems of philosophy [*ṣaṭtarka*], Grammar, Prosody, the collection and explanation of Vedic words and names, poetry, and the drama; who practised the observances of Vyāsa, Agastya, Durvāsa, Viśvāmitra, Nārada, and other holy saints; whose body was sprinkled with ashes; who wore a small piece of cloth around the loins [*kaupīna*], and the hairy skin of an antelope; who carried a rosary of Rudrākṣas; who

[41]Ed. Panchamukhi, I, 33–38.

[42]Ed. and trans. Fleet, *JBBRAS,* XII, 1–50 (no. IV). Re-edited by Panchamukhi, I, 71–74.

[43]They are listed as *yama, niyama, svādhyāya, dhyāna, dhāraṇā, maunānuṣṭhāna, tapas,* and *samādhi.*

preserved [the observances of the *Lākulāgama*;[44] and] who was a very incarnation of the Jaṅgama-liṅga . . .[45]

The subjects studied by Sarveśvara are much the same as those taught at the Kōḍiya-maṭha in Belagāve. As we have noted above,[46] this passage contains the only significant physical description of a Kālāmukha priest. His costume is that of a typical Śaivite ascetic.

One other Kālāmukha priesthood in Belgaum District existed at the village of Hadli, ancient Paldala. A Kālāmukha priest named Nyānaśakti (Jñānaśakti), a pupil of Devaśakti-paṇḍita, donated some land to the god Gavaṟeśvara there in the year A.D. 1084.[47] The temple of Mallikārjuna at Saundatti must also have been staffed by priests of this sect since it is connected with the Mallikārjuna shrine at Śrīśaila. In about A.D. 1230 a local feudatory named Kesirāja, having three times visited the Śrīśaila shrine, built the Saundatti temple for a *liṅga* which he had brought back with him from that famous site.[48] The priest of the temple was Vāmaśakti, also called Liṅgayya and Liṅgaśiva, who was the pupil of Devaśiva, the pupil of an earlier Vāmaśakti.

Bellary District

Several inscriptions found in this district record donations to temples staffed by members of the Siṃha-pariṣad.[49] Other Kālāmukha temples existed at Chinnatumbalam, Kurgōḍ and Sindigeri, and perhaps at Gudihalli, Kuruvatti and other places as well.

At Chinnatumbalam a grant was made in A.D. 1068 to Candrabhūṣaṇa-paṇḍita, a disciple of Anantaśakti-paṇḍita, the disciple of the Kālāmukha *ācārya* Nirañjana-paṇḍita.[50] It was for service to the god Dakṣiṇa-Someśvara of Tumbuḷa (Chinnatumbalam).

An inscription found at Kurgōḍ registers several grants to a temple of the god Svayambhū there, which had been built by a minister of Rācamalla I, the Sinda feudatory of the Kalyāṇa

[44]*Lākuḷāgama same(ma)ya samuddha(ddhā)raruṃ*. Fleet's translation, which is based on the reading *ākuḷāgama* for *Lākuḷāgama*, is less satisfactory.

[45]Trans. Fleet, *JBBRAS*, XII, 40. The important term *Jaṅgama-liṅga* will be discussed below, pp. 171–72.

[46]See above, p. 6.

[47]Ed. G.S. Gai, *SII*, XX, no. 57.

[48]Ed. J.F. Fleet, *JBBRAS*, X, 167–298 (no. VII).

[49]See above, pp. 143–44.

[50]Ed. Sastry and Rao, *SII*, IX, Part I, no. 133. See also ibid., no. 218.

Cālukyas.[51] In A.D. 1173 Rācamalla I made a donation for service of the god to the *sthānācārya* Bāla-Śivācārya, who maintained the *Lākulīśvarāgama* and the Kālāmukha doctrine *(darśana)* and practised the usual yogic virtues. Several years later, in 1181, Rācamalla gave a village to the same temple and trustee (here called Bāli-Śiva-deva). This gift was 'for the god Svayambhū's personal enjoyment, theatrical entertainment, offerings of food, restoration of worn-out *(buildings)*, the *Caitra* and *pavitra*, scriptural study, lectures on the Vaiśeṣika, class-reading of the *Śiva-dharma-purāṇa*, and charitable gifts of food.'[52] The inscription ends with a third grant by the two wives of the minister who had built the Svayambhū temple. They donated some land to the temple while mounting the funeral pyre of their dead husband.[53] Another inscription from Kurgōḍ mentions a Kālāmukha priest named Amṛtāśi-deva (? =Amṛtarāśi-deva).[54]

Two inscriptions dated A.D. 1144 and found near the Malleśvara temple in Sindigeri register gifts for feeding houses for pilgrims.[55] Both gifts were entrusted to the priest Nirvāṇa-deva, who was descended from Vāmadeva, also called Erkōṭi-cakravarti, the *ācārya* of the Svayambhū temple at Muḷugunda. Vāmadeva is described as the supporter of the Kālāmukha doctrine *(samaya)*, the possessor of all the usual yogic virtues, and a master of a great many *śāstras* including grammar, logic, Siddhānta (? = Lākula-siddhānta), poetry, two types of drama, Vedic names, rhetoric, *śruti* (?), *smṛti* (?), Purāṇa, *itihāsa*, Mīmāṃsā, and *nītiśāstra*.[56] Vāmadeva's disciple was Trilocana-deva, whose disciple was Kumāra-deva, whose disciple was Nirvāṇa-deva.

In A.D. 1065 an official named Bijjaladeva granted a village to the temple of the god Noḷambeśvara at Gudihalli while washing the feet of Divyaśakti-paṇḍita-deva of the Lākula sect, who belonged to the maṭha of the lineage *(santati)* of Agastēśvara (? = Agastyeśvara)

---

[51]Ed. and trans. L.D. Barnett, 'Two Inscriptions from Kurgod,' *EI*, XIV, 265–84 (no. A).

[52]Trans. ibid., p. 277. The text reads : 'śrī-Svayaṃbhu-dēvar = aṃga-bhōgaṃ(ga)-raṃga-bhōga-naivēdya-jīrṇṇ-ōddhāra-Caitra-pavitra-svādhyāya-Vaiśēṣika-byākhyāna-khaṇḍika-Śiva-dharmma-purāṇa-paṭhanav = anna-dānav . . .' It is not possible to identify the *Śiva-dharma-purāṇa*.

[53]Ibid., pp. 273, 277–78.

[54]See V. Rangacharya, *Inscriptions of the Madras Presidency*, no. 108.

[55]Ed. Sastry and Rao, *SII*, IX, Part I, nos. 235 and 237.

[56]Ibid., no. 235.

of Śrīparvata.[57] In 1111 another gift was issued to the Noḷambeśvara temple while the donor washed the feet of Vareśvara-paṇḍita, the disciple of Vāmaśakti-paṇḍita, who was the disciple of the same Divyaśakti-paṇḍita.[58] It seems almost certain that these priests were Kālāmukhas.

Another line of priests who were probably Kālāmukhas controlled the Abhinava-Someśvara temple in the village Kurivatti.[59] The founder of this line was Kaśmīra-deva, whose pupil was Someśvara-paṇḍita, whose pupil was Jñānaśakti-paṇḍita-deva, whose pupil was Lakulīśvara-paṇḍita. This last priest was in charge in A.D. 1099 when the two-hundred *mahājanas* of Kuruvatti and their chief, the Brahman Kālidāsa, made a grant for the service of the god. The official governing the district in which the village was situated was himself a priest named Sureśvara-paṇḍita-deva, the disciple of Vādideva-paṇḍita-deva.

Bijāpur District

This district has yielded Kālāmukha inscriptions of both the Simha- and Śakti-pariṣads. A record in Sanskrit and Kannada from Bijāpur itself contains a lengthy Sanskrit eulogy of the spiritual lineage of the Kālāmukha *ācārya* Yogeśvara-paṇḍita-deva.[60] In A.D. 1074–75 a *daṇḍanāyaka* of Someśvara II of the Kalyāṇa Cālukyas built a temple of the god Śrī-Svayambhū-Siddheśvara for Yogeśvara and his pupils and donated some land for its upkeep. Yogeśvara is given the following genealogy :

Bhujaṅga-devācārya or -munipa
|
Bhaujaṅga, also called Bhuvana and Trilocana
|
Bālasūrya-munipa, also called Trailocana
|
Kāśmīra-sūrīśvara
|
Śrī-Vādimahāpralaya-Kālabhairava-paṇḍita-deva,
also called Tatpuruṣa-munipati and Bhairava-muni
|
Yogeśvara- or Yogīśvara-paṇḍita-deva

---

57 Ibid., no. 128.
58 Ibid., no. 186.
59 See ibid., no. 165.
60 Ed. and trans. Fleet, *IA*, X, 126–32.

We have already mentioned the possibility that Bhujaṅga was the founder or a member of the Bhujaṅgāvali of the Śakti-pariṣad.[61] He is described as 'the *tilaka* on the face *(mukha)* of the Kālāmukha (sect),' as 'the leader of the Kālāmukhas,' as 'the crest-jewel of yogins,' and as 'the possessor of the *mantra* for subjugating the beautiful woman Liberation *(mukti)*.'[62] By means of Yoga he assumed a hundred different forms and established twelve *liṅgas* of the god Jhañjheśvara, including one at Bijāpur. In his lineage *(santāna)* many excellent *munis* appeared who possessed the yogic powers *(guṇas, = siddhis)* of becoming small *(aṇiman)* and so forth. His disciple Trilocana is said to have been expert in the Vedas and Vedāṅgas and in the *āgama* received from Śrī-Lākula. Yogeśvara's preceptor Kālabhairava is depicted as an eclectic sage of the same type as Someśvara-paṇḍita of the Kedāreśvara temple in Belagāve :

> Through his intelligence that Tatpuruṣa-munipati assumes the status of being a Bhairava to opponents. His terrifying trident is the Mīmāṃsa. He agitates the hearts of his proud opponents with the sound of his drum which is Sugata (Buddhist doctrine). He has the battle drum *(bhaya-kṛt)* of Triṇayana, which is Viśeṣa (*i e.* the doctrine of the Vaiśeṣikas), and the upraised skull of Kāpila (the Sāṃkhya doctrine of Kapila). He (causes even) the inner parts of space, the sky and the earth to be deafened by the sound of his huge bell which is Nyāya.[63]

His disciple was the donee Yogeśvara, 'whose form was purified by actions which were capable of washing away the mud of the Kali age.'[64] This mighty ascetic uprooted the tree of Love itself after reflecting on the loathsomeness *(bībhatsa)* of the net of *saṃsāra*. He is further described, in Kannada, as the possessor of the yogic virtues of *yama, niyama, āsana, prāṇāyāma, pratyāhāra, dhyāna, dhāraṇā,* and *samādhi*.[65] He was a veritable *rājahaṃsa*

---

[61]See above, p. 140.

[62]Fleet, *IA,* X, 127–28 (my translations).

[63]Ibid., p. 128 (my translation). Much of Fleet's translation of this passage seems to be incorrect.

[64]Ibid., (Fleet's translation).

[65]This is the list given in *Yoga-sūtra* ii. 29, It is slightly different than the one given in most of these inscriptions.

among the clusters of lotuses of the Kālāmukha family *(kula)* and an ear-ornament of the goddess Sarasvatī. He had obtained the excellent grace *(prasāda)* of the god Trilocana and had captivated the mind *(citta)* of the woman Liberation *(mukti)*.

The same line of ascetics beginning with Kāśmīra is praised in two grants from Muttagi in the same district, dated A.D. 1147 and 1158.[66] Both register gifts to the temple of Śivaliṅga-deva in the town, made with the approval of the Kalacuri Bijjala, first as a subordinate of Jagadekamalla II of the Kalyāṇa Cālukyas and second as emperor in his own right. The donee of these gifts was the priest Lakulīśvara-vratīśvara or Lakulīśa-vrati. He is said to be proficient in the *Lākulāgama* and a veritable crest-jewel among those who observe perpetual chastity *(naiṣṭhikas)*. His preceptor was the *muni* Yogīśvara-deva (II), whose preceptor was Vareśvara-deva, whose preceptor was the Yogīśvara-deva, mentioned in the Bijāpur grant. The inscription of A.D. 1147 adds the important information that this line of ascetics came to Bijāpur from Kashmir.[67] If the first priestly migrant was Bhujaṅga, he must have left this northern region about the middle of the tenth century.

Dharwar District

This district is located directly south of Bijāpur and Belgaum Districts and north of Shimoga District. Not surprisingly it also was a center of Kālāmukha activity. The Śakti-pariṣad controlled temples at Ablūr, Āḍūr, Gadag, Haḷe-Niḍnēgila, Hoṃbal, Kūyibāl, Lakshmēśvar, Rōṇ, and perhaps also at Sūḍi and Sātēnahaḷḷi. Other Kālāmukha temples existed at Kalkēri and Sāṃsi.

In A.D. 1076 a governor of the Cālukya king Someśvara II donated a village for the Kālāmukha temple of the god Svayambhū Someśvara in Kalkēri.[68] The priest in charge of the temple was Dēvasiṅga-jīya. In 1144 some leading citizens of the Savasi (Sāṃsi) *agrahāra* made some gifts to the Kālāmukha priest Īśānaśakti-paṇḍita-deva, the *ācārya* of the local temple of the god Gavaṟēśvara.[69]

Chikmagalur (Kadur) District

This district is located just south of Shimoga District. Only two

---

[66]Ed. Desai, *SII*, XV, nos. 32 and 97 respectively.

[67]See above, pp. 108–109.

[68]Ed. Gai, *SII*, XX, no. 49.

[69]Ibid., no. 112.

Kālāmukha sites have been identified. In about A.D. 1108 a feudatory of the Hoysala *mahāmaṇḍaleśvara* Ballāla I granted some land for a Śiva temple at the village Bāṇūru. The donee was the Kālāmukha priest Gīrvāṇaśakti-paṇḍita-deva.[70] In 1139 some local officials of Beraṭiyakere, modern Belṭikere, donated some land to the local Kālāmukha priest Dharmarāśi-paṇḍita.[71] Another twelfth century Kālāmukha priesthood may have existed at Jammāpura.[72]

Chitradurga (Chitaldrug) District

This district is situated immediately east of Shimoga District. Kālāmukha inscriptions have been found at Asagoḍa and Chadurugoḷa. In A.D. 1054 an official of the Pallava feudatory of the Cālukya king Someśvara I granted a village for the temple of the god Svayambhū in Asagoḍa.[73] The temple establishment is described as 'a *Kālāmukha-sthāna,* the *Naiṣṭhika-vedi-karttara-matha.'* The full implications of the latter term are unclear although *naiṣṭhika* obviously refers to the sexual continence of the priests of the maṭha. The temple is said to have been built by Karttāra, who was evidently a spiritual ancestor of the priestly donee, Trailokya-karttāra-bhaṭṭāraka. An official of a feudatory of the Cālukya king Vikramāditya VI made another grant to the temple in A.D. 1108 while washing the feet of Trailokya's disciple Bhuvana-karttāra-paṇḍita-deva.[74] Three years later another grant was made to this temple and was entrusted to Kālabhairava-deva, a disciple of Dharma-karttāra-paṇḍita-deva.[75]

A fragmentary inscription found at Chadurugoḷa records a donation made in the year A.D. 1166 'for the god . . . deśvara.' The donee was 'the Kālāmukha-vratin Tejonidhi-paṇḍita-deva's son Sarveśvara-paṇḍita-deva.'[76]

Hassan District

In addition to the Śakti-pariṣad priesthood at Haḷebiḍu,[77]

---

[70]Ed. *ARMAD* 1925, pp. 56–57.

[71]Ed. and trans. Rice, *EC,* VI, Kd. 80.

[72]See *ARMAD* 1943, pp. 91–99.

[73]Ed. and trans. Rice, *EC,* XI, Jl. 10.

[74]Ibid., Jl. 12.

[75]Ibid., Jl. 9.

[76]Ibid., Jl. 8.

[77]See above, p. 138.

there were Kālāmukha temples at Arasikere, Jājūr, Halkūr, Kaṇikaṭṭe, and Rājana Sirivūr. At Arasikere some local officials gave several plots of land for the temple of the god Gōjēśvara in A.D. 1183.[78] The donee was Amṛtarāśi-paṇḍita, the son of Dharmarāśi-paṇḍita, who was a pupil of Aghoraśakti-paṇḍita. Aghoraśakti is described as a supporter of the doctrine *(samaya)* of the *Lākulāgama* and a member of the Kālāmukha order.

An inscription of about A.D. 1195 found in the Kallēdēva temple at Jājūr praises two Kālāmukha priests named Candrabhūṣaṇa and Śivaśakti, who were ruling a place called Rājavūr in connection with the *Śaiva-sthāna* of Arasikere.[79] They are given the following genealogy :

Gaṅgarāśi-paṇḍita

Tribhuvanaśakti	Amṛtarāśi
Trailokyaśakti	Śivaśakti
Candrabhūṣaṇa	Kalyāṇaśakti

Candrabhūṣaṇa was expert in the proper characteristics of images and temples and in the rules for the performance of Īśa (Śiva) worship. He uprooted opposing doctrines and energetically propagated the Kālāmukha doctrine.

A line of Kālāmukha ascetics which extended over at least seven generations was located at Halkūr.[80] The first priest was Kēta-jīya whose disciple was Devendraśakti-paṇḍita. Devendraśakti had a female lay disciple named Dēkavve as well as a regular disciple named Rāmaśakti. Rāmaśakti's disciple was Kalyāṇaśakti, whose disciple was Vāmaśakti, whose disciple was Mahādeva-jīya, whose disciple was Cikkakavi-jīya, who was alive in A.D. 1177. These ascetics are described as Kālāmukhas who uphold the doctrine *(samaya)* of the *Lākulāgama* and worship the feet of the god Rāmanātha.

Several grants found at the village of Kaṇikaṭṭe entrust gifts of land and money to Kālāmukha ascetics. In about A.D. 1158

---

[78] Ed. *ARMAD* 1928, pp. 26–8.

[79] Ed. and trans. Rice, *EC,* XIV, Ak. 216. See also *ARMAD* 1911, p. 45.

[80] Ed. and trans. Rice, *EC,* V, Ak. 62.

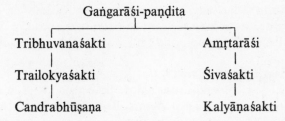

a donation seems to have been made to two priests called Kālā-mukha-dīkṣita and Jagateśvara for service of the god Kamma-ṭēśvara.[81] In about 1189 various prominent citizens and officials gave lands and taxes to a temple of Jagateśvara which they had earlier built in Kaṇikaṭṭe.[82] The donee was Kalyāṇaśakti-paṇḍita, a disciple of Śivaśakti-deva, who was a disciple of the Kālāmukha teacher Nāgarāśi-paṇḍita. Śivaśakti was the donee in a grant dated A.D. 1152.[83]

A fragmentary Hoysala inscription from the village of Rājana Siruvūr records some gifts to a temple of Dharmeśvara there.[84] A Kālāmukha priest of the *Atri-gotra* named Rudraśakti gave some money. References to the *gotras* of Kālāmukhas are rare. A Hoysala record of Vīra Ballāla II found at Rāmapura registers a grant to what may have been another Kālāmukha temple.[85] The donee was Somarāśi's son Bammarāśi, the head of the town's Mūlasthāna Śiva temple and a follower of the *Lākụlāgama.*

Kolar and Tumkur Districts

Very few Kālāmukha inscriptions have been found in these two districts of south-eastern Mysore. Two grants from Nandi Hill in Kolar District are of considerable importance, however, since they are by far the oldest Kālāmukha inscriptions yet discovered. In A.D. 810 Ratnāvali, a queen of the Bāṇa chieftain Vidyādhara-rāja, gave some land to a Śiva temple that she had built at Nandi Hill, now a well-known hill station.[86] The head of the maṭha on the hill was Īśvaradāsa, the chief disciple of the Kālāmukhya *(sic)* teacher Kāḷaśakti. Īśvaradāsa is described as compassionate towards all beings, devoted to performing good deeds and endowed with the virtues of observing vows *(vrata),* fasting *(upavāsa)* and *niyama.* Four years earlier, in 806, the Rāṣṭrakūṭa king Govinda III donated a village to this Īśvaradāsa, 'the lord of the *sthāna* on Nandi Hill,' for incense, lamps, perfume, *bali,* and *caru* in the temple of Śiva.[87]

These two records indicate that at least a few Kālāmukha ascetics

---

[81]Ibid., Ak. 42.
[82]Ibid., Ak. 48.
[83]Ibid., Ak. 52.
[84]Ed. *ARMAD* 1940, pp. 143–44.
[85]Ed. *ARMAD* 1937. pp. 135–42.
[86]Ed. *ARMAD* 1914, pp. 29–30, 35–37.
[87]Ed. ibid., pp. 30–32, 39–41.

had established themselves in Karṇāṭaka by the end of the eighth century. The ascetics must have originally migrated from somewhere in the North, the home of Lakulīśa and his disciples, but we do not know precisely when they arrived. The early presence of Kālāmukha monasteries in the Mysore region was probably an important factor in the later migration of Kālāmukha priests from Kashmir during the tenth and eleventh centuries.[88]

Ratnāvali's grant of A.D. 810 concludes with the following unusual imprecation: 'May he who destroys this incur the sin of having turned Śrīparvata upside down, of having cut off the heads of the sages there, of having cut off the heads of a thousand tawny cows and a thousand Brāhmaṇas at Bāraṇāsi (Benares) and of having killed in Jambu-dvīpa sages and Brāhmaṇas versed in the 4 Vedas, 18 *pramāṇas* and *siddhāntas*.'[89] The prominent mention of Śrīparvata indicates that this site was already an important holy center for the Kālāmukhas. The praising of Brāhmaṇas versed in the Vedas, cows and the city of Varanasi emphasizes the relative orthodoxy of these priests' beliefs.

A grant of A.D. 1169 found at Karadālu in Tumkur District registers a gift to the temples of Sobbēśvara, Mācēśvara, Bammēśvara, and '. . . śvara.'[90] The donee was Bamma-jīya's son Gaṅgarāśi-jīya, 'a moon to the Kālāmukhas' and 'the obtainer of a boon from the goddess Śāradā.'

The Kriyāśaktis of Vijayanagar

A priesthood the heads of which each bore the name or title Kriyāśakti played an important part in the religious life of the early Vijayanagar empire.[91] Many Kālāmukha and Pāśupata priests called themselves by this name and there is little doubt that the Kriyāśaktis of Vijayanagar also belonged to one of these two related sects. The term *kriyāśakti*—like *jñānaśakti*, another common Pāśupata-Kālāmukha name—denotes an important concept in Pāśupata theology.[92] One of these Kriyāśaktis is said to have

---

[88]See above, pp. 108–109.

[89]Trans. *ARMAD* 1914, p. 36.

[90]Ed. and trans. Rice, *EC*, XII, Tp. 91.

[91]The most detailed accounts of this line appear in *ARMAD* 1941, pp. 168–70, and *Mysore Gazetteer*, ed. C.H. Rao, II, Part III, 1442–44, 1474–78, 1650–54.

[92]These two *śaktis* are also found in the theologies of Kashmir Śaivism (Trika) and Vīraśaivism, but the names do not seem to have been common among the followers of either system.

induced his disciple Mādhava-mantrin to give a village to eighty learned Brāhmaṇas from Kashmir, another fact which suggests a connection with the Kālāmukhas.[93]

It must be admitted, however, that a few sources imply the existence of a close relation between these Kriyāśaktis and the *advaita* gurus of the famous Śriṅgeri maṭha founded by Śaṃkarācārya. Vidyāraṇya, the famous scholar and Vijayanagar guru, was one of the heads of this maṭha. A Sanskrit work called *Vidyāraṇya-kālajñāna* actually claims that Kriyāśakti was the disciple of Vidyāraṇya and states that these two were revered by the first thirteen kings of Vijayanagar, who were worshippers of the god Virūpākṣa.[94] An inscription of A.D. 1390 seems to record a grant by Immaḍi Bukka, son of Harihara II, to a shrine of Vidyāśaṃkara erected in memory of the guru Kriyāśakti, who had died the previous year.[95] Vidyāśaṃkarācārya was the title of the guru Vidyāraṇya's predecessor at Śriṅgeri, Bhārati-Kṛṣna-Tīrtha. Another reading of this record, which is evidently badly edited, concludes that Immaḍi Bukka made his grant with the permission of, rather than in memory of, Kriyāśakti.[96] A grant of Harihara II dated A.D. 1384 states that the king listened to the teachings of both Vidyāraṇya and Kriyāśakti.[97] A grant issued in the year 1403 registers gifts of land both to Kriyāśakti-deva-rāya-voḍeyar and to the guru of the Śriṅgeri maṭha.[98]

The Pāśupatas and Kālāmukhas were philosophical dualists and for this reason were regarded with disfavour by *advaita* theologians such as Śaṃkarācārya and Sāyaṇa-Mādhava, the author of the *Sarvadarśanasaṃgraha*. This latter priest has been identified as either Vidyāraṇya himself or his nephew.[99] If Kriyāśakti was a Pāśupata, it is highly unlikely that he was Vidyāraṇya's disciple or that a temple of Vidyāśaṃkara was set up in Kriyāśakti's memory. On the other hand, there is no need to assume that the two groups were overtly hostile to each other. Relations between the various Hindu sects in the early Vijayanagar empire were generally cordial. One Kriyāśakti was tolerant enough to grant

[93]Ed. and trans. Rice, *EC*, VII, Sk. 281.

[94]See *ARMAD* 1932, p. 105.

[95]See *ARMAD* 1941, p. 169.

[96]See *Mysore Gazetteer*, II, Part III, 1652.

[97]See *ARMAD* 1941, p. 169.

[98]See ibid., p. 170.

[99]*Mysore Gazetteer*, II, Part III, 1433–42.

land to a temple of Varadarāja (Viṣṇu) in A.D. 1377.[100] This cordiality was probably greatest between the Kālāmukha and Vīraśaiva schools since the latter appears to have gradually absorbed the former.[101] Some of the royal disciples of the Kriyāśakti priests are in fact claimed by the Vīraśaivas.[102] It is possible that the Kriyāśaktis were Vīraśaivas, but we feel that the evidence favors their identification as Pāśupatas or Kālāmukhas.

The dates of the Kriyāśakti epigraphs extend from A.D. 1347 to 1431, indicating that there were at least two and probably three or four priests by this name. As we have noted, one may have died in the year 1389. Several variants of the name occur, including Kāśīvilāsa-Kriyāśakti (1368), Kriyāśaktyācārya (1378), Vāṇīvilāsa-Kriyāśakti (1379), Kriyāśakti-deva (1398, 1399, 1431), Kriyāśakti-guru-munīśvara and Kriyāśakti-deva-rāya-voḍeyar (1403), Kriyāśakti-guru (1410), and Kriyāśakti-deśika (1410). In Mādhava-mantrin's *Tātparyadīpikā* the author identifies his guru as Kāśīvilāsa-Kriyāśakti, and Gaṅgādevī does likewise in her *Kamparāya-carita*.

Like several Kālāmukha priests,[103] Kriyāśakti is given the title *rājaguru* in a number of records. In some he appears as the guru of Mādhava-mantrin, a minister of Prince Mārapa.[104] Other records praise Kriyāśakti as the *kula-guru* or *rājaguru* of Harihara II, of a governor called Viṭṭhanna Oḍeyar (1403), of Devarāya I and his son Vijaya-bhūpati (1410), and possibly also of Devarāya II (1429). In the *Vīra-Kamparāya-carita* he is also called the *kula-guru* of Kampana II.[105] Since the term *kula-guru* means family preceptor, it is likely that these priests were held in high esteem by most of the early Vijayanagar rulers.

Many inscriptions describe Kriyāśakti as a worshipper of the god Śiva in the form Svayambhū-Triyambakadeva. Evidently this was the tutelary divinity of the priesthood. A grant made by Devarāya II in 1429 to some Brāhmaṇas headed by Kriyāśakti-guru at Cōḷiśaṭṭipalli in Kolar District states that this priest belonged

---

[100]See ibid., pp. 1651–53.

[101]See ibid., p. 1654, and below, pp. 167–72.

[102]Ibid., p. 1654.

[103]See above, p. 123.

[104]Mārapa was a brother of Harihara I and Bukka I and governor of the province Āraga in the western part of the Vijayanagar empire.

[105]See *Mysore Gazetteer,* II, Part III, 1651–52, and *ARMAD* 1941, pp. 169–70.

to the Kāśyapa-gotra and followed the *Yajur Veda*.[106] Since the donated village was renamed Tryambaka-pura, there is little doubt that this Kriyāśakti was a member of the same priesthood.

Apart from their devotion to Tryambaka, however, little is known about the religious beliefs of these priests. The best source is an inscription of Mādhava-mantrin dated A.D. 1368 which registers his gift of the village of Muchchaṇḍi in Shimoga District to eighty learned Kashmir Brāhmaṇas.[107] The lengthy eulogy of this minister asserts that he, 'through the astonishing favour of his master Kāśīvilāsa Kriyāśakti, a manifest incarnation of Girīśa, gained celebrity as a Śaiva [*śāmbhava*].' He also 'cleared and made plain the ruined path of the *upaniṣads*,' and 'on the advice of the Śiva guru Kāśīvilāsa Kriyāśakti, he worshipped in the manner of the *Śaivāmnāya* the god of gods embodied in his own favourite liṅga [*iṣṭa-liṅga*], Tryambaka-nātha, by means of daily special ceremonies, and by a number of rites and practices.' The grant to the eighty Brāhmaṇas was made to mark the completion of a 'great Śaiva vow' *(mahac-chaiva-vrata)* lasting one year which he had undertaken in accordance with the directions of the *Śiva-saṃdhyā*. Unfortunately the specific details of this great vow and the other rites and practices are never spelt out. The 'great Śaiva vow' is conceivably the Mahāvrata of the Kāpālikas although for reasons already stated we prefer not to make this identification.[108] The donees in the present grant must have had some connection with Kriyāśakti since they are described as 'pre-eminent by their virtues and the country of their birth [Kashmir], travellers to the farthest point of the *Cārāyaṇīya-aticaraṇāmnāya,* daily observers of all the rites appointed in the pure *Śivāmnāya,* ever devoted to the worship of the Aṣṭamūrti.'[109] From a record of A.D. 1347 we learn that Kriyāśakti's disciple Mādhava-mantrin aided Prince Mārapa in the compilation of a work called *Śaivāgama-sārasaṃgraha*.[110] The minister was also the author of the *Sūtasaṃhitā-tātparya-dīpikā* on the *Sūtasaṃhitā* of the *Skanda Purāṇa*.[111]

---

[106]Ed. and trans. *ARMAD* 1941, pp. 157–70.

[107]Ed. and trans. Rice, *EC,* VII, Sk. 281.

[108]See above, pp. 81–82.

[109]Ibid. *Cārāṇīya* is a school of the *Black Yajur Veda,* the Veda followed by the Kriyāsakti of 1429.

[110]Ed. and trans. Rice, *EC,* VIII, Sb. 375.

[111]*Mysore Gazetteer,* II, Part III, p. 1444.

Andhra Pradesh and Madras

The two chief centers of Kālāmukha activity in what is now Andhra Pradesh were Vijayawāda-Amarāvatī and Śrīparvata. These we have already discussed.[112] At least a few other Kālāmukha sites must have existed in the region. An inscription of A.D. 1021 found at Mēlpāḍi in Chittoor District registers a grant by some shepherds of the town for ghee for a lamp in the temple of Ariñjīśvara.[113] The head of the maṭha of the temple was a priest called Lakulīśvara-paṇḍita, who was probably a Kālāmukha. A Mahāvratin Lakulīśvara-paṇḍita, who was possibly the same teacher, is mentioned in an inscription of A.D. 1068–69 found at Jambai in South Arcot District, Madras.[114]

Although the Kālāmukhas were much less influential in Madras State than in Mysore, Kālāmukha temples existed in Chingleput, North Arcot, Thanjavūr (Tanjore), and Tiruchchirappali (Trichinopoly) Districts. Tamil inscriptions of A.D. 1127, 1205 and 1231 found in the Tiruvālīśvara temple at Tiruvānaikkōyil in Chingleput District mention the Kālāmukha priests Śailarāśi-paṇḍita and Ñānarāśi-paṇḍita. They controlled the *kāṇi* (land-revenue) of the temple.[115] A Tamil record of A.D. 926 from Vēḍal in North Arcot District refers to a Kālāmukha Daśapuriyan of the *Hārīta-gotra* and the *Āpastamba-sūtra*.[116] In A.D. 1123 Gōmaḍattu Aruḷāḷa Bhaṭṭan, a Kālāmukha, sold some land to a temple at Kōyil Tēvarāyanpēṭṭai in Thanjavūr District.[117]

An important Sanskrit inscription from Koḍumbāḷūr in the southern part of Tiruchchirappalli District shows that the Kālāmukhas had penetrated into the heart of Madras State by at least the middle of the tenth century.[118] The Koḍumbāḷūr chieftain Vikrama-kēsarī, a contemporary of Sundara Cōḷa Parāntaka II (957–73), erected there three temples *(vimāna-traya)* named after himself and his two queens. After enshrining the god Maheśvara he donated the Big Matha *(bṛhan-maṭha)*, together with the eleven

---

[112]See above, pp. 136–37 and 141–43.

[113]Ed. and trans. E. Hultzsch and H.K. Sastri, *SII*, III, no. 18.

[114]See K.A.N. Sastri, *The Cōḷas* (1st edition), I, 603. Sastri summarizes the evidence on the Madras Kālāmukhas in ibid., II, 493–94.

[115]See ibid., II, 623, 702 and 739.

[116]See ibid., I, 420, and Rangacharya, *Inscriptions* . . ., II, 1162.

[117]See K.A.N. Sastri, *The Cōḷas* (1st edition), II, 610.

[118]Ed. and trans. K.A.N. Sastri, 'The Koḍumbāḷūr Inscription of Vikrama-Kēsarī,' *JORM*, VII, 1–10.

villages attached to it, to the chief ascetic *(yati)* of the *Kālāmukhādāna,* Mallikārjuna. Vikrama-Kēsarī also seems to have made provision for the feeding of 50 *Asita-vaktra* ascetics resident there and for offerings, perfume, incense, flowers, lamps and betel for the service of the god of the three temples. *Asita-vaktra,* Black-face, is a synonym for Kālāmukha. This tends to show that Kālamukha, rather than Kālāmukha, is the correct Sanskrit form of the name. Mallikārjuna's own name may reflect devotion to the god of Śrīparvata. According to the inscription Mallikārjuna was a member of the *Ātreya-gotra,* a resident of Mathurā, a master of the Vedas, and a pupil of Vidyārāśi and Taporāśi. Mathurā might be either of two famous cities—Uttara-mathurā (modern Mathura in U.P.) or Dakṣiṇa-mathurā (modern Madurai in Madras). The latter city is more probable since it is less than 100 miles from Kòḍumbāḷūr, but the former is also possible since many Kālāmukhas were emigrating from the North at about this time.

Inscriptions found at Paḷḷimaḍam in Rāmanāthapuram (Ramnad) District and Tiruvoṟṟiyūr in Chingelput District refer to Mahāvratin ascetics who must have been Kālāmukhas. At Paḷḷimaḍam some sheep were given for a lamp in the maṭha of Mahāvratigaḷ attached to the Sundarapāṇḍya-īśvara temple.[119] The grant was issued during the reign of Vīra Pāṇḍya and has been tentatively dated at about the middle of the eleventh century.

At Tiruvoṟṟiyūr an important maṭha of Mahāvratins was founded or brought to prominence by Vaḷabha, a general of Cōḷa Rājāditya, in about the middle of the tenth century.[120] When Rājāditya died in A.D. 948 during the battle of Takkōlam, Vaḷabha was not at his side. In grief and shame the general went to bathe in the Ganges and resolved to become an ascetic. He returned to the South and entered a cave named after the guru Nirañjana at Tiruvoṟṟiyūr. There he obtained enlightenment and devoted himself to the performance of the Mahāvrata for the sake of the protection of the maṭha. He assumed the spiritual name or title, Caturānana-paṇḍita, and, in about A.D. 959, made a gift of some gold to the assembly *(sabhā)* of Narasiṃha-maṅgala for a special service to the god Śiva on the day of Dhaniṣṭhā, the star of his own birth.

---

[119]Ed. *SII,* XIV, no. 88.

[120]The story of the founding of the maṭha is contained in the Sanskrit and Tamil inscription of A.D. 959 edited and translated by V. Raghavan (*EI,* XXVII, 292–303). Raghavan's introduction gives a complete history of the maṭha.

Mahāvratins are mentioned in inscriptions from Tiruvoṟṟiyūr dated as early as A.D. 942.[121] The priest Caturānana is first referred to in a grant of 957.[122] The maṭha continued under a succession of teachers by this name until at least 1172.[123] V. Raghavan notes (*EI,* XXVII, 300) that the *Tiruvoṟṟiyūrp-Purāṇam* tells of a Toṇḍaimāṉ of Kāñcī who erected a Śiva temple at Tiruvoṟṟiyūr and established 500 Śiva *liṅgas*. He also brought from the banks of the Ganges 500 Brāhmaṇa Mahāvratins and dedicated several images of Kālī and Bhairava and one of Śiva in the form of a teacher of the Mahāvratins. Some of these images can still be identified and seem to date from later Pallava times.

Kālāmukhas and Vīraśaivas

A considerable amount of circumstantial evidence points to the existence of a close historical link between the Kālāmukhas and the Vīraśaivas. A definitive analysis of the problem would require extensive research both in the field and in the library. In particular, the voluminous hagiology of the Vīraśaivas, mostly written in Kannada and Telugu, would have to be digested and painstakingly compared with the available epigraphic data. We will be content to draw attention to some of the more important clues which have turned up in the course of our investigation of the Kālāmukhas.

The early history of the Vīraśaivas is buried in a maze of legends.[124] The principal early leader of the sect was Basava (Sanskrit *vṛṣabha* = bull), a minister of the Kalacuri king Bijjala (*c.* 1145–67). Vīraśaiva tradition claims that the sect antedates Basava, who was merely a major reformer. Modern authorities disagree about this point, but it seems probable that to most intents and purposes Basava was the founder. Not only is there no epigraphic evidence of the existence of Vīraśaivas before Basava, but the epigraphic allusions to Vīraśaiva activity in the two or three centuries after Bijjala are few and far between. This is not to say, of course, that the sect had no antecedents. The evidence suggests that it was a reformist schism from the Kālāmukha church

---

[121]See K.A.N. Sastri, *The Cōḷas* (1st edition), I, 433, and Rangacharya, *Inscriptions* . . ., I, 445.

[122]See K.A.N. Sastri, *The Cōḷas* (1st edition), I, 433–444.

[123]See ed. H.K. Sastri, *SII,* V, no. 1358.

[124]The most readable account of the life of Basava in English is still that in R.G. Bhandarkar's *Early History of the Dekkan* (pp. 101–104). See also Yazdani (ed.), *The early History of the Deccan,* I, 461–65, and *Mysore Gazetteer,* II, Part II, 873–93.

with Basava cast in the role of Luther.[125]

The chief Vīraśaiva sources for their own early history are two Kannada works—the *Basava Purāṇa,* written in about A.D. 1370,[126] and the *Canna-Basava Purāṇa,* written in about 1585.[127] A quite different account of the life of Basava is contained in a Jain work, the *Bijjalarāyacarita*. The *Basava Purāṇa* avers that Basava was the son of a Brahman named Māḍirāja and his wife Mādalāmbikā of Bāgevāḍi (in Bijāpur District). Basava was married to the daughter of Baḷadeva, Bijjala's chief minister, and was appointed to Baḷadeva's position after the latter's death. Basava's sister Nāgalāmbikā had a son named Canna-Basava. After Basava's appointment, he and his nephew began propounding the new Vīraśaiva doctrine and won a great number of converts. In the process they rapidly depleted Bijjala's treasury with munificent gifts to the *jaṅgamas,* the Vīraśaiva priests. This alienated the king who sought to punish Basava, but before he could do so the latter fled. The king set out to capture him, but Basava gathered together a large number of his followers and defeated the king in battle. The king then reinstated Basava to his old position but their relations were never again the same. Basava eventually commissioned one of his followers to murder the king. After the murder Basava hurried to the shrine of Saṅgameśvara at the confluence of the Malaprabhā and Krishna rivers and was absorbed into the godhead.

The major portion of the Jain version is similar, but there are several important differences. After the regicide, for instance, the murdered king's son is said to have chased Basava to Ulavi on the Malabar coast, where the former minister ignominiously committed suicide by throwing himself into a well. Basava's nephew Canna-Basava was later reconciled with the new king and became sole leader of the Vīraśaivas.

Both these sources are relatively late and there is no solid epigraphic confirmation of the story. For this reason J.F. Fleet

---

[125]S.C. Nandimath, in his *A Handbook of Virasaivism* (p. 9), notes that the Kālāmukha maṭha at Hūli is now an important Vīraśaiva maṭha and tentatively concludes that the transformation of Kālāmukha maṭhas into Vīraśaiva maṭhas may have occurred elsewhere as well: 'Slowly and imperceptibly they were absorbed into Vīraśaivism.' The *Mysore Gazetteer* (II, Part II, 885) offers the opinion that the Śaivite revival under Basava and the other early Vīraśaivas 'seems to have followed as the natural result of the work of these Śaiva teachers of the Pāśupata [*sic* for Kālāmukha] school at Balagami [=Belagāve].

[126]Trans. G. Würth, *JBBRAS,* VIII (1865–66), 65–97.

[127]Trans. G. Würth, *JBBRAS,* VIII, 98–221.

thought it best to ignore it (*EI,* V, 242–45). K.A.N. Sastri feels that Fleet went too far in this rejection and cites a genealogy contained in a subsequently edited Arjunawada inscriptions of the Yādava Kannara (A.D. 1260) which mentions 'Basava or Saṅgana-Basava as the younger son of Mādirāja described as *Tardavāḍi-madhyagrāma-Bāgavādi-puravarādhīsvara.*'[128] These two persons, Sastri believes, must be the famous Vīraśaiva and his father. Although this identification is perfectly plausible, there is still no epigraphic corroboration of the legendary biographies or even of Basava being a minister of Bijjala.

An inscription of about A.D. 1200 found at the Somanātha temple at Ablūr in Dharwar District provides better evidence about a Śaivite priest named Ēkāntada Rāmayya,[129] who is described as a Vīraśaiva saint in the *Canna-Basava Purāṇa.*[130] A great contest was held in the town between him and the Jains. He vanquished them by offering his own head to Śiva, who restored it as good as new after seven days. The losers still refused to destroy their image of Jina and establish one of Śiva in its place. Ēkāntada Rāmayya destroyed their shrine and built a large temple of Vīra-Somanātha in its place. The Jains appealed to Bijjala for retribution but declined his offer of a second contest for bigger stakes. Bijjala therefore dismissed their appeal and 'bestowed on Ēkāntada Rāmayya, in the public assembly, a *jayapatra* or certificate of success.'

This record contains an important clue to the possible relations existing between the Vīraśaivas and Kālāmukhas. In it Ēkāntada Rāmayya is said to have delivered a sermon in the Brahmeśvara temple at Ablūr. As we have seen,[131] this temple was headed by Kālāmukha priests of the Mūvara-kōṇeya-saṃtati until at least A.D. 1144. There is no reason to assume that it was not still in their hands when Ēkāntada Rāmayya visited it a few years later. Evidently Ēkāntada Rāmayya and these Kālāmukha priests

[128]In Yazdani (ed.), *The Early History* . . ., I, 463.

[129]Fleet, *EI,* V, no. E.

[130]Trans. G. Würth, *JBBRAS,* VIII, 198. The story of 'Yēkānta Rāmeiya' in this work differs considerably from the epigraphic account, but the essentials are similar enough to confirm that he is the same priest. According to the Purāṇa, 'Yēkānta Rāmeiya, a great saint,' heard of the fame of Basava and went to Kalyāṇa to see him. This suggests that Ekāntada Rāmayya became a Vīraśaiva after his reputation was already established. This Ablūr inscription gives no specific indication that he belonged to this sect.

[131]See above, p. 118.

maintained cordial relations. It is even possible that at the time of delivering his sermon Ēkāntada himself was a member of the Kālāmukha sect.[132] The Brahmeśvara temple is today known as the temple of Basaveśvara and is a Vīraśaiva shrine.[133]

Many other former Kālāmukha temples are now controlled by the Vīraśaivas. The exact number and percentage is not known[134] but they include the Kedāreśvara temple in Belagāve, the Trikūṭeśvara temple at Gadag (Dharwar District), and the Kālāmukha temples at Hūli (Belgaum District). Belagāve, the former seat of the Śakti-pariṣad, is now a center of Vīraśaiva activity and is visited by Vīraśaiva pilgrims from the surrounding areas.[135] Of the five most sacred Vīraśaiva maṭhas, one is at Śrīparvata in Kurnool District and one at Kedāranāth in the Himalayas—both sites with important Kālāmukha associations. Even more significant, perhaps, is the fact that few Vīraśaivas are found in areas not formerly dominated by the Kālāmukhas.

The similarities we can trace between Kālāmukha and Vīraśaiva cult and philosophy are regrettably few. This is not altogether surprising since very little is in fact known about the early Vīraśaivas apart from the broad outlines of their history. Our information about the Kālāmukhas is not much greater except insofar as we assume that they followed the doctrines and rituals of the Pāśupatas.

The most characteristic feature of later Vīraśaiva philosophy, the doctrine of *ṣaṭ-sthala,* is not mentioned in the early *vacanas.* According to S.N. Dasgupta, the philosophical content of Basava's *vacanas* is negligible.[136] One of the earliest Vīraśaiva philosophical works, Revaṇārya's *Siddhānta-śikhāmaṇi,* written in about the thirteenth century, does present certain similarities to Kālāmukha—or at least Pāśupata—doctrine. This work states that Śiva-Brahman is without any form or differentiation, yet is endowed with will by which he creates and destroys the world.[137] This corresponds to the view of the Kālāmukha priest Bonteyamuni of Hoṃbaḷ that the Creator *(kartṛ)* is formless.[138] The idea that the distribution of the fruits of *karman* is managed and controlled by God, rather

[132]See above, note 130.

[133]See Fleet, *EI,* V, 213.

[134]A systematic collection of this information would be of considerable interest.

[135]Information gathered from local informants at Belagāve in March, 1966.

[136]*History of Indian Philosophy,* V, 44.

[137]Ibid., pp. 48–49.

[138]See above, pp. 132 and 134.

than being automatic and autonomous, is, according to Dasgupta, a doctrine which Revaṇārya borrowed from the Pāśupatas.[139] We should also note here that Śrīpati Paṇḍita, a fourteenth century Vīraśaiva commentator on the *Brahma-sūtra,* quotes approvingly Haradatta, the author of the Pāśupata *Gaṇakārikā.*[140]

The social doctrines preached by the early Vīraśaivas included contempt for the caste system and child marriage as well as approval of widow remarriage. We know virtually nothing about Kālāmukha social attitudes, but it seems probable that they were more orthodox.[141]

Two important similarities between the respective cults of the Kālāmukhas and Vīraśaivas are the organization into large maṭhas and the emphasis placed on *liṅga* worship. The former needs no comment. There is no epigraphic evidence that the Kālāmukhas ever followed the Vīraśaiva practice of each devotee wearing a small *liṅga,* but the *Basava Purāṇa* itself admits that this practice existed even before Basava. In any case, the Kālāmukhas valued *liṅga* worship very highly. In the Kedāreśvara record of *c.* A.D. 1164, for instance, the Belagāve priest Kedāraśakti asserts that 'Whoso sets up but one *liṅga,* obtains a myriad-fold all the merit described in the *āgamas.*'[142]

The priests of the Vīraśaivas are called *jaṅgamas,* a term they explain as '*liṅgas* in movement.'[143] In a number of inscriptions the same word, with the same interpretation, is applied to Kālāmukha priests. The A.D. 1192 record from Gadag describes the Kālāmukha Candrabhūṣaṇa-paṇḍita-deva as the fourth, and moving *(jaṅgama) liṅga* of the god Trikūṭeśvara.[144] The donor of the A.D. 1189 grant from Hoṃbaḷ, the Kālāmukha priest Rudraśakti, is called a *jaṅgama,*[145] and the Kālāmukha ascetic Sarveśvara-deva, who headed the Jagadīśvara temple at Munavaḷḷi in A.D. 1252, is called a *jaṅgama-liṅgāvatāra,* an incarnation of a moving *liṅga.*[146] In the Vīraśaiva Purāṇas the relations between Basava and the *jaṅgamas,* especially the profligate twelve thousand, are not altogether

---

[139]*History* . . ., V, 49–50.

[140]Ibid., pp. 9–10.

[141]We have alluded to the Kālāmukha attitude to caste above, p. 149.

[142]Ed. and trans. Rice, *EC,* VII, Sk. 108.

[143]L. Renou and J. Filliozat, *L'Inde classique,* I, 638.

[144]See above, pp. 120–21.

[145]Ed. Desai, *SII,* XV, no. 73 (1. 50).

[146]See above, pp. 152–53.

clear.[147] It appears, however, that the *jaṅgamas* were organized even before the saint's appearance. It is by no means inconceivable, we feel, that these early *jaṅgamas* were none other than the Kālāmukhas.

[147]See *Basava Purāṇa*, trans. G. Würth, *JBBRAS*, VIII, pp. 68 and 71.

CHAPTER VI

LAKULĪŚA AND THE PĀŚUPATAS

We have noted more than once that Rāmānuja describes four sects as following the doctrine of Pāśupati : the Kāpāla, the Kālāmukha, the Pāśupata, and the Śaiva. The Pāśupata sect is the oldest of the four and was the spiritual parent of the Kālāmukha sect, if not of the others. In the period of Kālāmukha dominance in Mysore, which is also the time in which Rāmānuja preached, the epigraphs of the Pāśupatas and Kālāmukhas display many similarities. Both sects revere the legendary teacher Lakulīśa. The ascetics of both bear similar or identical names and undertake pilgrimages to Kedāranāth and Śrīparvata.[1] The philosophical content of the *Īśvara-kartṛ-vāda* propounded by the Kālāmukha priest Bonteyamuni of Hoṃbaḷ[2] can be little different from the Pāśupata doctrine of *Īsvara* as Cause *(kāraṇa)* of the Material Universe *(karyā)*. We have quoted above the passage from inscriptions at Nēsargi and Sirasangi which seems to equate Kālāmukha, Mahāvratin and Mahāpāśupata.[3] Most sources, however, describe the Kālāmukhas and Pāśupatas as separate, though closely allied, Śaivite sects.[4]

A number of modern scholars have written about the history, ritual and philosophy of the Pāśupatas. Since these topics lie somewhat at the periphery of our study, we will be content to summarise and review these scholars' arguments and to comment on possible reflections of Pāśupata beliefs and practices in Kālāmukha epigraphs.

The best discussions of the early history of the Pāśupatas are those by J.N. Banerjea.[5] Other contributions in this field have

---

[1]See above, pp. 107–109.

[2]See above, p. 134.

[3]See above, pp. 151–52.

[4]See above, pp. 7–12.

[5]In K.A.N. Sastri (ed.), *The Mauryas and Satavahanas*, pp. 393–403; in his own *Development of Hindu Iconography*; and his article 'Lakulīśa—The Founder or the Systematiser of the Pāśupata Order' in Indian History Congress, *Proceedings of the Fourteenth Session, Jaipur*, pp. 32–36.

been made by D.R. Bhandarkar, who first noted the purāṇic data on Lakulīśa and enabled scholars to establish his approximate date,[6] and by J.F. Fleet, R.G. Bhandarkar, M. Hara and others.[7] Studies more concerned with later developments have been made by G. Bühler, K.K. Handiqui, H.D. Sankalia and others.[8]

The earliest references to the Pāśupatas are probably those in the *Mahābhārata*. The most important mentions five religious doctrines—Sāṃkhya, Yoga, Pāñcarātra, the Vedas, and Pāśupata—and says that the last was propounded by Śiva, who is also called Lord of Umā, Lord of Beings, Śrīkaṇṭha, and Son of Brahmā.[9] Extrapolating from a very tentative suggestion of R.G. Bhandarkar, who first noted the passage,[10] V.S. Pathak has attempted to prove that a historical person named Śrīkaṇṭha was the founder of the Pāśupata order.[11] The passage in question, however, clearly refers to the god Śiva and not to a divinised human being. Of the allusions

[6]'An Eklingjī Stone Inscription and the Origin and History of the Lakulīśa Sect,' *JBBRAS*, XXII (1904–07), 151–65; 'Lakulīśa' in Archaeological Survey of India, *Annual Report*: 1906–7, pp. 179–92; 'Some Published Inscriptions Reconsidered,' *IA*, XXXII (1913), 57–64; and 'Mathura Pillar Inscription of Chandragupta II: G.E. 61,' *EI*, XXI (1931–32), 1–9.

[7]J.F. Fleet, 'Śiva as Lakulīśa,' *JRAS for* 1907, pp. 419–26; R.G. Bhandarkar, *Vaiṣṇavism* . . . ; M. Hara, 'Pāśupata kenkyū II—*Pañcārthabhāṣya* ad *Pāśupatasūtra* I, i,' *Hikata Hakushi koki kinen ronbunshū*, pp. (65)–(80); R.N. Mehta, 'Karavan—The Seat of the Lakulīśa Sect' in Indian History Congress, *Proceedings of the Fourteenth Session, Jaipur*, pp. 71–76, and his 'Avākhal: the Traditional Ulkāgrāma of *Kārvaṇa Māhātmya*,' *JOIB*, VII (1957), 169ff.; P.C. Divanji, 'Lakulīśa of Kārvān and his Pāśupata Culture,' *JGRS*, XVII (1955), 267–74; A.P. Karmarkar, *The Vrātya or Dravidian Systems*; and V.S. Pathak, *History of Śaiva Cults in Northern India*.

[8]G. Bühler, 'Cintra Praśasti of the Reign of Sāraṅgadeva,' *EI*, I (1888), 271–87; K.K. Handiqui, pp. 337–54, 467–510; H.D. Sankalia, *The Archaeology of Gujarat*; T.V. Mahalingam, 'The Pāśupatas in South India,' *JIH*, XXVII (1949), 43–53, and his 'A Family of Pāśupata Gṛhasthas at Jambukeśvaram,' *JORM*, XXV (1957), 79–85; B.P. Majumdar, 'Lakulīśa Pāśupatas and their Temples in Medieval India,' *JBRS*, XXXIX (1953), 1–9; H.K. Narasimhaswami, 'Dommara-Nadyala Plates of Punyakumara; 10th Year,' *EI*, XXVII, 268–76, and his 'Bhairavakonda Inscription of Vikramaditya,' *EI*, XXXIII, 78–81; N. Venkataramanayya in G. Yazdani (ed.), *The Early History of the Deccan*, II, 704–13; and A.K. Vyas, 'Paldi Inscription of Guhila Arisimha; V.S. 1173,' *EI*, XXX, 8–12. Relevant material is also found in the works mentioned in the previous note.

[9]*Śāntiparvan*, Part III, ed. V.S. Sukthankar and S.K. Belvalkar, xii. 337. 59 and 62: 'sāṃkhyaṃ yogaṃ pāñcarātraṃ vai// . . . umāpatir bhūtapatih śrīkaṇṭho brahmaṇaḥ sutaḥ/ uktavān idam avyagro jñānaṃ pāśupataṃ śivaḥ//.'

[10]*Vaiṣṇavism* . . ., p. 116.

[11]*History of* . . ., pp. 4–8.

to Śrīkaṇṭha which Pathak cites in support of his argument, most seem to denote the god Śiva-Śrīkaṇṭha and only one makes any connection between Śrīkaṇṭha and Pāśupata doctrine. This passage, from the *Tantrāloka* of Abhinavagupta (*c.* A.D. 1000), merely says that Śrīkaṇṭha and Lakuleśvara are the two authorities on Śiva-śāsana. This is hardly conclusive, or even very useful, evidence.

Also following R.G. Bhandarkar, but more plausibly, J.N. Banerjea has suggested that the Śiva-bhāgavatas mentioned by Patañjali (*c.* 150 B.C.) in his comments on Pāṇini v. 2. 76 were pre-Lakulīśa Pāśupatas.[12] Banerjea sees Lakulīśa as the 'systematiser' of this earlier Pāśupata order. Unfortunately, this theory finds no support in either of the two extant Pāśupata texts—the *Pāśupata-sūtra* with the *Pañcārtha-bhāṣya* of Kauṇḍinya[13] and the *Gaṇakārikā* with the *Ratnaṭīkā* attributed to Bhāsarvajña.[14] In his gloss on *Pāśupata-sūtra* i. 1, Kauṇḍinya (pp. 3–4) says that the Lord assumed the body of a Brāhmaṇa and came to earth at Kāyāvataraṇa. Then he went to Ujjayinī where he imparted the *sūtras* to a disciple named Kuśika. This, as we shall see, is a clear allusion to the legend of Lakulīśa. The *Ratnaṭīkā* instructs the devotee to honor the *tīrthakaras* beginning with Lord Lakulīśa and ending with Rāśīkara. Thus by as early as the Gupta period, the time to which Kauṇḍinya is generally assigned, Lakulīśa was regarded as the founder of the order by the Pāśupatas themselves. Banerjea's theory must be viewed as pure speculation. It is certain that Śaivite ascetics existed before Lakulīśa, and some of these undoubtedly inculcated similar beliefs and practices. Religious orders are never founded in a vacuum. Wine and wineskins are never completely new. Nonetheless this does not justify calling these early Śaivite ascetics Pāśupatas.

Lakulīśa was in all likelihood the founder of the Pāśupata order. The sources for his personal history are fairly numerous and varied

---

[12]Indian History Congress, *Proceedings of the Fourteenth* . . ., pp. 32–36. See also his, *The Development* . . ., pp. 448–52 and his discussion in K.A.N. Sastri (ed.), *The Mauryas* . . ., pp. 396–400.

[13]Ed. R.A. Sastri.

[14]Ed. C.D. Dalal. The authorship is disputed. The colophon attributes the *Gaṇakārikā* and not the *Ratnaṭīkā* to Bhāsarvajña. We agree with most authorities, however, that it is the commentary and not the text that this famous tenth century Naiyāyika logician composed. The author of the *Gaṇakārikā* was perhaps named Haradattācārya. See R.A. Sastri's introduction to *Pāśupata-sūtra*, p. 4.

but not very complete or consistent. In addition to the allusion in Kauṇḍinya's *bhāṣya,* legends of his birth and priesthood appear in the *Vāyu*[15] and *Liṅga Purāṇas,*[16] the *Kāravaṇa Māhātmya,*[17] and three early mediaeval inscriptions.[18] The *Kāravaṇa Māhātmya,* a comparatively late work, gives the most complete version. According to it Śiva was born as the son of a Brāhmaṇa couple named Viśvarāja and Sudarśanā in the village of Ulkāpurī. The divine infant performed several superhuman feats but died at only seven months. His mother put him into the water of a nearby *tīrtha,* and from there he was taken by tortoises to the Jāleśvara-liṅga. He was brought back to life after this initiatory journey to the underworld and later went to Kāyāvarohaṇa where he took up his priestly mission. In the *Vāyu* and *Liṅga Purāṇas* Śiva predicts, in purāṇic fashion, that he will become incarnate as the *brahmacārin* Lakulin by entering a corpse found in a cremation ground at Kāyārohaṇa *(Vāyu)* or Kāyāvatāra *(Liṅga)*. This was to occur in the twenty-eighth *yuga* when Kṛṣṇa was incarnate as Vāsudeva. The stone inscription of A.D. 971 from the Ēkliṅgjī temple near Udaipur states that in the country of Bhṛgukaccha, the region around modern Broach, the sage Bhṛgu was once cursed by Viṣṇu. The sage propitiated Śiva for aid and the god became incarnate as an ascetic holding a club *(lakula)*. This occurred at Kāyāvarohaṇa.[19] The Paldi inscription of A.D. 1116, also found near Udaipur, says that when Śiva saw the tree of *dharma* being destroyed by the axes of the *Kali-yuga,* he descended to earth at Kāyāvarohaṇa in Bhṛgukaccha.[20] The Cintra *praśasti* of Sāraṅgadeva, a late thirteenth century record from Somnāth in Gujarat, relates how Śiva came to Lāṭa and dwelt at Kārohaṇa as Lakulīśa 'in order to bestow favour on the universe' and also 'to favour the offspring of Ulūka, who long were deprived of sons in consequence of a curse of their father . . .'[21]

---

[15]Ānandāśram edition, xxiii. 219–224.

[16]Ed. J. Vidyasagara, i. 24. 124–34.

[17]Ed. C.D. Dalal in *Gaṇakārikā,* pp. 37–57. It is well summarised by D.R. Bhandarkar in Archaeological Survey of India, *Annual Report* : 1906–7, pp. 180–83.

[18]D.R. Bhandarkar, *JBBRAS,* XXII, 151–65; Vyas, *EI,* XXX, 8–12; and Bühler, *EI,* I, 271–87.

[19]D.R. Bhandarkar, *JBBRAS,* XXII, 166. Was this club used to do battle with Viṣṇu? Bhṛgu is usually portrayed as a Vaiṣṇava.

[20]Vyas, *EI,* XXX, 11.

[21]Trans. Bühler, *EI,* I, 274. Fleet (*JRAS for* 1907, p. 419) offers an alternative interpretation in which Śiva-Lakulīśa, 'in order to favour the boys of Ulūka, who

It is evident that not much solid historical information can be derived from these accounts. They are, however, unanimous on two points—that Lakulīśa was an incarnation of Śiva, and that he settled at a place called Kāyāvarohaṇa, Kāyāvatāra, Kārohaṇa, or Kāyārohaṇa located in the Lāṭa or Bhṛgukaccha region. It also seems that Lakulīśa belonged to a Brāhmaṇa family and that he travelled at least as far as Ujjain to preach his doctrines.

Kāyāvarohaṇa is unanimously identified with the modern village of Kārvāṇ about 19 miles north of Baroda.[22] Ulkāpurī, Lakulīśa's birthplace in the *Kāravaṇa Māhātmya* version, is modern Avākhal in the same region. The legend of the sons or offspring of Ulūka alluded to in the Cintra *praśasti* is not mentioned in other sources. Ulūka may be somehow connected with Ulkāpurī.[23] The name Ulūka also appears in the purāṇic lists of the *avatāras* of Śiva who preceded Lakulīśa and is associated with Kaṇāda, the founder of the Vaiśeṣika system of philosophy. Fleet's attempt (*JRAS for* 1907, pp. 425–26) to connect the inscriptional Ulūka with the *Mahābhārata* story of Śakuni, the son of a king of Gandhara named Subala, and Śakuni's son Ulūka is not altogether convincing.

The name Lakulīśa—with its variants Nakulīśa, Lakuleśa, Lakulin, and Lakulīśvara—is derived from the word *lakula, laguḍa* or *lakuṭa* meaning 'club.' This is clearly shown in the expression 'whose hand was characterised by a club *(lakulopalakṣita-kara)*' from the Ēkliṅgjī inscription[24] and in the epithet Lakuṭa-pāṇi from the *Kāravaṇa Māhātmya*.[25] Lakulīśa is thus the Lord *(īśa)* who bears a club *(lakulin)*. A plain club—not the *khatvāṅga* suggested by Bühler (*EI*, I, 274)—is in fact the identifying mark of Lakulīśa sculptures. D.R. Bhandarkar quotes a verse from a work called *Viśvakarmāvatāra-vāstu-śāstra* which specifies that sculptures of Nakulīśa should show him seated in the *padmāsana*, with his penis erect, and with a citron *(mātuliṅga)* in his right hand and a club *(daṇḍa)* in his left.[26] Most known sculptures

---

were for a long time without sons in consequence of a curse laid upon *(his)* father, . . . settled *(adhyuvāsa)* at Kārohaṇa.'

[22]See Bühler, *EI*, I, 274. The name variants Kāyāvarohaṇa (descending of the body) and Kāyārohaṇa (ascending of the body) have opposite meanings but it is clear that both represent the same place. See Hara, 'Pāśupata kenkyū II . . .'

[23]See Bühler, *EI*, I, 274.

[24]D.R. Bhandarkar, *JBBRAS*, XXII, 166.

[25]*Gaṇakārikā*, p. 37.

[26]Archaeological Survey of India, *Annual Report*: 1906–7, p. 186.

depict him in this pose.[27]

Recently Daniel H.H. Ingalls has pointed out the striking resemblances between the religious practices of the Pāśupatas and those of the Cynics.[28] He notes that 'one cannot avoid the suspicion that the name Lakulīśa is derived both semantically and phonetically from the patron saint of Cynicism,' Hercules ('Ηρακλῆs), another man-god who wielded a famous club.[29] The physical resemblance, though not the phonetic one, between Lakulīśa and Hercules was recognised much earlier by Fleet (*JRAS for* 1907, p. 424). He suggests that the Indian god ancient Greek writers called Hercules might be Śiva and not Kṛṣṇa as scholars usually assume. Whether or not this is true in every case, he adds, 'we can hardly doubt that the club of Śiva as Lakulīśa is the club of Hēraklēs.' He also points out that in about the first century A.D. the figure of Hercules on the coins of the Kuṣāṇas was being replaced by Śiva. On one of the coins of Huviṣka Śiva is shown holding a club.

In spite of the similarities in the cult practices of the Pāśupatas and the Cynics and the resemblances between Lakulīśa and Hercules, Ingalls (*HTR*, LV, 296) is forced to 'doubt that the evidence permits one to speak of a genetic relation.' Thus he rejects the conclusion of F. Sayre, who, without being aware of the Pāśupata parallels, sought to derive Cynicism from India.[30] On the whole we are inclined to agree with Ingalls since, as he indicates (*HTR*, LV, 296), there is virtually no direct evidence of a foreign background within either cult. Nonetheless there are one or two circumstantial details not noted by either scholar which point to some sort of relationship.

Sayre has well documented the Greek evidence for the migration of Indian religion and philosophy to Greece but ignored the evidence for migration in the other direction. His statement (p. 45) that 'the Greeks were receptive of ideas from other nations while the Indians were not' has been amply refuted by R.A. Jairazbhoy.[31]

---

[27]See ibid., pp. 184–89. For a recent discussion of some variant sculpture poses, see R.C. Agrawala, 'Two Standing Lakulīśa Sculptures from Rajasthan,' *JOIB*, XIV, (1965), 388–91.

[28]'Cynics and Pāśupatas : The Seeking of Dishonor,' *Harvard Theological Review*, LV (1962), 281–98.

[29]Ibid., p. 296. See also pp. 292–93.

[30]*Diogenes of Sinope : A Study of Greek Cynicism*, pp. 38–47.

[31]*Foreign Influence in Ancient India*. For the impact of Greek culture on India see especially chapter five.

One must agree with Ingalls (*HTR,* LV, 296) that if there were any borrowings, 'there exists a stronger possibility that the Pāśupatas were influenced by the Cynics.' Sayre (pp. 39–40) stresses that Sinope, the home of Diogenes, the effective founder of the Cynic cult, was an entrepôt on the ancient trade route between India and Greece. This, we might add, was also true of the Broach or Bhṛgu-kaccha region where Lakulīśa taught. At the time of the author of the *Periplus* (first century A.D.), Barygaza (Broach) was the chief trading port in western India. It seems to have held this position from as early as Mauryan times.[32] Gautama or Akṣapāda, the traditional author of the *Nyāya-sūtra,* is also believed to have resided in this region, and one modern authority has claimed that his logic borrows extensively from Aristotle.[33] As we have seen, both the Pāśupatas and the Kālāmukhas are known to have had close connections with the Nyāya and Vaiśeṣika schools of philosophy. It is also perhaps significant that Kashmir, the region from which many Kālāmukhas migrated to the South, was on another important trade route to the West and had been exposed to Greek culture under the Indo-Greeks.

Much controversy has centered around the date of Lakulīśa. Fleet (*EI,* VI, 228) originally identified him with the Kālāmukha priest Lakulīśvara-paṇḍita who presided over the Pañcaliṅga temple in Belagāve in A.D. 1035. Fleet later abandoned this opinion (*JRAS for* 1907, p. 420) in the light of the discoveries of D.R. Bhandarkar. In view of the references to Lakulīśa in the *Vāyu Purāṇa,* a work usually assigned to the early Gupta period, Bhandarkar (*JBBRAS,* XXII, 157) placed him 'as early as the first century A.D. at the latest.' R.G. Bhandarkar dated the rise of the Pāśupata system mentioned in the *Mahābhārata,* and presumably Lakulīśa as well, 'about a century after the rise of the Pāñcarātra system, i.e. about the second century B.C.'[34] In 1931 D.R. Bhandarkar published the Mathura pillar inscription of Candragupta II (*EI,* XXI, 1–9). This records a donation by the Māheśvara teacher Uditācārya of two *liṅgas* named after his teacher, *Bhagavat* Kapila, and teacher's teacher, *Bhagavat* Upamita. Uditācārya is described as tenth in descent from *Bhagavat* Kuśika and fourth in descent

[32]See R. Thapar, *Aśoka and the Decline of the Mauryas,* pp. 80–83, 229, and also K.A.N. Sastri (ed.), *The Mauryas . . .,* pp. 307–308, 437–46.

[33]See S.C. Vidyabhusana, 'Influence of Aristotle on the Development of the Syllogism in Indian Logic,' *JRAS for* 1918, pp. 471, 486–88.

[34]*Vaiṣṇavism . . .,* p. 117.

from *Bhagavat* Parāśara. Bhandarkar identified this Kuśika with Kuśika, the disciple of Lakulīśa. Since the inscription dates from A.D. 380, he assigned Lakulīśa to the first half of the second century A.D.

This date has justifiably commanded acceptance by most scholars, but there are a few problems and uncertainties about it which many have unfairly ignored. First, neither the word Lakulīśa nor Pāśupata occurs in the record. It was issued as a request to future Māheśvaras to protect and honour the two *liṅgas*. Māheśvara is normally simply a generic term for those who worship Śiva. Sāyaṇa-Mādhava, for instance, applies it to the adherents of both the Pāśupata and Śaiva doctrines.[35] Śaṃkarācārya seems to use it for the Pāśupatas alone,[36] but Vācaspati Miśra and Bhāskarācārya divide the Māheśvaras into four distinct sects.[37] The only reliable means of identifying Uditācārya's sectarian allegiance are the inscription's concluding line of praise to Lord Daṇḍa, who bears the staff of Rudra *(Rudra-daṇḍa)*, and the Lakulīśa-like standing figure engraved on the pillar. These render it reasonable to assume that this is a Lakulīśa-Pāśupata record, but there is still a problem about the identification of *Bhagavat* Kuśika. As V.S. Pathak has noted,[38] there are at least two Kuśikas among the spiritual descendants of Lakulīśa. Kuśika I was his chief disciple and is mentioned in a number of epigraphic and literary sources.[39] Kuśika II is mentioned in Rājaśekhara's *Ṣaḍdarśana-samuccaya* (*c.* 1350),[40] in the commentary of Guṇaratna (*c.* 1375) on Haribhadra's work of the same name,[41] and indirectly in the Pāśupata *Ratnaṭīkā*

---

[35] *Sarvadarśana-saṃgraha*, ed. U.S. Sharma, pp. 297, 320.

[36] *Brahma-sūtra-bhāṣya* ii. 2. 37.

[37] Vācaspati Miśra, *Bhāmatī* on *Brahma-sūtra* ii. 2. 37. Bhāskarācārya, *Brahma-sūtra-bhāṣya* ii. 2. 37.

[38] *History of Śaiva Cults* . . ., p. 9.

[39] In addition to the reference in Kauṇḍinya's *bhāṣya* on *Pāśupata-sūtra* i. 1, Kuśika I is named in the Cintra *praśasti* (Bühler, *EI*, I, 273 and 281), the Ekliṅgji inscription (D.R. Bhandarkar, *JBBRAS*, XXII, 152 and 167), the Paldi inscription (Vyas, *EI*, XXX, 9 and 11), the A.D. 987 Udeypur inscription of Naravāhana (cited by Pathak, pp. 9–10), the *Vāyu Purāṇa*, xxiii. 223, the *Liṅga Purāṇa*, i. 24. 131, and, as Kuṇika, in the *Kūrma Purāṇa* i. 53 (p. 443). He also appears as Kauśika and Sauṣya-Kauśika in the works by Rājaśekhara and Guṇaratna cited below.

[40] Extract edited by Dalal in *Gaṇakārikā*, pp. 35–36.

[41] Extract edited and translated by D.R. Bhandarkar in Archaeological Survey of India, *Annual Report*: 1906–7, pp. 190–92. This is the same as the extract edited by Dalal in *Gaṇakārikā*, pp. 29–30 although the readings vary slightly.

commentary on the *Gaṇakārikā*.[42] Kuśika II is tenth in a list of seventeen or eighteen *tīrtheśas* or *tīrthakaras* beginning with Lakulīśa. Although the list is not in strict chronological order—Lakulīśa's four disciples appear to succeed one another—Kuśika II must have lived some time after Kuśika I. If the Mathura inscription refers to Kuśika II, then Lakulīśa's date must be pushed back about another one hundred years. A Kuśika III or IV is, of course, also by no means impossible.

Lakulīśa had three other important disciples besides Kuśika. The names of all four disciples are given, with variations, in the *Kūrma, Vāyu* and *Liṅga Purāṇas*,[43] by Rājaśekhara and Guṇaratna,[44] and in the Cintra *praśasti*. This last record describes Lakulīśa's arrival at Kārohaṇa in Lāṭa and then continues :

> His four pupils—Kuśika, Gārgya, Kauruṣa, and Maitreya—arrived *(avateruḥ)* at this place in order to (learn) the special conduct *(caryā)* of the Pāśupata vow. The fourfold lineage *(jāti)* of those ascetics then came into being (and) adorned (all) the land girded by the four oceans.[45]

The abbot *(sthānādhipa)* Kārttikarāśi, who became 'an ornament of the *gotra* of Gārgya,' is then introduced. He belongs to the early thirteenth century. By this time, it seems, the followers of the four disciples of Lakulīśa were organised into separate groups. From the evidence of the Mathura pillar inscription, this division probably goes back at least as far as the fourth century A.D.

No records survive of any priesthoods which traced their descent

---

[42]Ed. Dalal, p. 19. The *Ratnaṭīkā* merely mentions the *tīrthakaras* beginning with Lakulīśa and ending with Rāśīkara, who is the seventeenth *tīrtheśa* in the lists of Rājaśekhara and Guṇaratna. These two authors name eighteen *tīrtheśas* as follows (Rājaśekhara's reading is given first) : (1) Nakulīśa or Nakulin, (2) Kauśika or Sausya-Kauśika (= Kuśika I), (3) Gārgya, (4) Maitrya, (5) Kauruṣa or Akauruṣa, (6) Īśāna, (7) Pāragārgya, (8) Kapilāṇḍa, (9) Manuṣyaka, (10) Aparakuśika or Kuśika (= Kuśika II), (11) Atri, (12) Piṅgalākṣa or Piṅgala, (13) Puṣpaka or Puṣyaka, (14) Bṛhadācārya or Bṛhadārya, (15) Agasti, (16) Santāna, (17) Rāśīkara, and (18) Vidyāguru. Most of the names in Dalal's edition of the Guṇaratna extract coincide with those he gives for Rājaśekhara rather than with Bhandarkar's version of Guṇaratna.

[43]*Kūrma Purāṇa* i. 53 (Kuṇika, Garga, Mitraka, Ruru); *Vāyu Purāṇa* xxiii. 223 (Kuśika, Gargya, Mitraka, Ruṣṭa); and *Liṅga Purāṇa* i. 24. 131 (Kuśika, Garga, Mitra, Kauruṣya).

[44]See note 42 above.

[45]Ed. Bühler, *EI*, I, 281 (my translation).

from either Maitreya or Kauruṣa. R.G. Bhandarkar attempted to connect the third disciple, Kauruṣa, with the Kāruka-siddhāntins named as one of the four Śaivite sects by commentators on *Brahma-sūtra* ii. 2. 37.[46] These Kāruka-siddhāntins appear as Kāruṇika-siddhāntins in Vācaspati's (*c.* 850) *Bhāmatī*, as Kāṭhaka-siddhāntins in Bhāskarācārya's (*c.* 850) *Brahma-sūtra-bhāṣya,* and as Kālāmukhas in Rāmānuja's *Śrī-bhāṣya* and other commentaries on this *sūtra.*[47] We cannot accept Bhandarkar's theory. In the first place, the word *Kauruṣa* is not very close phonetically to Kāruka, Kāṭhaka or Kālāmukha. Secondly, there is no precedent or reason for connecting the names of any of the other three Śaivite sects—Pāśupata, Śaiva and Kāpālika—with the names of Lakulīśa's other three disciples. The followers of Kuśika and Gārgya both seem to have been Pāśupatas. Thirdly, if the Kāruka-, Kāruṇika- and Kāṭhaka-siddhāntins later became known as Kālāmukhas,[48] as appears likely, and if they were all descended from Kauruṣa, it is strange that no mention of this disciple is found in any Kālāmukha epigraph.

By the time of Harṣa-vardhana (606–647), and probably as early as Gupta times, there were Pāśupata temples in most parts of India.[49] The pilgrim Hsüan Tsang met or heard reports about 'ash-smeared (followers) of the outer way,' i.e. Pāśupata heretics,[50] at Jālandhara in East Panjab, Ahicchatrā in U.P., Malakuṭa in

---

[46]R.G. Bhandarkar, *Vaiṣṇavism* . . ., p. 121. We have not been able to trace any of these commentators, but Kāruka-siddhāntin is listed in M. Monier-Williams' *Sanskrit-English Dictionary.*

[47]See above, p. 1.

[48]There is a tenuous relation between Kāṭhaka-siddhānta and the *Pāśupata-sūtra.* Many of the *sūtras* in this work are based on the *Taittirīya Āraṇyaka* (see C. Chakravarti, *Pāśupatasūtra, IHQ,* XIX, 271). *Kāṭhaka* is a school of the *Black Yajur Veda,* the Veda to which the *Taittirīya Āraṇyaka* belongs.

[49]Although several small studies and surveys of the later history of the Pāśupata sect have been published, a complete work is still needed. The purāṇic material especially should be examined in more detail. Several of these works show definite Pāśupata influence. A preliminary study of this influençe on parts of the *Kūrma Purāṇa* has been made by R.C. Hazra, 'The Smṛti-chapters of the *Kūrma Purāṇa,*' *IHQ,* XI (1935), 265–86. The *Vāyu Purāṇa* has two chapters (xi and xiv) on Pāśupata-yoga. Their contents bear only a partial resemblance to the doctrines of the *Pāśupata-sūtra.*

[50]The characters are 塗灰外道 Hodous and Soothill, Beal, Watters, and others translate this as Pāśupata. There is no reason to quarrel with this interpretation, but it should be noted that the various Chinese phonetic equivalents of Pāśupata do not occur in Hsüan Tsang's text.

South India, Mālava, Khotan, Kapiśa (Nuristan) in East Afghanistan, Gandhara, Varanasi, and elsewhere.[51] Two early seventh century inscriptions registering grants to Pāśupata ascetics have been found as far afield as South-East Asia.[52] Important early references to Pāśupatas also occur in Mahendravarman's South Indian drama, *Mattavilāsa,* and, indirectly, in Varāhamihira's *Bṛhat-saṃhitā.*[53] Sanskrit writers from Bāṇa onwards mention them frequently, and from about the tenth century epigraphical references also become numerous. Post-Gupta sculptures of Lakulīśa have been found throughout India, although the center of gravity for both sculpture and epigraphy shifts to the South by about the end of the tenth century.[54]

No texts on the ritual regimen and religious philosophy inculcated by the Kālāmukhas have so far been discovered. There are, however, several works composed by or about the Pāśupatas. In the absence of contrary evidence we must assume that the Kālāmukhas maintained the Pāśupata regimen and theology more or less intact.

The first Sanskrit sources on the Pāśupata system to be noticed by modern scholars were the brief passages in the *Brahma-sūtra* commentaries, the 'Pāśupata vow' of the *Atharvaśiras Upaniṣad,*[55] and the 'Nakulīśa-Pāśupata-darśana' chapter of Sāyaṇa-Mādhava's *Sarvadarśana-samgraha.* Although Sāyaṇa-Mādhava wrote his account in the fourteenth century, it is still the best short summary of the subject. It was translated into English by A.E. Gough in 1882, into French by S. Lévi in 1889, into German by P. Deussen in 1908, and partly paraphrased again in English by R.G. Bhandarkar in 1913.[56] All these translations suffered from an inadequate text and an inability to understand some of the technical terminology. In 1920 C.D. Dalal published the first actual Pāśupata work, the *Gaṇakārikā* with the *Ratnaṭīkā* commentary now attributed to Bhāsarvajña. In 1940 R.A. Sastri published the newly discovered *Pāśupata-sūtra* with Kauṇḍinya's *Pañcārtha-bhāṣya.*[57]

---

[51]S. Beal (trans.), *Chinese Accounts of India,* pp. 118, 163, 209, 228, 291, 433, 453, 461, and 464–67.

[52]K. Bhattacharya, *Journal asiatique,* CCXLIII (1955), 479–81.

[53]See Banerjea, *Development* . . ., pp. 230–31.

[54]For an attempted explanation of this migration see above, pp. 108–109.

[55]Trans. R.G. Bhandarkar, *Vaiṣṇavism* . . ., p. 112. The whole Upaniṣad is translated by T.R.S. Ayyangar in *Śaiva Upaniṣads,* pp. 28–53.

[56]See M. Hara (trans.), 'Nakulīśa-Pāśupata-darśanam,' *IIJ,* II (1958), 8–9.

[57]A list of variant readings for some of the *sūtras* is given by C. Chakravarti, *'Pāśupatasūtra,' IHQ,* XIX, 270–71.

Since 1940 several scholars have attempted to re-evaluate the Pāśupata system in the light of the new evidence. The most important work is the critical translation of Sāyaṇa-Madhava's 'Nakulīśa-Pāśupata-darśana' chapter by M. Hara. (*IIJ,* II, 8–32). D.H.H. Ingalls has translated most of text and commentary of the third chapter of the *Pāśupata-sūtra.*[58] F.A. Schultz has published a valuable study of Pāśupata theology[59] and useful general surveys have been written by S.N. Dasgupta,[60] K.K. Handiqui (pp. 199–204, 234–44), and K.C. Pandey.[61]

The theology and ritual regimen or cult of the Pāśupatas are rightly regarded by Schultz and Ingalls as basically separate. Since the oldest extant and possibly original work of the sect, the *Pāśupata-sūtra,* is devoted almost exclusively to ritual, it is likely that philosophy was a secondary development. Already in the *Pañcārtha-bhāṣya,* however, Pāśupata philosophy is presented in a systematic form. Since the cult seems older we will outline its basic features first.

The ritual prescriptions of the *sūtras* do not have a very rigid arrangement or order. Kauṇḍinya and later writers attempted to remedy this situation and also to incorporate both theology and ritual into a single theoretical scheme. Two rather pedantic systems of classification were evolved—the first best represented by Kauṇḍinya and the second by the *Gaṇakārikā.*

Kauṇḍinya divides Pāśupata doctrine into five Principal Topics *(pañcārthas)* : Effect *(kārya),* Cause *(kāraṇa),* Union *(yoga),* Observance *(vidhi)* and End of Sorrow *(duḥkhānta).*[62] These five Topics are described as the central feature of Pāśupata (or Māheśvara) doctrine in the comments of Śaṃkarācārya, Vācaspati Miśra and Bhāskarācārya on *Brahma-sūtra* ii. 2. 37. Most of what may be called the Pāśupata cult falls under the heading of Observance.

The system of classification set out in the *Gaṇakārikā* is somewhat more complicated. In eight short mnemonic verses it divides Pāśupata doctrine into nine primary Groups *(gaṇas)*—eight Pentads *(pañcakas)* and one Group of Three. The third Pentad

---

[58] *HTR,* LV, 285–91. M. Hara is preparing a translation of the entire work.

[59] *Die philosophisch theologischen Lehren des Pāśupata-Systems nach dem Pañcārthabhāṣya und der Ratnaṭīkā.* See also M. Hara's review in *IIJ,* IV (1960), 165–70.

[60] In his *A History of Indian Philosophy,* V, 1–10, 130–49.

[61] *Bhāskarī,* Vol. III.

[62] *Pañcārtha-bhāṣya* on *Pāśupata-sūtra* i. 1. (p. 6).

consists of the five Stages *(avasthās)* in the initiate's spiritual development. These are: (1) the Marked *(vyakta)*, (2) the Unmarked *(avyakta)*, (3) Victory *(jaya)*, (4) Cutting *(cheda)*, and (5) Cessation *(niṣṭhā)*.[63] In the Marked Stage the Aspirant *(sādhaka)* adopts the marks of the sect and performs certain vows. He 'bathes' himself and lies down in ashes from a funeral pyre. He wears flowers taken from an image of Śiva. He lives in a temple and performs there six Acts of Worship *(upahāra)*: laughing, dancing, singing, uttering the auspicious sound *huḍuk* (or *ḍumḍum*), offering homage *(namaskāra)*, and pious incantation *(japya)*. All this is to be done only in the company of other Pāśupatas. In the Unmarked Stage the Aspirant leaves the temple, abandons the identifying marks of his sect, and actively encourages censure from the populace by means of several peculiar practices, notably the six so-called Doors *(dvāras)* : *krāthana* (snoring or acting as if asleep when one is not), *spandana* (shaking one's limbs as if afflicted by 'wind-disease'),[64] *mandana* (walking as if crippled), *śṛṅgāraṇa* (making amorous gestures in the presence of women), *avitatkaraṇa* (acting as if devoid of judgement), and *avitadbhāsaṇa* (uttering senseless or contradictory words). The third, Victory Stage is characterised by victory over the senses. In the fourth, Cutting Stage, the Aspirant presumably destroys all his remaining worldly ties.[65] The final, Cessation Stage marks the absolute cessation of all exertion, mental or physical, religious or profane.

Each of the five Stages is associated with a particular Place *(deśa)*, Strength *(bala)*, Impurity *(mala)*, Purification *(viśuddhi)*, Procedure *(upāya)*, Attainment *(lābha)*, and Aspect of Initiation *(dīkṣākārin)*. These form the remaining seven Pentads. The relationship of all these items is best seen in the table on next page.

The last of the nine Groups is called Means of Livelihood *(vṛtti)*. It is threefold: Alms *(bhaikṣya)*, Left-over Food *(utsṛṣṭa)*, and Food Acquired by Chance *(yathālabdha)*. According to the

---

[63]Most of the verses of the *Gaṇakārikā* are quoted by Sāyaṇa-Mādhava in the 'Nakulīśa-Pāśupata-darśana' chapter of the *Sarvadarśana-saṃgraha*. Our translations of these technical terms closely follow those given by Hara in his translation of the latter work (*IIJ*, II, 12–32). Hara also gives elaborate cross references to the other Pāśupata works.

[64]*vāyu-abhibhūta*. The wind humour is the cause of a great number of disorders according to Hindu medical works. See J. Filliozat, *The Classical Doctrine of Indian Medicine*, pp. 61–79, 196–228.

[65]The *Ratnaṭīkā* does not explain this term very clearly.

Stage	Marked	Unmarked	Victory	Cutting	Cessation
Place	With the Guru	Among Men *(jana)*	Cave *(guhā-deśa)*	Cemetery *(śmaśāna)*	With Rudra
Strength	Devotion to the Guru *(Guru-bhakti)*	Tranquility of Mind *(Mati-prasāda)*	Victory over Opposites *(dvandva-jaya)*	Merit *(dharma)*	Constant Caution *(apramāda)*
Impurity	False Knowledge *(mithyā-jñāna)*	Demerit *(adharma)*	Cause of Attachment *(sakti-hetu)*	Deviation *(cyuti)*	Creaturehood *(paśutva)*
Purification	Removal of Ignorance *(ajñāna-hāni)*	Removal of Demerit	Removal of Attachment Causes	Removal of Deviation	Removal of Creaturehood
Procedure	Impregnation with Doctrine *(vāsa)*[66]	Prescribed Conduct *(caryā)*	Pious Incantation and Meditation *(japa* and *dhyāna)*	Constant Recollection of Rudra *(sadā Rudra-smṛti)*	Grace *(prasāda)*
Attainment	Knowledge *(jñāna)*	Penance *(tapas)*	Constant Association with God *(deva-nityatva)*[67]	Fixedness (in Rudra) *(sthiti)*	Magical Perfection *(siddhi)*
Aspect of Initiation	Material *(dravya)*	Time *(kāla)*	Ritual *(kriyā)*	Divine Image *(mūrti)*	Guru

Ratnaṭīkā these are the only sources of nourishment approved by the *āgamas*.

The *Ratnaṭīkā* attempts to combine this system of classification with the five Principal Topics of Kauṇḍinya by including these Topics under the heading of Knowledge, the first of the five Attainments. Since the Principal Topic of Observance *(vidhi)* has little to do with knowledge, however, it is mainly subsumed under the Procedure of the Unmarked Stage, Prescribed Conduct *(caryā)*.[68]

The most important of the five Stages are the first two, the Marked and the Unmarked. The other three seem to denote mental states as much as courses of behaviour. The most notable feature of the Marked Stage is the 'six-limbed' Act of Worship *(upahāra)*: laughing, dancing, singing, and so forth. As we have seen, the

[66] The meaning and reading of this term is not certain. See Hara, *IIJ*, II, 15–16, and S.N. Dasgupta, *A History* . . ., V, 148.

[67] See M. Hara, 'A Note on the Sanskrit Word *Ní-tya-*,' *JAOS*, LXXIX (1959), 90–96.

[68] See *Gaṇakārikā*, pp. 9–15, 17–19.

Kālāmukha priest Vāmaśakti from the Kedāreśvara temple in Belagāve was known as 'the most skilled in the world in daily performing pleasant dances.'[69] This might well be a reference to the Pāśupata Act of Worship. It should also be recalled that several other Kālāmukha priests are described as experts in drama and music.

The curious custom of courting dishonour by disreputable behaviour during the Unmarked Stage is the most distinctive feature of the Pūśapata cult. It is described in some detail in the third chapter of the *Pāśupata-sūtra* and in Kauṇḍinya's commentary thereon.[70] According to these two sources the chief rationale for this behaviour is the transfer of good and bad *karman*. The *sūtras* explain it thus : 'Because of the censure of others, he gives his (accumulated) demerit (*pāpa* or *adharma*) to them, and he takes the (accumulated) merit *(sukṛta* or *dharma)* from them.'[71] Without the censure of others these actions would result simply in the increase of the performer's own demerit.[72] The idea of exchanging good and bad *karman,* as Ingalls notes (*HTR,* LV, 293) is common in classical Sanskrit literature. The idea of intentionally courting dishonour for this purpose, however, is very unusual and difficult to explain.

Ingalls (*HTR,* LV, 295–98) seeks the origin of some of the ascetics' peculiar behaviour in the beast-vows mentioned by the *Jaiminiya-Brāhmaṇa* and later Sanskrit literature and in other techniques of spiritual possession practised by shamans in primitive societies throughout the world. Without wishing to discard Ingalls' hypothesis entirely, we believe that most of the psychological and historical foundation for these practices can be found, without going so far afield, in the dominant asceticism complex of Indian religion itself.

Courting the censure of one's fellow humans is, after all, an efficient means of cutting oneself off from them, of achieving isolation and worldly detachment. Under various names this state of detachment is an essential ingredient of Jainism, Buddhism and Upaniṣadic Hinduism. As we have seen, Removal of Attachment Causes *(saṅgakara-hāni)* is one of the five Purifications in

[69]See above, p. 128.

[70]Most of this chapter and its commentary have been translated by Ingalls, *HTR,* LV, 285–91.

[71]*Pāśupata-sūtra* iii. 7, 8 and 9.

[72]Kauṇḍinya's *Pañcārtha-bhāṣya* on *sūtra* iii. 7.

Pāśupata doctrine. Kauṇḍinya himself makes it clear that the cultivation of detachment as much as the transfer of merit is the motive behind the Pāśupata's actions. Under *sūtra* iii. 3, 'Dishonored *(avamataḥ)*,' for instance, he quotes a verse which declares: 'For he who is despised lies happy, freed of all attachment.'[73] His comments on *sūtra* iii. 11 are equally explicit. The *sūtra* declares: 'He should go about like an outcaste *(preta)*.'[74] Kauṇḍinya comments:

> He should appear as though mad, like a pauper, his body covered with filth, letting his beard, nails and hair grow long, without any bodily care. Hereby he becomes cut off from the respectable castes and conditions of men, *and the power of passionless detachment is produced.*[75]

This type of idea has no place in the world of the shaman. His babblings, animal noises and so forth do cut him off from his fellow men, but both he and they regard this behaviour as a sign of his superior spiritual power. However much the shaman controls his trance, he believes that he is in communication with the spiritual world. The Pāśupata's mad behaviour, on the other hand, is completely feigned and wins only contempt from ordinary men. It is possible that the ultimate source of some of his practices may be found in shamanism, but their psychological basis has changed completely. For this reason we prefer to consider the Pāśupata's courting of dishonour mainly as an extension, albeit a highly original one, of the search for worldly detachment through ascetic penance.[76]

---

[73]Trans. Ingalls, *HTR,* LV, 286.

[74]Trans. ibid., p. 289. The usual meaning of *preta* is, of course 'dead person' or 'ghost.' This may well have been the meaning intended by the *sūtra* although Kauṇḍinya seems to interpret it as 'outcaste.'

[75]Trans. ibid., except for the passage put into italics. Ingalls translation at this point seems significantly misleading. The whole of the Sanskrit sentence reads: 'ato varṇāśrama-vyucchedo vairāgyotsāhaś ca jāyate.' Ingalls renders the italicised passage as 'and gives rise to disgust.' In the present context *vairāgya* seems more likely to denote the positive quality of 'freedom from all worldly desires.' This is the meaning used by Kauṇḍinya elsewhere in his commentary. Under *sūtra* i. 42, for instance, we find the compound *dharma-jñāna-vairāgyaiśvaryādharmājñānā-vairāgyānaiśvaryānām*. 'Freedom from all worldly desires' would naturally arise in the worshipper, not in those who see him.

[76]The acceptance, if not the courting, of dishonour is prescribed for Jain ascetics

One other point about the cult of the Pāśupatas should also be noted. This is the great emphasis placed by Kauṇḍinya, and to a lesser extent by the *Ratnaṭīkā,* on the ten *yamas* and *niyamas* or 'major and minor restraints.' Kauṇḍinya defines the five *yamas* as non-injury *(ahiṃsā),* celibacy *(brahmacarya),* truthfulness *(satya),* non-trade *(asaṃvyavahāra),* and non-theft *(asteya).* He defines the *niyamas* as non-anger *(akrodha),* attentiveness to the teacher *(guru-śuśrūṣā),* purity *(śauca),* abstemious diet *(āhāra-lāghava),* and constant caution *(apramāda).*[77] Other Sanskrit works define these *yamas* and *niyamas* somewhat differently.[78] They form the first two of five 'limbs' of Yoga named in *Yoga-sūtra* ii. 29[79] and invariably head the similar lists of yogic virtues repeatedly attributed to Kālāmukha ascetics in epigraphy. The five *yamas* also appear to be associated with the epithet Mahāvratin as it is applied to Kālāmukha ascetics. According to *Yoga-sūtra* ii. 31, when the five *yamas* are maintained under all circumstances—without regard for caste, place, time, or occasion—they are called the Mahāvrata.[80]

The theology of the Pāśupatas is a large and rather complicated subject which we do not feel qualified to discuss in detail.[81] Its basic outlines are summed up in the five Principal Topics (minus the third, Observance, which denotes the cult). The first Topic is Effect *(kārya).* This is divided into three categories : (1) Cognition *(vidyā)* including various types of conscious and unconscious mental activity; (2) World and Body Parts *(kalā)* including the physical elements and human organs, senses and mental faculties; and (3) the Individual Soul *(paśu).* All Effect is said to be dependent *(asvatantra).*

---

in the following passage from the *Ācārāṅga-sūtra* (trans. H. Jacobi, iv. 16. 2–3): 'A mendicant, living thus, self-controlled towards the eternal (world of living beings), the matchless sage, who collects his alms, is insulted with words by the people assailing him, like an elephant in battle with arrows. Despised by such-like people, the wise man, with undisturbed mind, sustains their words and blows, as a rock is not shaken by the wind.'

77 *Pañcārtha-bhāṣya* on *Pāśupata-sūtra* i. 9 (pp. 16–33).

78 See P.V. Kane, *HDS,* V, Part II, 1418–24.

79 'yama-niyamāsana-prāṇāyāma-pratyāhāra-dhāraṇā-dhyāna-samādhayoṣṭāv aṅgāni.' See also above, p. 111.

80 'ahiṃsā-satyāsteya-brahmacaryāparigrahā yamāḥ/ jāti-deśa-kāla-samayānavacchinnāḥ sārva-bhaumāḥ mahāvratam.' *Yoga-sūtra* ii. 30–31. See also above, p. 81.

81 The reader is referred especially to the work of F.A. Schultz, to Hara's translation of the 'Nakulīśa-Pāśupata-darśana' chapter of Sayana-Madhava's *Sarvadarśana-saṃgraha,* and to S.N. Dasgupta's, *A History . . .,* Vol. V.

The second Topic is Cause *(kāraṇa)*. This is defined quite simply as God or Īśvara. The Pāśupata faith is thoroughly theistic and consequently God functions as the linchpin of its metaphysical system. He is described as the creator, destroyer and supporter of the universe.[82] He has two major aspects—one which is immanent and manifold *(sakala)* and one which is transcendent and formless *(niṣkala)*. Both are characterised by unlimited Power of Knowledge *(jñāna-śakti)* and Power of Action *(kriyā-śakti)*.[83] Speech is incapable of expressing his formless aspect.[84] In his manifold aspect, however, he is called by various names in accordance with his several attributes and functions such as *patitva, sattva, ādyatva, ajātatva,* and so forth.[85] In this aspect he is also said to pervade all Effect (defined as the twenty-five categories or *tattvas* of Sāṃkhya).[86]

This doctrine of God as Cause must be very similar to the Īśvara-kartṛ-vāda taught by the eleventh century Kālāmukha priest Bonteyamuni of Hoṃbaḷ. Although little is known about his doctrine apart from its name, one of the stories describing the miracles he performed during his travels provides the additional information that the *Kartṛ* of his doctrine also had a formless aspect. At a great debate his opponents 'questioned him how the *Kartṛ* he defended could be formless.' In reply 'he stood invisible (became formless) for a while and made them speechless . . .'[87]

One of the most distinctive features of Pāśupata doctrine as propounded by Kauṇḍinya and the *Ratnaṭīkā* is the belief in God's absolute independence *(svatantratā)*.[88] In practical terms this independence means that God acts without regard for human *karman (karmādinirapekṣa)*. God's will is thereby placed over and above even the moral order *(dharma)*. Sāyaṇa-Mādhava contrasts this view with that of the Māheśvaras who follow the Śaiva-darśana. They reject this Pāśupata doctrine 'because it is blemished by the faults of cruelty and injustice' and hold that 'the Supreme Lord, the Cause, (acts) in conformity with (human) *karman,* etc.'[89] In other words, the Śaiva-darśana God cannot

---

[82] *Ratnaṭīkā* in *Gaṇakārikā,* p. 11.

[83] Kauṇḍinya on *Pāśupata-sūtra* ii. 27 and v. 27.

[84] Ibid., v. 27. See also *Ratnaṭīkā* in *Gaṇakārikā,* p. 11.

[85] *Ratnaṭīkā* in *Gaṇakārikā,* p. 11.

[86] Kauṇḍinya on *Pāśupata-sūtra* ii. 5.

[87] Ed. Desai, *SII,* XV, no. 73. Translated for us by H.S. Biligiri. See also above.

[88] Kauṇḍinya on *Pāśupata-sūtra* v. 47 and *Gaṇakārikā,* p. 15.

[89] 'karmādisāpekṣaḥ parameśvaraḥ kāraṇam iti.' *Sarvadarśana-saṃgraha,* p. 320.

act arbitrarily but must reward good deeds and punish evil ones. H. Jacobi points out that the Nyāya logician Uddyotakara (*c.* 620), who calls himself a Pāśupatācārya, adopts the Śaiva-darśana point of view on this point.[90] This shows that at least one important doctrinal split had occurred in the Pāśupata sect by the seventh century. This is by no means surprising since the radical view of Kauṇḍinya and the *Ratnaṭīkā* strikes at the heart of nearly all Indian ethical systems, the theory of *karman*. Sāyaṇa-Mādhava allows the Pāśupatas a rebuttal to the charge that their doctrine of God as an independent Cause would lead to a situation in which 'human deeds *(karma)* would produce no result and all effects would be produced at the same time,'[91] but their reply, at least as Sāyaṇa-Mādhava presents it, is not altogether clear or convincing. It does appear, however, that they were forced to temper this doctrine somewhat, although not to such a degree that it is possible to agree with Jacobi (p. 53) that the difference between Uddyotakara and Lakulīśa *(sic)* is only apparent.

Salvation in Pāśupata doctrine is the state called End of Sorrow *(duḥkhānta)*, the last of the five Principal Topics. As is to be expected in such an uncompromisingly theistic system, it is achieved only by the grace of God. *Sūtra* v. 40 declares : 'He who has constant caution attains the end of sorrows through the grace of God.'[92] Preliminary to this final liberation, however, is Yoga, the fourth Topic, which Kauṇḍinya repeatedly defines as 'the union of the *ātman* and Īśvara.'[93] The soul does not become absorbed or dissolved in Īśvara or Brahman as in monistic Vedānta, but remains inseparably tied to God in the state the *sūtras* call *Rudra-sāyujya*.[94]

The designation of Salvation as End of Sorrow has a rather negative ring. Bhāskarācārya claims that the Pāśupatas, Vaiśeṣikas, Naiyāyikas, and Kāpālikas all hold End of Sorrow and *mokṣa* to be identical. In this condition, he adds, the *ātmans* are without attributes and resemble only stones.[95] Much the same claim is made by Yāmunācārya.[96] This does not seem to be any more true for the Pāśupatas than for the Kāpālikas. It is certainly not the

[90]*Die Entwicklung der Gottesidee bei den Indern*, p. 53.

[91]Trans. Hara, *IIJ*, II, 31.

[92]'apramādī gacched duḥkhānām antam īśa-prasādāt.'

[93]See, for instance, his commentary on *sūtras* i. 1 (p. 6), i. 20, and v. 2.

[94]*Pāśupata-sūtra* v. 33.

[95]*Brahma-sūtra-bhāṣya* ii. 2. 37.

[96]See Handiqui, p. 235.

view of Kauṇḍinya or the author of the *Ratnaṭīkā*. The latter work distinguishes between two types of End of Sorrow—the Impersonal *(anātmaka)* and the Personal *(sātmaka)*. Impersonal End of Sorrow does resemble the state referred to by Bhāskara and Yāmuna. It is characterised only by the absolute extirpation of all sorrows. Personal End of Sorrow, however, is a state of 'Perfection *(siddhi)* characterized by the Power of Lordship *(aiśvarya)* of Maheśvara.'[97] This Perfection consists of Power of Knowledge or Perception *(jñāna-* or *dṛk-śakti)* and Power of Action *(kriyā-śakti)*. These two are also divided into a number of specific superhuman abilities. The Power of Knowledge is fivefold and comprises extraordinary powers of seeing, hearing, thinking, discrimination, and omniscience. Power of Action is threefold and comprises the ability to act with the swiftness of the mind *(manojavitva)*, the ability to assume forms at will *(kāmarūpitva)* and the ability to act without physical organs *(vikaraṇadharmitva)*. In addition, the *ātman* who has attained Personal End of Sorrow gains ten other Perfection characteristics including such qualities as fearlessness, agelessness, deathlessness, and lordship *(patitva)*.[98] He possesses, in short, nearly all the attributes of Īśvara himself.

[97] *Ratnaṭīkā* in *Gaṇakārikā*, pp. 9–10.

[98] Ibid. See also Sāyaṇa-Mādhava's 'Nakulīśa-Pāśupata-darśana,' trans. Hara, *IIJ*, II, 19–21.

BIBLIOGRAPHY

Aiyangar, S. Krishnaswami. *Maṇimekhalai in its Historical Setting*. London: Luzac and Co., 1927.

Agrawala, R.C. 'Two Standing Lakulīśa Sculptures from Rajastan,' *JOIB,* XIV (1965), 388–91.

Agrawala, Vasudeva S. *Vāmana Purāṇa—A Study*. Varanasi: Prithivi Prakashan, 1964.

Ānandagiri. *Śamkara-vijaya*. Ed. J. Tarkapanchānana. ('Bibliotheca Indica.') Calcutta: Baptist Mission Press, 1968.

Ānandarāyamakhin. *Jīvānanda*. Ed. M. Duraiswami Aiyangar. ('Adyar Library Series,' No. 59). Adyar: 1947.

———. *Vidyāpariṇayana*. Ed. Śivadatta and K.P. Parab. 2nd ed. ('Kāvyamālā,' No. 39) Bombay: Nirṇaya Sāgar Press, 1930.

Annigeri, A.M. (ed.) *Karnatak Inscriptions,* Vol. IV. Dharwar: Kannada Research Institute, 1961.

Āpastambīya Dharmasūtra. With Haradatta's *Ujjvala* commentary. Ed. Mahādeva Śāstrī and K. Raṅgāchārya. Mysore: Government Press, 1898.

Āpastambīya Dharmasūtra. Trans. G. Bühler. Vol. II of *SBE*. Oxford: The Clarendon Press, 1879.

Atharvaśiras Upanisad. Ed. G.S. Murti and trans. T.R.S. Ayyangar in their *Śaiva Upaniṣads*. Madras: Adyar Library, 1953.

Atiya, A.S. *Crusade, Commerce and Culture*. Bloomington, Ind.: University Press, 1962.

Bādarāyaṇa. *Brahma-sūtra*. See Bhāskarācārya, Rāmānuja, Śaṃkarācārya, and Vācaspati Miśra.

Balfour, Henry. 'The Life History of An Aghorī Fakir,' *Journal of the Anthropological Institute* [London], XXVI (1897), 340–57.

Bāṇa. *Harṣa-carita*. Ed. P.V. Kane. Two parts in one volume. 2nd ed. Delhi: Motilal Banarsidass, 1965.

———. *Harṣa-carita*. Trans. E.B. Cowell and F.W. Thomas. Photo reprint of 1897 edition. Delhi: Motilal Banarsidass, 1961.

———. *Kādambarī*. 'Pūrvabhāga.' Ed. P.V. Kane. 2 parts. Bombay: by the editor, 1920–21.

———. *Kādambarī*. 'Uttarabhāga.' Ed. P.V. Kane. Bombay: Nirṇaya Sāgar Press, 1913.

———. *Kādambarī*. Trans. C.M. Ridding. London: Royal Asiatic Society, 1896.

Banerjea, Jitendra Nath. *Development of Hindu Iconography*. Calcutta: University of Calcutta, 1956.

———. 'Lakulīśa—the Founder or the Systematiser of the Pāśupata Order,' Indian History Congress, *Proceedings of the Fourteenth Session, Jaipur* (1951), pp. 32–6.

Bārhaspati-sūtra. Ed. and trans. F.W. Thomas. Lahore: Moti Lal Banarsi Dass, 1921.

Barnett, Lionel David (ed. and trans.). 'Inscriptions at Yewur,' *EI,* XII, 268–98 and 329–40.

———. (ed. and trans.). 'Inscriptions of Huli,' *EI*, XVIII (1925–26), 170–218.

———. (ed. and trans.). 'Inscriptions of Sudi,' *EI*, XV (1919–20), 73–112.

———. (ed. and trans.). 'Three Inscriptions of Lakshmeshwar,' *EI*, XVI (1921–2), 31–52.

———. (ed. and trans.). 'Two Inscriptions from Kurgod,' *EI*, XIV, 265–84.

———. (ed. and trans.). 'Two Inscriptions from Ron, of Śaka 944 and 1102,' *EI*, XIX, 222–36.

Barrow, H.W. 'On Aghorīs and Aghorapanthīs,' *JAnSB*, III (1893), 197–251.

Basava Purāṇa. Trans. G. Würth in *JBBRAS*, VIII (1864–6), 65–97.

Basham, A.L. *History and Doctrines of the Ājivikas: A Vanished Indian Religion*. London: Luzac & Co., 1951.

———. *The Wonder That Was India*. London: Sidgwick and Jackson, 1954.

Baudhāyana Dharmaśāstra. Trans. G. Bühler. Vol. XIV of *SBE*. Oxford: The Clarendon Press, 1882.

Beal, Samuel (trans.). *Chinese Accounts of India*. 4 vols. New edition. Calcutta: Susil Gupta (India) Ltd., 1957–8. (First published in 1883.)

Bhandarkar, D.R. (ed.) 'An Ekliṅgjī Stone Inscription and the Origin and History of the Lakulīśa Sect,' *JBBRAS*, XXII (1904–7), 151–65.

———. 'Lakulīśa,' Archaeological Survey of India, *Annual Report*: 1906–7, pp. 179–92.

———. (ed. and trans.). 'Mathura Pillar Inscription of Chandragupta II: G.E. 61,' *EI*, XXI (1931–2), 1–9.

———. (ed.). 'Some Published Inscriptions Reconsidered,' *IA*, XLII (1913), 57–64.

Bhandarkar, R.G. *Early History of the Dekkan: Down to the Mahomedan Conquest*. Reproduced from the *Bombay Gazetteer*, Vol. I, Part II (1896). Calcutta: Susil Gupta (India) Private Ltd., 1957.

———. (ed. and trans.). 'A Revised Transcript and Translation of a Chālukya Copper-plate Grant,' *JBBRAS*, XIV (1878–80), 16–28.

———. *Vaisṇavism, Śaivism and Minor Religious Systems*. Photo reprint of 1913 edition. Varanasi: Indological Book House, [1965].

Bharati, Agehananda. *The Ochre Robe*. London: G. Allen and Unwin, 1961.

———. *The Tantric Tradition*. London: Rider and Co., 1965.

Bhāsarvajña. See *Gaṇakārikā*.

Bhāskarācārya. *Brahma-sūtra-bhāṣya*. Ed. Vindhyeśvarī Prasāda Dvivedin. ('Chowkhambā Saṅskrit Series,' Nos. 70, 185 and 209.) Benares: Vidya Vilas Press, 1915.

Bhattacharya, Kamaleswar. 'La Secte des Pāçupata dans l'ancien Cambodge,' *Journal asiatique* [Paris], CCXLIII (1955), 497–90.

Bhavabhūti. *Mālatī-Mādhava*. With Jagaddhara's commentary. Ed. R.G. Bhandarkar. Bombay: Government Central Book Depot, 1905.

———. *Mālatī-Mādhava*. Ed. and trans. C.R. Devadhar and N.G. Suru. Poona: By the editors, 1935.

al-Bīrūnī. *Tarīkh al-Hind*. Trans. Edward Sachau as *Alberuni's India*. Two volumes in one. New edition. London: Kegan Paul, Trench, Trübner & Co. Ltd., 1910. (First published in 1888.)

Bloomfield, Maurice, 'On False Ascetics and Nuns in Hindu Fiction,' *JAOS*, XLIV (1924), 202–42.

Böhtlingk, O., and Roth, R. *Sanskrit Wörterbuch*. 7 vols. St. Petersburg: 1855–75.

Brahmāṇḍa Purāṇa. Bombay: Veṅkaṭeśvara Press, 1913.

Briggs, George Weston. *Gorakhnāth and Kānphaṭā Yogīs*. Calcutta: Y.M.C.A. Publishing House, 1938.

Brown, Norman O. *Hermes the Thief*. Madison : University of Wisconsin Press, 1947.
Bühler, G. (ed. and trans.). 'The Cintra Praśasti of the Reign of Sarangadeva,' *EI*, I (1888), 271–87.
Caṇḍapāla. See Trivikrama-bhaṭṭa.
Canna-Basava Purāṇa. Trans. G. Würth in *JBBRAS*, VIII (1864–6), 98–221.
Carstairs, George Morrison. *The Twice Born*. London : Hogarth Press, 1957.
Chakravarti, Chintaharan, 'The Soma or Sauma Sect of the Śaivas,' *IHQ*, VIII (1932), 221–3.
———. *Tantras : Studies on their Religion and Literature*. Calcutta : Punthi Pustak, 1963.
Chandra, Pramod. 'The Kaula-Kāpālika Cults at Khajurāho,' *Lalit Kalā*, Nos. 1–2 (1955–56), pp. 98–107.
Chattopadhyāya, Sudhakar. *The Evolution of Theistic Sects in Ancient India*. Calcutta : Progressive Publishers, 1962.
Chaudhuri, Nirad C. *The Continent of Circe*. London : Chatto and Windus, 1965.
Choudhary, Radhakrishna, 'Heretical Sects in the Purāṇas,' *ABORI*, XXXVII (1956), 234–57.
Cousens, Henry. *The Chālukyan Architecture of the Kanarese Districts*. ('Archaeological Survey of India,' New Imperial Series, Vol. XLII.) Calcutta : Government of India, Central Publication Branch, 1926.
Crooke, William. 'Aghorī,' *ERE*, I, 210–13.
Cunningham, A. *Report of a Tour in the Punjab in* 1878–79. ('Archaeological Survey of India Reports,' Old Series, Vol. XIV.) Calcutta : Office of Superintendant of Government Printing, 1882.
Daṇḍin. *Daśakumāra-carita*. Ed. and trans. V. Satakopan, V. Anantacharya, and N. Bhaktavatsalam. Madras : V. Ramaswamy Sastrulu and Sons, 1963.
Dasgupta, Shashi Bhusan. *An Introduction to Tāntric Buddhism*. 2d ed. Calcutta : University of Calcutta, 1958.
———. *Obscure Religious Cults*. 2d ed. Calcutta : Firma K.L. Mukhopadhay, 1962.
Dasgupta, Surendranatha. *A History of Indian Philosophy*. 5 vols. Cambridge : Cambridge University Press, 1922–55.
Desai, P.B. (ed.) *South Indian Inscriptions*, Vol. XV. Madras : Government Press, 1964.
Devaṇṇa Bhaṭṭa. *Smṛticandrikā*. Ed. L. Srinivasacharya. 6 vols. Mysore : Government Press, 1914–21.
Devendra Gaṇī. Commentary on *Uttarādhyayana*. Trans. J.J. Meyer in his *Hindu Tales*. London : Luzac & Co., 1909.
Dhanapatisūri. See Mādhavācārya.
Divanji, P.C. 'Lakulīśa of Kārvān and his Pāśupata Culture,' *Journal of the Gujarat Research Society*, XVII (1955), 267–74.
———. 'The Māheśvara Cult and its Offishoots,' *Journal of the Asiatic Society of Bombay*, XXX (1955), Part II, 6–22.
Eliade, Mircea. *Cosmos and History : The Myth of the Eternal Return*. Translated by W.R. Trask. New York : Harper Torchbooks, 1959. (First published in 1949 as *Le Mythe de l'eternel retour : archetypes et repetition*.)
———. *Yoga : Immortality and Freedom*. Translated by W.R. Trask. London : Routledge & Kegan Paul, 1958. (First published in 1954 as *Le Yoga : Immortalité et Liberté*.)
Filliozat, Jean. *The Classical Doctrine of Indian Medicine*. Translated by D.R.

Chanana. Delhi: Munshiram Manoharlal, 1964. (First published in 1949 as *La Doctrine classique de la Médecine indienne.*)

Fleet, John Faithful (ed. and trans.). *Corpus Inscriptionum Indicarum*, Vol. III. Calcutta: 1888.

———. (ed. and trans.). 'Inscriptions at Ablur,' *EI*, V (1898–9), 213–65.

———. (ed. and trans.). 'Notes on Inscriptions at Gaddak in the Dambaḷ Tālukā of the Dhārwāḍ District,' *IA*, II (1873), 296–303.

———. (ed. and trans.). 'Sanskrit and Old-Canarese Inscriptions,' *IA*, IX (1880), 123–5.

———. (ed. and trans.). 'Sanskrit and Old-Canarese Inscriptions,' *IA*, X (1881), 126–32.

———. (ed. and trans.). 'Sanskrit and Old-Canarese Inscriptions Relating to Yādava Kings of Dēvagiri,' *JBBRAS*, XII (1876), 1–50.

———. 'Śiva as Lakulīśa,' *JRAS for* 1907, pp. 419–26.

———. (ed. and trans.). 'Sravana Belgola Epitaph of Marasimha II,' *EI*, V (1898–99), 151–80.

———. (ed. and trans.). 'A Series of Sanskrit and Old-Canarese Inscriptions Relating to the Raṭṭa Chieftains of Saundatti and Beḷgaum,' *JBBRAS*, X (1871–74), 167–298.

Gai, G.S. (ed.), *South Indian Inscriptions*, Vol. XX, Mysore: Government Press, 1965.

Gait, Edward Albert. 'Human Sacrifice (Indian),' *ERE*. VI, 849–53.

Gaṇakārikā. Often ascribed to Haradattācārya. With *Ratnaṭīkā* commentary often ascribed to Bhāsarvajña. Ed. C.D. Dalal. ('Gaekwad's Oriental Series,' No. 15.) Baroda: Central Library, 1920.

Gautama Dharmaśāstra. Trans. G. Bühler. Vol. II of *SBE*. Oxford: The Clarendon Press, 1879.

Ghurye, G.S. *Indian Sadhus*. 2d. ed. Bombay: Popular Prakashan, 1964.

Gokulanātha. *Amṛtodaya*. Ed. Śivadatta and K.P. Parab. 2d ed. revised. ('Kāvyamālā,' No. 59.) Bombay: Nirṇaya Sāgar Press, 1935.

Gorakṣa-siddhānta-saṃgraha. Ed. Gopi Nath Kaviraj. ('Princess of Wales Saraswati Bhavana Texts,' No. 18.) Benares: Vidya Vilas Press, 1925.

Guṇaratna. See Haribhadra.

Hāla. *Gāthāsaptaśatī*. With Gaṅgādhara's commentary. ('Kāvyamālā,' No. 21.) Bombay: Nirṇaya Sāgar Press, 1889.

Haldar, R.R. (ed.) 'Inscription of the Time of Hammir of Ranthambhor, Dated (V.S.) 1345,' *EI*, XIX, 45–52.

Handiqui, Krishna Kanta. *Yaśastilaka and Indian Culture*. Sholapur: Jaina Saṃskṛti Saṃrakshaka Sangha, 1949.

Hara, Minoru. 'Pāśupata Kenkyū I,' *Journal of Indian and Buddhist Studies* [Tokyo], XII (1964), 57–73.

———. '*Pāśupata* kenkyū II—*Pañcārthabhāṣya* ad *Pāśupatasūtra* I, i,' *Hikata Hakushi koki kinen ronbunshū* [Fukuoka: 1964], pp. (65)–(80).

———. 'A Note on the Sanskrit Word *ni-tya-*,' *JAOS*, LXXIX (1959), 90–6.

———. Review of *Die philosophisch-theologischen Lehren des Pāśupata-Systems nach dem Pañcārthabhāṣya und der Ratnaṭīkā* by F.A. Schultz, *IIJ*, IV (1960), 165–70.

Haradattācārya. See *Gaṇakārikā*.

Haribhadra. *Ṣaḍdarśana-samuccaya*. With Guṇaratna's *Tarkarahasya-dīpikā* commentary. Ed. Luigi Suali. ('Bibliotheca Indica.') Calcutta: 1905–14.

———. *Samarāiccakahā*. Ed. H. Jacobi. ('Bibliotheca Indica.') Calcutta : 1926.

Hauer, J.W. *Der Vrātya*. Stuttgart : W. Kohlhammer, 1927.

Hazra, Rajendra Chandra. 'The *Kālikā-Purāṇa*,' *ABORI*, XXII (1941), 1–23.

———. 'The Smṛti-chapters of the *Kūrma-Purāṇa*,' *IHQ*, XI (1935), 265–86.

Heesterman, J.C. 'Vrātya and Sacrifice,' *IIJ*, VI (1962–3), 1–37.

Hemacandra. *Triṣaṣṭiśalākapuruṣa-caritra*. Trans. Helen M. Johnson. 6 vols. ('Gaekwad's Oriental Series.' Nos. 51, 77, 108, 125, 139 and 140) Baroda : Central Library, 1931–62.

Hultzsch, E. (ed. and trans.) 'Sravana Belgola Epitaph of Mallishena,' *EI*, III (1894–95), 184–207.

Hultzsch, E., and Sastri, H. Krishna (ed. and trans.). *South Indian Inscriptions*, Vol. III. Madras : Government Press, 1929.

Indraji, Bhagvānlāl, and Bühler, G. (ed. and trans.) 'Inscriptions from Nepal,' *IA*, IX (1880), 163–94.

Ingalls, Daniel H.H. 'Cynics and Pāśupatas : The Seeking of Dishonor,' *HTR*, LV (1962), 281–98.

Jacobi, Hermann. *Die Enteicklung der Gottesidee bei den Indern und deren Beweise für das Dasein Gottes*. Bonn : K. Schroeder, 1923.

Jairazbhoy, R.A. *Foreign Influence in Ancient India*. New York : Asia Publishing House, 1963.

Jambhaladatta. *Vetālapañcaviṃśati*. Ed. and trans. M.B. Emeneau. ('American Oriental Series,' Vol. IV.) New Haven : American Oriental Society, 1934.

Jātakā. Ed. V. Fausbøll. 7 vols. Photo reprint of 1st edition of 1877–97. London : Luzac and Co., Ltd., 1962–4.

Joshi. Purushottam Balkrishna. 'On the Rite of Human Sacrifice in Ancient, Mediaeval and Modern India and Other Countries,' *JAnSB* III (1893), 275–300.

Kalhaṇa. *Rājataraṅginī*. Ed. M.A. Stein. Bombay : Education Society Press, 1892.

———. *Rājataraṅginī*. Trans. M.A. Stein. 2 vols. Photo reprint of 1900 edition. Delhi : Motilal Banarsidass, 1961.

Kālikā Purāṇa. Chapter entitled 'Rudhirādhyāya.' Trans. W.C. Blaquiere in *Asiatick Researches*, V (1797), 371–91.

Kane, Pandurang Vaman. *History of Dharmaśāstra*. 5 vols. Poona : Bhandarkar Oriental Research Institute, 1930–62.

Kāṇhapāda. See Shahidullah.

Kāravaṇa Māhātmya. Edited by C.D. Dalal in his edition of the *Gaṇakārikā*. See above.

Karmarkar, A.P. *The Vrātya or Dravidian Systems*. Vol. I of a projected *The Religions of India*. Lonavla (India) : Mira Publishing House, 1950.

Kathākośa. Ed. Jagdish Lal Shastri. Lahore : Shanti Lal Jain, 1942.

Kathākośa. Trans. C.H. Tawney. London : Royal Asiatic Society, 1895.

Kavikarṇapūra. *Caitanyacandrodaya*. Ed. Kedāranātha and W.L. Śāstrī. ('Kāvyamālā,' No. 87.) Bombay : Nirṇaya Sāgar Press, 1906.

Keith, A. Berriedale. *A History of Sanskrit Literature*. Photo reprint of 1920 edition. London : Oxford University Press, 1961.

———. *The Sanskrit Drama*. Photo reprint of 1924 edition. London : Oxford University Press, 1964.

Kielhorn, F. (ed.) 'Gadag Inscription of the Yadava Bhillama ; Śaka-Samvat 1113,' *EI*, III (1894–5), 217–220.

———. (ed.). 'Twenty-one Copper-plates of the Kings of Kanauj; [Vikrama-] Samvat 1171 to 1233,' *EI*, IV, 97–129.

Koestler, Arthur. *The Lotus and the Robot*. London : Hutchinson, 1960.

Kosambi, Damodar Dharmanand. *Myth and Reality*. Bombay : Popular Prakashan, 1962.

Krishnamacharlu, C.R. *List of Inscriptions Copied by the Office of the Superintendent for Epigraphy, Madras*. Delhi : Government Press, 1941.

———. (ed.). *South Indian Inscriptions*, Vol. XI, Part I. Madras : Government Press, 1940.

Krishnarao, Bhavaraj V. (ed.) 'Tandikonda Grant of Ammaraja II,' *EI*, XXIII, 161–70.

Kṛṣṇamiśra. *Prabodhacandrodaya*. With *Candrikāvyākhyā* and *Prakāśaṭīkā* commentaries. Ed. V.L. Paṇśīkar. 6th ed. Bombay : Nirṇaya Sāgar Press, 1965.

Kṣemendra. *Daśāvatāra-carita*. Ed. Durgāprasād and K.P. Parab. Bombay : Nirṇaya Sāgar Press, 1891.

———. *Deśopadeśa and Narmamālā*. Ed. Madhusūdan Kaul Shastri. Poona : Āryabhūshan Press, 1923.

Kṣemīśvara. *Caṇḍakauśika*. Ed. and trans. Sibani Das Gupta. Calcutta : The Asiatic Society, 1962.

Kudalkar, J.S. (ed. and trans.) 'A Note on Tilakwādā Copper-plate Inscriptions of the Time of King Bhoja Paramāra of Mālwā,' All India Oriental Conference, *Proceedings and Transactions of* 1*st session, Poona*, 1919, Vol. II, pp. 319–26.

Kulārṇava-tantra. Edited, with a rough paraphrase, by Tārānātha Vidyāratna. Madras : Ganesh and Co. (Madras) Private Ltd., 1965.

Kūrma Purāṇa. Ed. Nilamani Mukhopadhyaya. ('Bibliotheca Indica') Calcutta : Giriśa-Vidyāratna Press, 1890.

Lal, Rai Bahadur Hira, 'The Golakī Maṭha,' *Journal of the Bihar and Orissa Research Society*, XIII (1927), 137–44.

Lalitavistara. Ed. P.L. Vaidya. ('Buddhist Sanskrit Texts,' No. 1.) Darbhanga : Mithila Institute, 1958.

Liṅga Purāṇa. Ed. Jīvānanda Vidyāsāgara. Calcutta : Nūtana Vālmīki Press, 1885.

Lüders, H. (ed.) 'Gadag Inscription of Vira-Ballala II; Saka-Samvat 1114,' *EI*, VI (1900), 89–97.

Mādhavācārya. *Śaṃkara-digvijaya*. With Dhanapatisūri's *Ḍiṇḍima* commentary. (Ānandāśram Sanskrit Series,' No. 22.) Poona : Ānandāśram Press, 1915.

Mahābhārata (critical edition). Vols. III–IV : *Āraṇyakaparvan*. Ed. V.S. Sukthankar. Poona : Bhandarkar Oriental Research Institute, 1942.

Mahābhārata (critical edition). Vols. XIII–XVI : *Śāntiparvan*. Ed. V.S. Sukthankar and S.K. Belvalkar. Poona : Bhandarkar Oriental Research Institute, 1949–54.

Mahābhārata (critical edition). Vol. XI : *Śalyaparvan*. Ed. R.C. Dandekar. Poona : Bhandarkar Oriental Research Institute, 1961.

Mahalingam, T.V. 'A Family of Pāśupata Gṛhasthas at Jambukēśvaram,' *JORM*, XV (1957), 79–85.

———. 'The Pāśupatas in South India,' *JIH*, XXVII (1949), 43–53.

Mahānirvāṇa-tantra. Ed. and trans. John Woodroffe as *The Great Liberation (Mahānirvāṇa Tantra)*. 3d ed. Madras : Ganesh & Co. (Madras) Ltd., 1953.

Mahendravarman. *Mattavilāsa*. Ed. T. Gaṇapati Sāstrī. ('Trivandrum Sanskrit Series,' No. 55.) Trivandrum : Government Press, 1917.

———. *Mattavilāsa*. Trans. L.D. Barnett in *BSOS*, V (1930), 697–710.

Maitrāyaṇīya Upaṇīṣad. Ed. and trans. J.A.B. van Buitenen. The Hague : Mouton and Co., 1962.

Majumdar, B.P. 'Lakulīśa Pāśupatas and their Temples in Medieval India,' *JBRS*, XXXIX (1953), 1–9.

Majumdar, Ramesh Chandra (ed.). *The Age of Imperial Kanauj*. Vol. IV of *The History and Culture of the Indian People*. Bombay : Bharatiya Vidya Bhavan, 1955.

———. (ed.). *The Age of Imperial Unity*. Vol. II of same series. Bombay : Bharatiya Vidya Bhavan, 1951.

———. (ed.). *The Classical Age*. Vol. III of same series. Bombay : Bharatiya Vidya Bhavan, 1954.

———. (ed.). *The Struggle for Empire*. Vol. V of same series. Bombay : Bharatiya Vidya Bhavan, 1957.

Manu-smṛti. Trans. G. Bühler. Vol. XXV of *SBE*. Oxford : Oxford University Press, 1886.

Matsya Purāṇa. ('Ānandāśram Sanskrit Series,' No. 54.) Poona : Ānandāśram Press, 1907.

Mehta, R.N. 'Karavan—The Seat of the Lakulīśa Sect,' Indian History Congress, *Proceedings of the Fourteenth Session, Jaipur* (1951), pp. 71–76.

Mitra, Rajendralāla. 'On Human Sacrifices in Ancient India,' *JRASB*, XLV (1876), 76–118.

Monier-Williams, Monier. *A Sanskrit-English Dictionary*. Photo reprint of 1899 1st edition. Delhi : Motilal Banarsidass, 1963.

Mysore Gazetteer. New edition edited by C. Hayavadana Rao but mostly based on B.L. Rice's original edition. 5 vols. Bangalore : Government Press, 1927–30.

Nandimath, S.C. *A Handbook of Viraśaivism*. Dharwar : L.E. Association, 1942.

Narasimhachar, R. (ed. and trans.) *Epigraphia Carnatica*, Vol. II (revised edition). Bangalore : Mysore Government Press, 1923.

Narasimhaswami, H.K. (ed.) 'Bhairavakonda Inscription of Vikramaditya,' *EI*, XXXIII (1959–60), 78–81.

———. (ed.). 'Dommara-Nandyala Plates of Punyakumara; 10th Year,' *EI*, XXVII (1947–8), 268–76.

Pañcatantra. Ed. Nārāyaṇa Rāma Āchārya. Bombay : Nirṇaya Sāgar Press, 1959.

Panchamukhi, R.S. (ed.) *Karnatak Inscriptions*, Vol. I. Dharwar : Kannada Research Office, 1941.

Pandey, Kanti Chandra. *Bhāskarī*. Vol. III. ('Princess of Wales Sarasvati Bhavana Texts,' No. 84.) Lucknow : Superintendent, Printing and Stationery, U.P., 1954.

Panigrahi, Krishna Chandra. *Archaeological Remains at Bhubaneswar*. Bombay : Orient Longmans, 1961.

Pāśupata-sūtra. With Kauṇḍinya's *Pañcārthabhāṣya* commentary. Ed. R. Anantha-krishna Sastri. ('Trivandrum Sanskrit Series,' No. 143.) Trivandrum : University of Travancore, 1940.

Pāśupata-sūtra. Variant readings of several *sūtras* edited by C. Chakravarti in *IHQ*, XIX, 270–1.

Patañjali. *Yogasūtra*. Ed. and trans. J. Ballantyne. 4th reprint. Calcutta : Susil Gupta (India) Private Ltd., 1963.

Pathak, V.S. *History of Śaiva Cults in Northern India from Inscriptions*. Varanasi : Dr Ram Naresh Varma, 1960.

———. *Ancient Historians of India—A Study in Historical Biographies*. Bombay: Asia Publishing House, 1966.

Pillai, J.M. Somasundaran. *Two Thousand Years of Tamil Literature*. Madras: By the author, 1959.

Pires, Edward A. *The Maukharis*. B.G. Paul & Co., 1934.

Raghavan, V. (ed. and trans.) 'Tiruvorriyur Inscription of Chaturanana Pandita: 20th Year of Krishna III,' *EI*, XXVII (1947–8), 292–303.

Rahamāna, Abdula. *Saṃdeśa-rāsaka*. Ed. and trans. Śri Jina Vijaya Muni. Bombay: Bharatīya Vidyā Bhavan, 1944.

Rājaśekhara. *Karpūramañjarī*. Ed. Sten Konow and trans. Charles Rockwell Lanman. ('Harvard Oriental Series,' Vol. IV.) Cambridge, Mass.: Harvard University, 1901.

Rāmacandra. *Kaumudī-mitrānanda*. Ed. Muni Punyavijaya. Bhavanagar: Jaina Ātmānanda Granthamālā, 1917.

———. *Nalavilāsa*. Ed. G.K. Shrigondekar and Lalchandra B. Gandhi. ('Gaekwad's Oriental Series,' No. 29). Baroda: Central Library, 1926.

Rāmānuja. *Śrībhāṣya*. Ed. and trans. R.D. Karmarkar. 2 vols. Poona: University of Poona, 1959–62.

Rangacharya, V. *Inscriptions of the Madras Presidency*. 3 vols. Madras: Government Press, 1919.

Rangaswamy, M.A. Dorai. *The Religion and Philosophy of Tēvāram*. 4 vols. in 2 books. Madras: University of Madras, 1958–59.

Rao, N. Lakshminarayan (ed.). *South Indian Inscriptions*, Vol. XI, Part II. Madras: Government Press, 1953.

Rao, R. Rama. 'Origin and Development of Śiva-Worship with Special Reference to Vīraśaivism,' *QJMS*, IV (1924), 190–210 and 282–301.

Rao, T.A. Gopinatha (ed.). 'The Huzur Treasury Plates Belonging to the Viṣṇu Temple at Tiruvalla,' *TAS*, II (1910), 131–207.

———. *Elements of Hindu Iconography*. 2 vols. Madras: The Law Printing House, 1914–16.

Renou, Louis, and Filliozat, Jean. *L'Inde classique*. 2 vols. Paris: Payot, 1947–53.

Rice, B. Lewis (ed. and trans.). *Epigraphia Carnatica*. 12 vols. Bangalore: Mysore Government Press, 1886–1904.

Sakhare, M.R. *History and Philosophy of Lingāyat Religion*. Belgaum: Mahavir Press, 1942.

Śaktisaṅgama-tantra. Ed. Benoytosh Bhattacharya. 3 vols. (Gaekwad's Oriental Series,' Nos. 61, 91 and 104.) Baroda: Central Library, 1932–47. (An intended final volume was never published.)

Saletore, Bhasker Anand. *Mediaeval Jainism: With Special Reference to the Vijayanagara Empire*. Bombay: Karnatak Publishing House, [1938].

Śaṃkarācārya. *Brahma-sūtra-bhāṣya*. Published together with Vācaspati Miśra's *Bhāmatī*, Āmalānanda-Sarasvatī's *Kalpataru*, and Appayadīkṣita's *Parimala*. 2d ed. Ed. Bhārgav Śāstrī. Bombay: Nirṇaya Sāgar Press, 1938. (1st edition edited by Anantkṛiṣṇa Śāstrī.)

———. *Brahma-sūtra-bhāyṣa*. Trans. G. Thibaut. Vols. XXXIV and XXXVIII of *SBE*. Oxford: Oxford University Press, 1904.

Sankalia, Hasmukh D. *The Archaeology of Gujarat*. Bombay: Natwarlal and Co., 1941.

Śaṅkhadhara. *Laṭaka-melaka*. Ed. Durgāprasād. 3d ed. ('Kāvyamālā,' No. 20.)

Bombay : Nirṇaya Sāgār Press, 1923.

Sansom, G.B. *Japan : A Short Cultural History*. Revised edition. New York : Appleton-Century-Crofts, Inc., 1943.

Sarkar, Jadunath. *A History of Dasnami Naga Sanyasis*. Allahabad : Śri Panchayata Akhara Mahanirvani, 1958.

Sastri, K.A. Nilakanta. *The Cōḷas*. 2 vols. Madras : University of Madras, 1935–7.

———. *The Cōḷas*. 2d ed. revised. Madras : University of Madras, 1955.

———. *Development of Religion in South India*. Bombay : Orient Longmans, 1963.

———. *A History of South India*. London : Oxford University Press, 1958.

———. (ed. and trans.). 'The Koḍumbāḷūr Inscription of Vikrama-Kēsarī,' *JORM*, VII (1933), 1–10.

———. (ed.). *The Mauryas and Satavahanas*. Vol. II of *A Comprehensive History of India*. Bombay : Orient Longmans, 1957.

Sastry, R. Shama, and Rao, N. Lakshminarayan (ed.). *South Indian Inscriptions*, Vol. IX, Parts I and II. Madras : Government Press, 1939–41.

Ṣaṭ-cakra-nirūpaṇa. With *Kālācaraṇa* commentary. Ed. and trans. J. Woodroffe as *The Serpent Power*. 7th ed. Madras : Ganesh & Co. (Madras) Private Ltd., 1964.

Sāyaṇa-Mādhava. *Sarvadarśana-saṃgraha*. Edited with a Hindi translation by Uma Shankar Sharma. Varanasi : Chowkhamba Vidyabhawan, 1964.

———. Chapter of *Sarvadarśana-saṃgraha* entitled 'Nakulīśa-Pāśupata-darśana.' Trans. Minoru Hara in *IIJ*, II (1958), 8–32.

Sayre, Farrand. *Diogenes of Sinope : A Study of Greek Cynicism*. Baltimore : [Printed by J.H. Furst Company], 1938.

Schultz, F.A. *Die philosophisch-theologischen Lehren des Pāśupata-Systems nach dem Pañcārthabhāṣya und der Ratnaṭīkā*. Walldorf-Hessen : 1958.

Shahidullah, M. (ed. and trans.) *Les Chants Mystiques de Kāṇha et de Saraha; les Dohā-koṣa et les Caryā*. Paris : Adrien-Maisonneuve, 1928.

Shāstri, Dakshinaranjan. 'The Lokāyatikas and the Kāpālikas,' *IHQ*, VII (1931), 125–37.

Śiva Purāṇa Vāyavīyasaṃhitā. Ed. Mallikārjunaśāstrī. 2 vols. Sholapore : Dattaprasāda Press, 1905–6.

Skanda Purāṇa. 7 vols. Bombay : Veṅkaṭeśvara Press, 1909–11.

Skanda Purāṇa Sūtasaṃhitā. With Mādhavācārya's commentary. Ed. V.S. Paṇaśīkara. 3 vols. ('Ānandāśrama-saṃskṛita-granthāvaliḥ,' No. 24.) Poona : M.C. Apte, 1893.

Somadeva. *Kathāsaritsāgara*. Ed. Durgāprasād and K.P. Parab. Bombay : Nirṇaya Sāgar Press, 1889.

———. *Kathāsaritsāgara*. Trans. C.H. Tawney as *The Ocean of Story*. 10 vols. London : Chas. J. Sawyer, 1924–8.

Sreenivasachar, P. (ed. and trans.) *A Corpus of Inscriptions in the Telingana Districts of H.E.H. the Nizam's Dominions*. Vol. XIII, Part II, of *HAS*. Hyderabad : 1940.

Śrīharṣa. *Naiṣadhacarita*. Translated, with extensive notes and extracts from several commentaries, by Krishna Kanta Handiqui. 2d ed. revised. ('Deccan College Monograph Series,' No. 14.) Poona : 1956.

Subandhu. *Vāsavadattā*. Ed. and trans. Louis H. Gray. Reprint of 1913 edition. New York : Ams Press Inc., 1965.

Subbiah, A. Venkata. 'A Twelfth Century University in Mysore,' *QJMS*, VII (1917), 157–96.

Thapar, Romila. *Aśoka and the Decline of the Mauryas*. London : Oxford University Press, 1961.

Trivikrama-bhaṭṭa. *Nalacampū*. With Caṇḍapāla's *Viṣamapadaprakāśa*. Ed. Durgāprasād and Śivadatta. 3d ed. Bombay : Nirṇaya Sāgar Press, 1931.

Tucci, Giuseppe. 'Animadversiones Indicae,' *JRASB*, n.s. XXVI (1930), 125–60.

Umāpati. *Śivaprakāśam*. Trans. Henry R. Hoisington as 'Siva-Pirakāsam,—Light of Siva' in *JAOS*, IV (1854), 125–244.

Upadhyay, Vasudeva. *Socio-Religious Condition of North India* (700–1200 A.D.). ('Chowkhamba Sanskrit Studies,' Vol. XXXIX.) Varanasi: Chowkhamba Sanskrit Series Office, 1964.

Vācaspati Miśra. See Śaṃkarācārya.

La Vallée Poussin, Louis de. 'Tāntrism (Buddhist),' *ERE*, XII, 193–97.

Vāmana Purāṇa, Bombay : Veṅkaṭeśvara Press, 1908.

Varāhamihira. *Bṛhajjātaka*, Ed. and trans. V. Subrahmanya Sastri as *Brihat Jataka*. Mysore : Government Branch Press, 1929.

———. *Bṛhajjātaka*. With Utpala's commentary. Bombay : 1863.

———. *Bṛhatsaṃhitā*. Ed. H. Kern. ('Bibliotheca Indica.') Calcutta : 1865.

———. *Bṛhatsaṃhitā*. Trans. H. Kern in *JRAS*, n.s. IV(1870), 430–79; n.s. V(1871), 45–90 and 231–88; n.s. VI (1873), 36–91; and n.s. VII (1875), 81–134. (Translation only up to chapter 134).

———. *Bṛhatsaṃhitā*. 2 vols. Ed. and trans. V. Subrahmanya Sastri. Bangalore: V.B. Soobbiah and Sons, 1947.

Vāsiṣṭha Dharmasūtra. Trans. G. Bühler. Vol. XIV of *SBE*. Oxford : The Clarendon Press, 1882.

Vāyu Purāṇa. ('Ānandāśram Sanskrit Series,' No. 45.) Poona : Ānandāśram Press, 1905.

Venkayya, V. (ed.) 'Triplicane Inscription of Dantivarman,' *EI*, VIII, 290–96.

Vidyābhūṣaṇa, Satis Chandra. 'Influence of Aristotle on the Development of the Syllogism in Indian Logic,' *JRAS for* 1918, pp. 469–88.

Vinayacandra. *Mallinātha-carita*. Ed. Hargovinddas and Bechardas. Benares: Harshchand Bhurabhai, 1911.

Viṣṇu Purāṇa. Trans. H.H. Wilson. 3d ed. Calcutta : Punthi Pustak, 1961. (First published in 1840.)

Viṣṇu-smṛti. With Nandapandita's *Keśavavaijayanti* commentary. 2 vols. Adyar: Library and Research Centre, 1964.

Viṣṇu-smṛti. Trans. J. Jolly. Vol. VII of *SBE*. Oxford : The Clarendon Press, 1880.

Vyas, Akshaya Keerty (ed.). 'Paldi Inscription of Guhila Arisimha, V.S. 1173,' *EI*, XXX, 8ff.

Vyāsācala. *Śaṃkara-vijaya*. Ed. T. Chandrasekharan. Madras : Government Press, 1954.

Watters, Thomas. *On Yuan Chwang's Travels in India*. 2 vols. London: Royal Asiatic Society, 1904.

Yājñavalkya-smṛti. With Vijñāneśvara's *Mitākṣara* commentary. Ed. N.R. Āchārya. 5th ed. Bombay : Nirṇaya Sāgar Press, 1949.

Yaśaḥpāla. *Moharājaparājaya*. Ed. Muni Chaturavijaya. ('Gaekwad's Oriental Series,' No. 9.) Baroda : Central Library, 1918.

Yazdani, G. (ed.) *The Early History of the Deccan*. 2 vols. London : Oxford University Press, 1960.

Zimmer, Heinrich. *The King and the Corpse*. New York : Pantheon Books, 1948.

INDEX

The following abbreviations are used; Kp: probable Kālāmukha priest and Kt: probable Kālāmukha temple.